THE BRITISH AT TABLE
1940–1980

THE BRITISH
AT TABLE
1940–1980

Christopher Driver

What greater restoratives
have we poor mortals than a good meal
taken in the company of
loving friends?

Flora Thompson, *Lark Rise to Candleford* (1945)
– in a passage on funeral teas.

CHATTO & WINDUS

THE HOGARTH PRESS
LONDON

Published in 1983 by
Chatto & Windus · The Hogarth Press
40 William IV Street
London WC2N 4DF

British Library Cataloguing in Publication Data

Driver, Christopher
The British at table 1940–1980.
1. Food habits—Great Britain
I. Title
394.1'0941   GT2853.G7

ISBN 0 7011 2582 9

Phototypeset by Wyvern Typesetting Limited
Printed in Great Britain by
Redwood Burn Ltd
Trowbridge, Wiltshire

Contents

List of illustrations

Preface

Thirty years ago, in a pleasurable book called *Pleasure*, Doris Langley Moore reported that 'a highly serviceable knowledge of human nature is to be acquired merely from observing its reaction to eating and drinking.' (Her father was both a journalist and a good cook.) The *aperçu* comes unbidden to mind when the moment arrives to express thanks for help with a book like this. The author is obliged to remember everyone who has ever fed him, beginning with his mother, and a good many of those whom he himself has fed. This makes it impractical to name names. Besides, at least as much is to be learnt from detestable meals as from good ones, and tact precludes . . .

But my chief debt is to the cluster of connections formed since I first met Raymond Postgate, in the year when Consumers' Association took over publication of his *Good Food Guide*. They include Hope Chenhalls and Neil Rhind, whose unpublished history of the *Guide* I have drawn upon in Chapter Four; thousands of correspondents during my own twelve years as editor; affectionate, protective colleagues; and my friend Aileen Hall who has suggested more lines of thought, and saved me from more errors of fact or judgement, than any other single person during the years of eating, reading, observing and writing that preceded this book. Others who have conducted investigations, opened sources, found books, read sections, answered questions or generally put themselves out for me include my daughter Catharine, Michelle Berriedale-Johnson, Jill Norman, Ishbel Speight, Dr Roland Harper, Martin Leighton, George Perry-Smith and Heather Crosbie, the librarians of the *Guardian* in Manchester and of the Preston-Leigh collection of food books in the Brotherton Library of the University of Leeds, and numerous secondhand booksellers, including Gillian Weall who manages my own Book in Hand shop in Shaftesbury. Sarah Wright helped me with the index. More formal acknowledgements for the use of printed material appear on page viii, but it has been a pleasure to transcribe into these pages the work of so many good writers. Lines appropriate (except in one rather important particular) to my wife Margaret's role will be found by anyone who manages to read to the end.

Highgate, London, January 1983

Acknowledgements

I would like to thank the following for permission to quote copyright material: Cambridge University Press (*Cooking, Cuisine and Class* by Jack Goody); Central Office of Information and Dr Roland Harper (*Spectrum* by Dr Roland Harper); Century Publishing Ltd (*With Love* by Theodora Fitzgibbon); Collier Macmillan Ltd (*Myself: My Two Countries* by Marcel Boulestin and *The Memoirs of the Rt Hon. the Earl of Woolton*); John Gifford Ltd (*Recipes of the 1940s* by Irene Veal); Hamish Hamilton Ltd (*Kitchen Book* by Nicholas Freeling); Hutchinson Books Ltd (*British Tastes* by D. Elliston Allen); Macmillan Publishers Ltd (*English Food* by Jane Grigson); Mitchell Beazley Ltd and Michael Broadbent (*Pocket Guide to Wine Tasting* by Michael Broadbent); Oxford University Press (*The Joyless Economy* by Tibor Scitovsky); Penguin Books Ltd (*The Philosopher in the Kitchen* by J.-A. Brillat-Savarin, translated by Anne Drayton); A. D. Peters & Co. Ltd (*The Age of Austerity* by Michael Sissons and Philip French); Gerald Priestland (*Frying Tonight*); Routledge & Kegan Paul Ltd (*The Social Impact of Oil* by Robert Moore and *In the Active Voice* by Mary Douglas and Michael Nicod); Scolar Press (*Plenty and Want* by John Burnett).

I would also like to thank the following for permission to reproduce illustrations: Noel Carrington, Faber & Faber Ltd, John Lehmann, Norman Mansbridge, A. D. Peters & Co. Ltd, and Gerald Priestland.

Introduction

This is a book about the way we eat now in the light of the way we used to eat within middle-aged memory. It is about ourselves as shoppers, cultivators, cooks and consumers. The perspective is that of a fifty-year-old Englishman who has lived in different parts of the United Kingdom, who travels here and there in the earth and likes to cook in more than one national style, but who owes most of his tastes in food, drink, art and apparel to the sedate professional class in which he was brought up. The chief prejudice expressed throughout is shared with a minority of British people, who are to be found in all walks of life but represented more strongly in some than in others. It is a prejudice in favour of eating well, even if it means taking time and paying attention. This taste for what should perhaps be called 'slow food' carries with it an attitude that in this country – though in very few others – is often confused with pretension or elitism. The theme will be developed later, but briefly, the opposite is true. You may neglect your diet altogether, but you still have to eat to live, and by settling for the shoddy because it is cheap or quick, you affect the quality of everyday materials, processes and services. Of course, civilised life does not depend on choosing invariably, or for that matter ever, the best pictures or the best music or the best food to live with. But it does depend on learning – most easily in childhood – how to distinguish, and why other people make different choices or submit to different compulsions.

Because the period of time covered by the book opens in a food world so different in many ways from the present, the approach is at first historical. It is not just that many foods, tastes and skills vanished from domestic and restaurant kitchens during the war years, to be replaced either then or subsequently by the products, techniques and influences discussed in these pages. The changes were themselves historically determined, not merely contingent on the outbreak of war. The characteristic achievements of nineteenth-century food science were margarine ('cartgrease', as countrymen called it in the 1890s) and the tin can, but the twentieth century was half over before the synthesis of flavours and nutrients began to affect the market on a large scale, and domestic refrigeration and mechanisation became so much part of British family life that avoiding them required effort or eccentricity. For instance, in my 1930s childhood, the household had a car, a telephone, a piano, and a maid, but there was no refrigerator, and food tradesmen called at the door daily, as milkmen still do. By 1980, over 40 per cent of British households possessed not only refrigerators but deep-freezes too, and I searched shops in vain for a meat-safe, which few households would have cared to be without even as late as the 1950s.

However, with most historical writing it is hard to know where to begin. During the 1939–45 war a serious national attempt was made, not just to save food and reduce imports, but to change and less consciously to democratise the way the British people as a whole ate and cooked. This policy and activity can be understood better with some sense, however inexact, of the cultural base on which the tastes and resources of the 1940s were built. I have tried to provide this in Chapter One.

After the war years a peacetime diet was very gradually restored, and the approach remains narrative-historical throughout Part One. Since the mid-1950s, abundance has reigned with recent checks but very few actual reverses. New technologies and more diverse tastes have appeared. This last quarter-century is too short and crowded for sequential narration, and Part Two contains essays on different themes: immigrant cuisines, food technology, the art and science of taste, the catering industry, and others.

The reader will by now expect this book, like most cultural history and comment, to concentrate on the tastes and habits of the social class whose dietary adaptability, output of cookery books, and disposable income have led most of the changes that have taken place in this sphere during the past three hundred years. In our own time, the fixed, even nursery tastes of the aristocracy can still be studied daily in the dining rooms of St James's. The mass market, as its middle-class persuaders have so often discovered to their own profit and discredit, is deprived by history of sound models and domestic education, and so often vulnerable to inferior substitutes for familiar things, yet at the same time wary of genuine novelty and differentiation. Working-class women, hard-pressed for time and energy, are noticeably averse in their shopping to foodstuffs that threaten trouble and 'mess'.

Indeed, I now realise more clearly than I did when I embarked on this book that the food history of our own time presents the middle class rediscovering, and the working class escaping, the mingled pleasure and enslavement of the physical world. Up till the 1940s, the bourgeoisie was protected by its domestic servants from kitchen tasks which it at first detested, later discovered ways round, and finally took to parading as a form of social display. The march of regulation and technology themselves assisted this process: to obtain good bacon, it is once again necessary to kill and cure your own pig, as in the eighteenth century. Progress takes odd forms.

*For M
and other table companions*

PART ONE
History – from lean to fat

CHAPTER ONE
French models and British cooks

An adequate diet can be had for 35p a day according to M. Jean Conil, who said that during the war he had cooked larks, rooks and seagulls. Boiled seagulls were very good. 'We waste tripes, intestines, which are made into chitterlings in Europe and Russia, and spleen, rind, tail, heads, ears. In this country these are made into pet food.'
Guardian, 11 January 1982.

Truly, I always declar'd 'twould be pity
To burn to the ground such a choice-feeding city ...
As to Marshals, and Statesmen, and all their whole lineage,
For aught that I care, you may knock them to spinage;
But think, Dick, their Cooks – what a loss to mankind!
What a void in the world would their art leave behind!
Their chronometer spits – their intense salamanders –
Their ovens – their pots, that can soften old ganders,
All vanish'd for ever – their miracles o'er,
And the *Marmite Perpetuelle* bubbling no more!
Thomas Brown the Younger, *The Fudge Family in Paris* (1818).

The origin of British industrial decline has often been traced to the period of high confidence or complacency that followed the Great Exhibition of 1851, although it was only in later years that our inferior performance *vis-à-vis* German, American and eventually Japanese rivals became visible to the naked eye. In household matters, by contrast, mercantile Britain's confidence in national skill and tradition had begun to ebb away under foreign influence at an earlier stage. The first half of the nineteenth century saw the rise of the railway, the steamship, the grand hotel and the public restaurant, and inspired the multiplying bourgeoisie with a well-documented passion for social entertaining. It also detached the executant-craftswoman from the owner-administrator in the domestic kitchen, and diminished the contentment

3

that women of previous generations had found in still-room and kitchen as well as in the drawing-room.

This change is distinct from the earlier dietary impoverishment of artisan and labouring families congregated in cities by the industrial revolution. The middle class controlled the rise of public education, adult literacy, and communication in print. They enjoyed a leisure and residential stability denied to men who had to migrate in search of work and labour cruelly long hours to keep their families fed on wickedly adulterated produce. Social horizons widened with the railway network, and as the French Revolution and the Napoleonic wars receded into memory, British cooks and food commentators slowly began to surrender their independence to the culture of the people their armies had defeated. Symbolically, to this day Marengo is remembered in Britain for a recipe, not a battle, and the dish is seldom cooked correctly either. It is true that in the previous century too, authors of cookery books written in English for the wives of the gentry had often recognised the superior system and technical sophistication of their French counterparts. But this did not seem to disturb eighteenth-century housekeepers, or make them feel like clumsy second-raters in their own time and country. Their own methods were adequate to the context and scale of British country life, and depended on materials which French observers themselves often acknowledged to be superior to their own, as well as more equitably shared between aristocrat and artisan.

After Waterloo, the climate gradually changed, and British cooking of the country house kind, represented in the previous century by Eliza Smith, Hannah Glasse and others, began to look old-fashioned. Technically, it belonged to an age that was passing away. Vaguely measured recipes were ill fitted to the new scale of entertaining, and could not be used by people who needed instruction rather than reminder. The French style, preached by professional and talented French chefs settling in London (as in our own day), appealed to middle-class would-be ladies who were trying to entertain in fashionable style without the easy manners and financial recklessness of the aristocracy. By the time Eliza Acton's *Modern Cookery* showed them a better indigenous example in the 1840s, it was too late. A gap had opened up between the fancy and the normal, and has lasted in British eating until this day. One can readily imagine what life was like in Victorian households during the days following one of these pretentious dinner parties. The children, the servants, and the servants' families would have been invited to pick over the unlovely remains of numerous entrees and removes, warmed over as

Cook thought best. (The dreadful progression of the English weekly joint through cold cuts to shepherd's pie and rissoles, a feature of scrupulously run households until very recent times, may well have the same historical origin.)

Lest this be thought an analysis built upon twentieth-century hindsight, a contemporary complaint on similar lines is worth disinterring. The anonymous author of *Dinners and Dinner Parties, or the Absurdities of Artificial Life* (2nd edn 1862) dedicates his book to 'the five millions of unmarried daughters of England and Wales, with a view to awakening the attention of their mothers, whom half a century of sleep and bad cookery have rendered so careless that they know not what they eat nor of what their soup is composed'. His thesis is that 'a century ago the art of cookery was fashionable among English girls and English women . . . Nowadays, the piano mania and reception rooms are all that are thought of; cookery is out of use, and only practised by the lower orders.' His verdict is a pre-echo of correspondents to *The Good Food Guide*, a century later, grumbling about grossly overcooked meat, and 'billsticker's paste' for sauce. The author does not hesitate to tender practical advice: 'If you ever get introduced into a house where the lady of the mansion looks to the cuisine, you need not be under the apprehension of poison'; but 'if the dame is incapable of giving instruction, let her employ a man-cook from Belgium. Although she will pay him 80*l.* a year, the highest wage known there, she will save her husband at least 100*l.* a year in the food that will be saved' – not to mention, he adds, the doctor's and apothecary's bills, and the risk of premature decease.

In the 1820s, as in the 1950s, the sudden freedom to travel on the Continent after an interlude of isolation played a significant role in the cultural conquest of the conqueror by the conquered. The classic account of what happened when peace arrived after the Napoleonic wars comes from that dandified but immensely shrewd and practical food critic Brillat-Savarin, who saw the economy of France transformed after the reparations demanded by the Second Treaty of Paris, and reported 'mathematical proof' through the rate of exchange that more money was coming into France than going out of it.

What divinity performed this miracle?
Gourmandism.
When the Britons, the Germans, the Teutons, the Cimmerians, and the Scythians poured into France, they brought with them a rare voracity and stomachs of uncommon capacity.
They were not content for long with the official cheer forthcoming from

forced hospitality; they aspired to more delicate pleasures; and before long the queen of cities had become a vast refectory. These intruders ate in restaurants, in hotels, in taverns, at street-stalls, and even in the streets. They stuffed themselves with meat, fish, game, truffles, pastry, and above all with our fruit.

It was a golden time for all who ministered to the pleasures of taste. Véry finished making his fortune; Achard laid the foundations of his; Beauvilliers amassed his third, and Madame Sulot, whose shop in the Palais-Royal was only a few feet square, sold up to twelve thousand tarts a day.[1]

It must not be deduced from all this that French infiltration of British food culture during the nineteenth century was more thorough than it was. Nor for that matter was it simply a question of preferring ragouts to roasts or *foie gras en croûte* to venison pasties if the choice presented itself. The commanding position enjoyed in London by chefs such as Ude, Soyer and Francatelli did not overawe Eliza Acton, Mrs Beeton's predecessor, model, and superior, when she compiled her *Modern Cookery* (1845) and her *Bread Book* (1857). These are books as English as their eighteenth-century predecessors, though more catholic in their range and systematic in their arrangement.

Isabella Beeton herself was a proper little Englander. When she and her husband visited Paris, her biographer records,

she displayed no curiosity about French cooking, and the only comments she made about their dinners were 'nice'. They were as conservative as possible in their choice of menu, and had chicken every night, almost always preceded by vegetable soup and fricandeau of veal, and followed by Russian or apple Charlotte. As at home they ate an enormous breakfast of steaks or chops, eggs, and potatoes; then they had a light lunch and a very early dinner – in contrast to the French custom of a large lunch and late dinner.[2]

However, Britons' rising expectation of memorable meals eaten in France or cooked by Frenchmen had long since begun to spread, and it pervaded polite society in a subtly lethal way. The famous chefs who crossed the Channel to England left behind them in France the secure simplicities of the *cuisine de terroir* which had nourished them in their youth, and which were equally vivid in the minds of most of their Paris clients. Settled in London, working for ducal houses or London clubs in an age which was just beginning to acquire the modern world's awful reverence for experts, the French connection implanted in ladylike Victorians the conviction – still commonly articulated in the present writer's hearing – that there is food (fuel food, that is) and 'good food', just as people who merely 'like their food' are to be distinguished from 'gourmets'. This dissociation of sensibility was unknown in France itself until very recent years, when the French in their turn became vulnerable to external influences, notably Anglo-American convenience foods and the taste of the media for showbiz cookery.

By the last quarter of the nineteenth century in Britain, the natural response to simple and simply cooked foods had been atrophied in socially ambitious circles. Ever since, every great French chef who has arrived to work in these islands has had to begin by saying, in Escoffier's phrase, *faites simple*, because he has only had to look around him to realise that most people who could afford it had convinced themselves that food, to be good, had to be made complicated. 'In England you taste your dinners, you do not eat them'[3], said Escoffier's successor at the Savoy, M. Joseph, to the turn-of-the-century restaurant critic Lieut. Col. Nathaniel Newnham-Davis, and, reading between the lines of Newnham-Davis's evocative descriptions of London restaurants at this period, it is easy to realise from the behaviour and preferences of his female companions what was expected of the grand restaurants by a clientele of whom only a tiny proportion, then as now, cared more for the eating than for the show. Escoffier himself, though England provided him with his livelihood, did not hide the personal cost:

What feats of ingenuity have we not been forced to perform, at times, in order to meet our customers' wishes? Those only who have had charge of a large modern kitchen can tell the tale. Personally, I have ceased counting the nights spent in the attempt to discover new combinations, when, completely broken with the fatigue of a heavy day, my body ought to have been at rest.[4]

A generation later, though much had been pruned by the 1914–18 War and the relative impatience of the men who survived it, the same message had to be delivered again by a very different kind of Frenchman, X. M. Boulestin, Colette's friend. Boulestin was a creative *bricoleur* (his own description) who in 1922 went to see a London publisher about his friend Laboureur's etchings, and emerged with a casual commission for a cookery book (this was three years before the opening of the restaurant, built on the book's success, that still bears his name).[5]

His method and attitude is admirably expressed in his autobiography:

I devoted myself entirely to my cookery book. I had never learnt anything, but I had eaten well all my life and, like all Frenchmen from the South-West of France, I instinctively knew how to cook. So my idea was to produce a book which, ignoring the rules and the jargon of cookery books, could be understood by anybody just gifted with a little common sense – a book written as simply as possible, containing not only simple and genuine recipes of French *cuisine bourgeoise*, but recipes of remarkable local dishes, handed down, like Homer's verses, from generation to generation, recipes which had not found their way yet even into French cookery books and were entirely ignored by the chefs of international hotels . . .

Cooking must be natural and exact science was no help. It would be better, I thought, to say to the novice: if you are in doubt, pinch a grain of rice between your fingers, cut a bit off the end of your steak, eat a fried potato – then you will know if they are all right. Common sense, practice and *gourmandise* were the only sound basis.[6]

Boulestin's enthusiasm, and his identification with the contemporary in music and the visual arts, took him straight to the heart of Bloomsbury and the Sitwell circle, who were delighted to find that they could eat well in London and say boo to Victorian and Edwardian vulgarity at the same stroke. At this level of society, more cultivated than the suburban public whose taste in cookery books was different, Boulestin represented the most influential style of the 1930s. Moreover, people who had imbibed his style were later better placed than others in the same income bracket to adapt to the gastronomic opportunism which was forced upon them by the war years. Boulestin's influence is also detectable in the prolific output of the English cookery journalist Ambrose Heath, whose span extended from his *Good Food* (1932), through *Kitchen Front Recipes* (1941) and the *Daily Mirror*'s 'Patsy' cookery strip (very adventurous for a 1940s working class audience in its range and treatment of vegetables), and back to the plenty of the early 1960s. Alas, Heath was by then unable to enjoy the new affluence very much: like many writers of the time, he had forgotten to provide himself with a pension when he signed away his copyrights.[7]

Before the war years were over Boulestin himself was dead. An anglophile who never lost his consciousness of being a missionary in a strange land, he had at least succeeded in clarifying to people who would listen what real French cooking was *not* as well as what it was. He also became the world's first TV cook. But the 1930s also saw the beginnings of a British regional or folk cookery movement, in the work of singular individuals such as Florence White and Dorothy Hartley.

Florence White shared some of the crustiness of the Sussex inn-keepers from whom she was descended, and her English Folk Cookery Association died with her in 1940. She was not an untutored patriot: she spent several years in Paris, wrote a history of the French Revolution, frequented cookery schools, and had an extensive French acquaintance.

A drawing by Edward Bawden

But after she had travelled Britain collecting regional recipes, rather as Cecil Sharp had collected regional tunes, she reached the unexpected but defensible conclusion that 'our kitchen has more in common with America than any other country . . . This is natural, as the foundations of both the English and American kitchens were the same up to 1620.'[8] Florence White's two collections, together with the evocative 1930s kitchen autobiography that opens the Yorkshirewoman Dorothy Hartley's rurally rooted *Food in England* (1954), and Hilda Leyel's eclectically original *The Gentle Art of Cookery* (with Olga Hartley, 1925), all in their different ways illustrate a thoroughly English, unsystematic, but in detail precise continuity, from the pre-technological practice of Georgian and early Victorian homes to country house and farmhouse cookery between the wars.

However, these stirrings of cultural patriotism or catholicity exerted little or no influence upon metropolitan cooking, as the comparable movement led by the gastronome 'Curnonsky' (Maurice Saillant) did in France.[9] The kitchens of London hotels and restaurants were still dominated by French and more particularly Italian survivors of the easy job market that had opened up to them or their fathers and uncles before and after 1900 (see Chapter Five). The modest scale and rural style of the cooking admired by White and Hartley – *Flowers as Food* was one of the former's titles – was incapable of satisfying a twentieth-century mass market, or of affecting the commercial developments in food production and marketing that were already beginning to take off and transform the tastes and habits of post-war generations. Nor were individualists of this kind ever likely to create – or capture – training schools and colleges in the public sector, and set about the daunting task of teaching young would-be professionals to approach with respect and develop with understanding Britain's own pre-industrial tradition of cookery.

Private institutions, such as the London Cordon Bleu cookery school run before 1939 by Rosemary Hume, were more successful organisationally than the 'folk cooks' could ever have been, but constituted in effect an English variant on the French style. They were also confined in practice to young ladies of the leisured classes, whose variable perseverance and self-criticism tended to make the phrase 'Cordon Bleu' as much of a risk as an invitation at the tables over which they subsequently presided. (This is no criticism of Rosemary Hume herself, an exact and professional cook who re-started her school after the war with her friend Constance Spry. The late fruit of their collaboration, *The Constance Spry Cookery Book* [1956] was thick and sound enough to acquire Beeton-like status among brides of the period.)

However, when allowances are made for the necessary modesty of all these enterprises, in a country and a class which regarded serious interest in food as a slightly vulgar eccentricity, it is possible to look back with the hindsight of the kitchen-mad 1980s and pay fair tribute to the 'rescue archaeology' which all these enterprising women did during the Twenties and Thirties on the Englishness of English food. Its time was to come; besides, during the 1940s there must have been people glad enough to find Florence White's more outré recipes for chrysanthemum salad and cowslip cake, even if they did not dare to follow her enthusiasm for L. C. R. Cameron's *Wild Foods of Great Britain* (1917), with its instructions for roasting a hedgehog and grilling a sea-gull.

But all these were the trend-setters, who lived comfortably, wrote books, and read them. The British middle class as a whole knew little about the diet of the labouring masses, though they could make no secret of their own. Professional and mercantile families drew their servants from working-class homes, to prepare food amongst other tasks; they seldom entered homes of this kind themselves unless they had a professional or voluntaristic reason for doing so, and would have been no more likely to enquire the intimate details of domestic economy in the households their Sallys or Bridgets dwelt in when off duty. In 1956, Constance Spry still thought it worth reminding her readers of the 'immensely better and fairer distribution of food among all grades of society' that had taken place. 'Remembering as I do the days of immensely long, boring, wasteful dinners, remembering too the starvation which was all too often at our very doors, I cannot forbear to remind you how much respect ought to be paid to food, how carefully it should be treated, how shameful waste is.'[10]

Among great English nineteenth-century novelists, only Dickens displays a detailed interest in what and how ordinary folk ate. The preoccupations of Thomas Hardy and later D. H. Lawrence, also lay elsewhere. The destructive and widespread malnutrition revealed by B. Seebohm Rowntree in his famous York study *Poverty* (1901) was noted with interest at the time by those drawn to the comparatively new science of social description allied to statistics, and it was one of the formative influences behind Lloyd George's radical budget of 1909. But it came too late to prevent the more generally alarming discovery, nearly twenty years later, that only one man in three of military age in Britain could be described as fit and healthy. By these grim standards, the incidence of actual malnutrition had undoubtedly fallen between the wars, and a much higher proportion of men satisfied Army medical officers in 1939. But the health of working-class women – the chief sufferers from bread-winners' unemployment – was deplorable, and a very substantial section of the population had neither the money nor – more important – the knowledge to acquire for themselves and their children a diet commensurate with the general prosperity of the land they lived in. The dietary historian John Burnett comments:

A nutritionally adequate diet was probably possible in the 1930s for five sixths of the population, but because of ignorance or prejudice, lack of time or lack of facilities, only half the population was able to receive it . . . Sugar consumption was so high in the poorer social classes partly because of their heavy use of cheap jams and syrups and the quantity that went into endless cups of tea: these, together with white bread, margarine and an occasional kipper, were the hallmarks of the poverty-line diet which George Orwell observed in *The Road to Wigan Pier*.[11]

At the other socio-political extreme lie the reminiscent accounts of Petronian excess which Evelyn Waugh, by his own admission, inserted into *Brideshead Revisited* to console himself for the kind of food he was actually eating while writing the novel during the war years.

However, it is as true of the national diet as it is of housing and other aspects of daily living that the 1930s, on other grounds such a dismal decade in British life, represented at least for those in work a substantial advance in nutritional health on conditions in the previous generation.

Most literate people's view of how the Twenties and Thirties ate, at the 'popular' level, is formed by a composite of their own memories, if they are old enough, and George Orwell's vignette of his lodgings in Wigan:

For breakfast you got two rashers of bacon and a pale fried egg, and bread-and-butter which had often been cut overnight and always had thumb-marks on it . . . For dinner there were generally those threepenny steak puddings which are sold ready-made in tins, and boiled potatoes and rice pudding. For tea there was more bread-and-butter and frayed-looking sweet cakes which were probably bought as 'stales' from the baker. For supper there was pale flabby Lancashire cheese and biscuits.[12]*

Orwell's *nostalgie de la boue*, and his nose for the very smell of depressed humanity, never lacked material to work upon in the Thirties, nor would during the Eighties in the right homes and the right places. But reportage so powerful needs to be set against actual working-class narratives, such as those provided by Hornsey railwaymen and Bermondsey housewives to London School of Economics researchers in the same period. Here, for instance, is the wife of an intermittently employed East End docker paid (in a good week) £2.19.0:

My husband has his breakfast, which consists of a cup of tea and bread and butter or dripping, and takes a lunch with him, for he may go to work. I have then to start with the children's breakfast and my own. They may have porridge one day, boiled egg the next, and I have to reverse it according to their wish . . . To get their dinner for 12 o'clock I must dish it up before going to get them from school and place it within two plates in the gas oven, with a very low glimmer so as not to spoil. I find it all right to give them minced meat on Mondays for their dinner, and gravy on Tuesdays. Wednesdays we have just a small meat pudding;

---

* Lancashire cheese took as long to recover from this slight as Cheddar did from its war-time nickname 'mousetrap'. Orwell clearly never tasted a mature farmhouse Lancashire. Neither is the 1980s reader likely to, though for different reasons.

Thursdays, a baked dinner with lamb chops and baked potatoes and cabbage and Yorkshire pudding. Fridays is a day of fish, which depends on which is the best to be had. On Saturday we usually have braised steak and potatoes and cabbage, or else we have liver and bacon. On Sunday I have only a small piece of meat, such as a piece of beef or a small half-shoulder of lamb, with baked potatoes, Yorkshire or suet pudding, with cabbage or greens that are in season. We do not have a large tea on Sundays, perhaps a little watercress or celery, and no supper. I make a very small rice pudding or tapioca or spaghetti each day for after dinner, which makes the children want very little tea, so should I have any milk pudding I warm it for them before they go to bed.

My husband, if at work, is home at 5 o'clock in the evening, then there is his tea. Monday, usually eggs and bacon; Tuesdays, lamb chop; Wednesdays, steak and onions; Thursday may be ham or a little meat left from dinner, and Friday he eats nothing but fish or eggs and cheese.[13]

Clearly this Catholic housewife was what used to be called 'a good manager', and her contemporary counterpart in Belfast – let alone Warsaw – would be unlikely to consider her deprived.

It is also striking, in this and other similar narratives, how strong a hearthstone tradition of actual cooking finds expression. Colour supplement readers and contributors in the 1980s might turn up their noses at the Oxo and Bisto references in these accounts of family eating, but they would be puzzled to know how to make a steamed sponge or suet pudding without referring to their Jane Grigson or Margaret Costa, while it is most unlikely that the Bermondsey housewives possessed a cookery book to consult. In families of the lowest social class, half of them spending less on food than the British Medical Association considered necessary for maintaining proper health, 80 per cent of housewives told the National Food Enquiry in the mid-thirties that they were 'very much' or 'moderately' interested in cooking, but only 15 per cent admitted using a cookery book.[14] Among those who did cook by the book, the most popular choices were those published by Be-Ro (a flour company) and the Gas Company. Even in the middle and upper classes, who took more interest in cookery and cookery books, only the name of Elizabeth Craig,* mentioned by 4 per cent, remotely challenged the ritual obeisance paid by ten times as many respondents to 'Mrs Beeton', whose progressive debasement under successive editors, revisers and

---

* Probably her *Cookery Illustrated and Household Management* (1936), the fat, down-to-earth kitchen manual of my own childhood, more ambitious in content than would appear from the first two photographic plates, illustrating how to use up hard-boiled eggs and cold fish respectively.

enlargers almost from the date of its first publication (1865) may either explain or be explained by the relative stagnation and want of refinement in the indigenous cooking of Britain between 1880 and 1930.

The war years forced more prosperous housewives than Bermondsey ones to learn the old techniques and depend on more modest resources. They had to go foraging for strange foodstuffs in shops they had never cared to explore, and learnt quickly enough how to compose and cook meals for their families after their cooks and kitchen maids had vanished into factories. But the break in mental set was of equal importance. In the early days of the war, middle-class women may have hoped, however vaguely, that not only abundance but also domestic servants would one day return to their kitchens.

However, by the time there was once again abundance of things to cook, their hands had acquired more cunning, and their minds were more open to suggestions about how this abundance might be exploited. A century of employing other people to cook wholesome English dishes for ordinary occasions and mock-French dishes for grand ones had fallen away. The end of an era in English domestic management was signalled by figures in the 1951 Census – the first since 1931 – which disclosed that only 1.2 per cent of private households in Great Britain had one or more domestic servants, compared with 4.8 per cent (England and Wales) in 1931. Not far short of 1 million people, over 90 per cent of them women, formerly occupied below stairs had found more profitable or congenial employment elsewhere: in 1931, there were 1,332,224 women and 78,489 men; in 1951, 509,728 women and 28,933 men. Middle-class houses continued to be cleaned, at least in part, by persons other than their owners. But no longer did these persons live in, or work full time, as cooks and housemaids.

During the war years, the French style which Britons had imitated or envied was less attainable than it had ever been. But its essential spirit had at last made the Channel crossing. British cooks discovered for themselves the doctrine '*rien se perd*', on which bourgeois French and most oriental food management both rest. They learnt that the art of eating well in good times, and at least tolerably in bad ones, is the product of intelligence and application first, and a full larder or a long pocket second.

It was not the Thirties generation themselves but their children who entered into this inheritance in full, partly because the children had been at impressionable ages when this daily battle to prepare edible meals had been fought in their presence, partly because it was in fact the

Fifties before abundance fully returned. Men and women born too late to remember pre-war diets and conventions were naturally the most open to the new range of influence (discussed in Chapter Five) which brought into our cookery what had always been our boast in other fields: our prowess on the global market as borrowers, opportunists, cultural *saladiers*.

But when the grocers' shelves were emptied and the siege economy took shape in 1940, this development could hardly have been foreseen.

CHAPTER TWO
The seven lean years

A partir de 1940, les Anglais sont restés seuls . . . avec leur cuisine.
Jean Cocteau

To give friends in foreign parts some idea of our meals: Meat ration lasts only for three evening meals. Cannot be made to go further, that is, Saturday, Sunday and Monday. Tuesday and Wednesday I cook a handful of rice, dodged up in some way with curry or cheese. But the cheese ration is so small there is little left. Thursday I have an order with the Dairy for a pound of sausage. These make do for Thursday, Friday and part of Saturday. No taste much of sausage, but are of soya bean flour. We just pretend they are the real thing. A little fish would help, but there are queues for it. All rather monotonous, but we are not hungry, and the authorities have done well for us, we consider. Vere Hodgson, *Few Eggs and No Oranges* (1976): entry for 7 May 1944 from her 1940–45 diary.

Painters learn to draw the fleshy curves of the human figure in action and repose by studying the bone structure underneath, and on this analogy the 1940s are the skeleton which the observer of contemporary British eating habits and choices does well to inspect. The 1980s abundance in shops and markets of almost every foodstuff that plane can fly and money buy may or may not last for ever, or even into the next century. It also blurs what dearth revealed about national and individual tastes and priorities on 'the kitchen front' during the last three or four years of the 1939–45 war and the first three or four years of peace. (The biblical 'seven lean years' of the chapter heading need not be taken too literally, but it is closer to reality than the dates of the war itself: severe rationing was slow to arrive and very slow to disappear.)

Even at its leanest, our wartime diet went well beyond bare essentials. It was dull rather than deleterious. The cupboard looked bare to André Simon and Louis Golding of the Wine and Food Society, who compiled in 1944 a reminiscent anthology called *We Shall Eat and Drink Again*. At this period British housewives went for months without seeing a lemon, queued for hours in hopes of a few onions, and had to cook meals their families would enjoy on a weekly ration of a single shell egg and half a pound of butter, margarine and cooking fat (in varying proportions) per head. Present-day consumption of the same things – 3.5 eggs and just under 10 ounces of fats – is a somewhat unfair comparison, because so much is now bought by so many people ready-baked or otherwise processed. Besides, we now eat 35 ounces of meat a week, which is more than twice the wartime level (ingeniously rationed by price, not weight).

But it is at least clear that rations of this kind compared rather well with the diet of unemployed men and their families in the early 1930s, with the diet of Germany in the early years of the post-war Occupation, and indeed with the diet of families wholly dependent on social security benefits in the 1980s. Historians and nutritionists are agreed that for three prime reasons – scientific knowledge, efficient administration, and a newly-discovered national sense of equity – Britain as a whole was more healthily fed during the 1940s than ever before (or since, some might add). Even supplies of fat, in the technical sense that includes consumption derived from milk, cheese, meat and fish as well as actual fats and oils, exceeded during the war years the 1909–13 level, though it fell some 30 per cent below the 1934–8 level, which was regained in 1950–4.[1] Sugar consumption, too, was restricted during the Second World War, but it fell only as far as the 1880–1928 level. Nutritionists who regard the five-fold increase in sugar consumption that took place between the 1840s and the 1940s as a physiological calamity were depressed at the British people's failure to recognise in the longer term what was good for it: by 1954, sugar consumption had again surpassed the 1934–8 level. (More recently, it has levelled off at about 11 ounces, above the wartime level but well below 1930s consumption.)

All this, however, merely serves as a reminder that nutritional well-being and psychological perception of eating better or worse are often two entirely different things. During the war, grasslands were put under the plough and food imports drastically reduced, to save merchant shipping tonnage for essential purposes that justified the risk of the voyages. This curtailed severely the kinds of food most appreciated by those who could afford them: 'red meat', as the carnivorous Winston Churchill called it, fish, butter, cream, and imported fruit, fresh or dried, along with palate stimulants such as blue cheese and anchovies. (Garlic did not at this date form a noticeable part of the British diet, even though it would have been quite possible to cultivate it domestically.)

The percentage loss of such foods was clearly much higher for the most prosperous and articulate sections of the community than it was for many urban working-class homes, which had been accustomed to bread and scrape during the Depression, and in many cases for much longer than that.[2]

Politicians, administrators, and scientists involved in the supply of food after the declaration of war faced a daunting task for which, surprisingly, they were rather better prepared than their counterparts in defence and diplomacy had been. As an American scholar observes, British politicians and administrators began the First World War 'with a mystical, unanalytical, laissez-faire belief which for a time kept them from taking advantage of the assistance that conscription, rationing and other forms of control might have made to their war effort'. But by 1939 Britain had become 'a nation much better able to understand the scientific, economic and administrative problems involved in a food shortage'. The result, according to the same author, was that 'the health of the British people actually improved during World War II'.[3]

The nature and quality of the scientific influences that achieved this result can be seen from a series of Royal Institution lectures on *The Nation's Larder*,[4] arranged by Sir William Bragg and delivered during the military reverses of 1940. Major-General Sir Robert McCarrison demonstrated that laboratory rats fed on the diet of a healthy north Indian tribe thrived, while there was disease, discontent and eventually cannibalism among a group of rats fed 'on a diet in common use by many people in this country: a diet consisting of white bread and margarine, tinned meat, vegetables boiled with soda, cheap tinned jam, tea, sugar, and a little milk: a diet which does not contain enough milk, milk products, green leaf vegetables and wholemeal bread for proper nutrition' (p. 24). Sir John Orr (later Lord Boyd-Orr) showed that even an iron ration, made up mostly of home-produced foods, could improve markedly on this latter diet. Both these and other contributors reveal the element of idealism for which so many scientists and doctors of the time were conspicuous:

The war will blow away a great many nineteenth-century ideas of the supreme importance of trade and money-making. We may assume that the post-war Government in dealing with food will have as its objective the welfare of the whole population. Supply will be regulated, not by trade interests, but according to the needs of the people, and in price-fixing, the price of essential foods will be fixed in accordance with the purchasing power of the poorest (pp. 63–4).

Sir John Orr's expectations read oddly now, in a hard-hearted decade which has recovered a taste for non-interventionist nineteenth-century economics. But his hopes were in part confirmed by successive post-war governments, which continued food subsidies and a cheap food policy until accession to the Treaty of Rome transferred the direct benefits from consumers to producers. However, by this time full employment had diminished the need to bend the laws of the market in favour of the British poor. No less important, the centralised communications of wartime, and a corporate focus on the wellbeing of the whole community, had done much – though in the long run, not enough – to improve popular nutritional understanding. This unexpected development was due above all to two men who might otherwise never have met each other, nor exerted comparable national influence, Sir Jack Drummond and Sir Fred Marquis (Lord Woolton). The consumption patterns, and to a remarkable extent the actual tastes, of the 1940s were shaped by this alliance between a fundamental scientist with a gust for food and drink and a rare gift for popular exposition, and a Liverpool retail business-man with a social conscience, whose own communicator's touch made him Churchill's most effective Minister on the Home Front during the war, and a famously shrewd chairman of the Conservative Party after it.

Outside a comparatively small circle, Drummond's fame was post-humous. His wartime role as the apostle of the best food for bad times only became widely known in August 1952, when with his second wife and collaborator (Anne Wilbraham) and their daughter he encamped for the night near the Dominici family farm at Lurs, Haute Provence, and was savagely murdered 'by a mad Italian farmer'. (The phrase is that of André Simon, unable to confer the name of Frenchman on the monster who had butchered his friends.)[5] By training a nutritional biochemist, Drummond's experimental work on butter and margarine substitutes and on infant feeding had earned him a biochemistry chair at the age of thirty-one. In 1939 the couple published *The Englishman's Food*, a 500-page pioneer study of the British diet since the Middle Ages. 'Small, neat, sprightly and gay,' as his biographer H. M. Sinclair called him,*[6] he was summoned in the second month of the war to advise the Ministry of Food, and the force of his internal memoranda on the application of recent nutritional knowledge to wartime diet, especially bread, had him confirmed as the Ministry's chief scientific adviser before the arrival of Lord Woolton as Minister in April 1940. History, science and personal experience had convinced Drummond that if a

* Not 'gay' in the 1980s sense, of course.

basic intake of essential protective foods was ensured, it mattered little what else was eaten. He had seen what took place when the uncooked, nutrient-rich 'Oslo health dinners' devised by Schiotz for Norwegian schools were given to East End children in the 1930s. One specific ambition of Drummond's, realised in full after his death, was expressed in his own contribution to the series of public lectures already mentioned:

I believe the time is coming when two types of bread will be on sale in every baker's shop. One will be baked from 80 to 85 per cent extraction flour, or even, perhaps, wholemeal; the other from the ordinary white flour we have to-day. People will buy some of each, eating the one as a health-giving food and the other when they feel they want a change. But, if this is to happen, we must get rid of the extraordinary idea that brown breads and wholemeal breads are luxuries for which a higher price can be charged.[7]

Drummond's luck, and Britain's, was that these lines of thought interwove with the mind of the incoming Minister of Food. Sir Fred Marquis, created Lord Woolton to give him a seat in Parliament, had had experience of wartime supply administration in the First World War, and as chairman of Lewis's of Liverpool he was one of the most powerful retailers in the land. But experience in the Liverpool Settlement before 1914 had convinced him that rickets, dental decay and other diseases of malnutrition and neglect could and should be prevented. He had also had the advantage of a scientific education – most unusual among Tory Ministers of the time – and he considered that this made him more open to the dietary advisers who calculated all the calories and vitamins needed for different age and occupational groups: the services, heavy manual workers, children, babies, pregnant and nursing mothers.

'That was large-scale and all-embracing planning, and I determined to use the powers I possessed to stamp out the diseases that arose from malnutrition, especially those among children.' Woolton's political skills provided the package for the policy. 'Under the force of necessity people will stand rationing during war-time, but it is no use telling them that they are going to be scientifically fed, because they at once begin to feel that they are really the victims of bureaucracy.'[8] If a conventional bonehead from the shires had been appointed to the Ministry of Food, it is a fair guess that the British people would have ended the war fed, no doubt, but discontented, as they afterwards became when the privations of peace had to be explained to them by a Labour Minister, John Strachey, whom they suspected of being 'too clever by half'.

The alliance of Woolton and Drummond (reinforced by the prune-like voice of the Radio Doctor, Charles Hill, another success in postwar Conservative politics), ensured that whatever it was prudent to explain was explained; and that whatever humour could be found in the situation was duly extracted. Woolton, according to Drummond, 'invariably balanced evidence and arguments on the psychological side against the recommendation of the scientists.' Hence the Minister's determination to keep rationing simple and confine it to goods whose supply could be guaranteed, with a safety margin in ample quantities of unrationed bread and potatoes ('I knew that if we had to ration bread my plans would have failed'). Hence his eager adoption of the 'points' system which one of his administrators, Martin Roseveare, borrowed from the Germans (a detail not disclosed to the British public) and which gave housewives an element of choice by establishing 'a sort of stock exchange' in such luxuries as sardines and sultanas, too scarce to be distributed in bulk as a ration-book entitlement. Hence his personal approach to Gert and Daisy (Elsie and Doris Waters) to persuade them to create sketches and songs for their music hall tours that would make people laugh about food rationing: 'Please leave my butter alone.' Hence, most illuminatingly, the care he took under the broadcaster Howard Marshall's tutelage in preparing his radio talks:

I realised – and I believe this to be the secret of good broadcasting – that my audience was not the aggregate of the public who were listening but the detail of the individual in front of the domestic receiving set. In fact, I always kept a picture in front of my mind of the man in a cottage house, sitting without a collar, with slippers on, at the end of the day's work with children playing on the rug, with his wife washing up in an adjoining room with the door open: that was my audience – and it was interrupted by a ring on the front-door bell, and a visitor arriving in the middle of my broadcast. If I was fortunate, and successful, the man said, 'Sit down and shut up; we are listening to Woolton.'[9]

This was the team that sold the British people the 85 per cent extraction National Loaf, whose healthiness was belied by its greyish colour,[*][10] and Woolton Pie, which Woolton's Liverpool friend Sir Sydney Jones described at a public meeting as 'looking on the outside

---

* 'White' flour normally represents about 72 per cent extraction: that is, 28 per cent of the original grain has been sifted off, including the highly nutritious germ as well as the bran. If the extraction rate is raised to 85 per cent, the calcium, iron and vitamin elements in bread are vastly increased, because some of the germ is allowed through the sieve. But it tends to look grey because of the bran also admitted. 'Wholemeal' bread represents at least 90 per cent extraction.

exactly like a steak and kidney pie, and on the inside just like a steak and kidney pie – without the steak and kidney'.[11] All the power of the Whitehall information machine was harnessed to tell housewives through radio chats and newspaper advertisements how to substitute potatoes for meat, turn surplus bread into rusks, use peapods for soup, make dried eggs behave like shell ones, and above all how to cook or make salads of green vegetables: it had been Drummond the nutritionist who wanted the vitamin C preserved, and Drummond the member of the Wine and Food Society who remarked 'Britain grows the best vegetables in the world – but does the worst cooking of them.'

In macro-economic terms, the success of all this effort is best measured on the supply side, where the credit belongs to British agriculture as well as to British food administration and processing: in 1939 the United Kingdom was importing annually 29.3 million tons of food, rather more than half its total consumption; by the end of the war, it was importing less than 10 million tons without serious diminution of food values. Apart from the vast increase in home production, shipping tonnage was saved by elementary – but commercially upsetting – processes of dehydration and compression. Fresh tropical fruit was confined to oranges and a few lemons; fruit for import was dried rather than tinned; carcases from the southern hemispheres were telescoped to save space or boned at source to save weight: no wonder housewives after the war had to re-learn what parts of what animal they had been eating.

But from the consumer's point of view, the principal influence on diet and taste was rationing itself. In a sense, as has already been suggested, it is inappropriate to speak of 'war-time' rationing. True, whereas in the 1914–18 war the introduction of rationing schemes was put off till the last moment, endangering the security of the nation and the health of the population, in 1939–45 rationing could be brought in with little delay. Munich, in this as in other respects, had served as a warning, and just as well, because the Stationery Office had let it be known that it would take six months merely to *print* 45 million ration books, without allowing for planning and distribution time. As it was, however, the Ministry of Food's predecessor, the Food (Defence Plans) Department, had obtained permission to print ration books as early as July 1937, and by August 1939 the books had been printed and deposited in dumps round the country.

But the 'phony war' was as phony in food consumption as it was in actual hostilities: butter, sugar, bacon and ham were not rationed until

8 January 1940, four months after war was declared. Meat followed in March, the month before Woolton replaced W. S. Morrison as Minister, and although Woolton came to be nicknamed 'Squirrel' by cartoonists for his policy of 'putting something in the cupboard' against days when supplies might fail, he thought it prudent to wait until July before rationing tea, cooking fats and margarine. By this time, Dunkirk had been evacuated, France had fallen, and the Battle of Britain was in full swing. The worst impact of rationing was felt after the war rather than during it, though by then the fear that matters might get worse had been lifted.

The time lag before shortages and the sheer boredom of wartime diet began to be felt is vividly reflected in the cookery books of the period. For instance, Susan Strong's *'Feed the Brute!' or Cookery for the Million*, was probably started before the war, then finished and published in 1942. It is a general cookery book, technically sound and quite imaginative in spite of its popular approach. It specifies without reserve the egg yolks, lemon juice and ground almonds needed to make this recipe or that. The only concession to the times was made by the publisher, who clearly took fright as 1942 wore on and printed an optimistic blurb: 'There are excellent recipes including several which will be valuable in wartime and which offer very good food, although with limited materials.'

The *Daily Express Wartime Cookery Book* had the distinction of passing through the press rather more rapidly than the ration books to which it served as a footnote: the initial edition is dated 1 November 1939. But as befitted the newspaper that had told its readers that there would be no war, optimism was unabated:

With an allowance of $\frac{1}{4}$ lb of butter, $\frac{1}{4}$ lb of bacon, and $\frac{3}{4}$ lb sugar per head per week, and other food unrationed, war time catering should not prove difficult for the economical housewife. Butter is a very valuable food and it is a relief to know that every human being in this country will be able to have at least $\frac{1}{2}$ oz of butter a day.

Ambrose Heath (see page 8) who had published early in 1939 a book called *Open Sesame*, entirely devoted to tinned foods, revised if for the 1943 season under the title, *Good Dishes from Tinned Foods*. He included corned beef and 'fresh Newfoundland tinned cod', which his middle-class readers might previously have overlooked in the immense range of canned goods available to the British public in 1939 (see Appendix One). His list, 'by no means comprehensive', includes boiled mutton, tripe and onions, mixed grill (*sic*), chop suey, enchiladas, samphire, and béarnaise sauce, among about 500 other items.

With Irene Veal's *Recipes of the 1940s*, finished in 1943 and published in 1944, the characteristic temper of the decade is finally reached. The author dedicates her book 'to Lord Woolton, who taught British women to cook wisely' and continues in her preface, with a Victorian affection for underlinings and an abiding assumption – shared by almost all her contemporaries – that cooking was woman's work: 'Never before have the British people been so *wisely* fed or British women so *sensibly* interested in cooking. We are acquiring an almost French attitude of mind regarding our food and its careful preparation, and the demand for good and practical recipes is continually increasing.'

This is possibly the first indication in print that the Ministry of Food's intervention in the affairs of hearth and home was stoking a cultural revolution that had to take place before Elizabeth David, Jane Grigson, and other continentally-minded cookery writers of the post-war years could find their audience. Besides, Irene Veal was consciously compiling facts and recipes for the record, 'to serve the dual purpose of being useful, now, to all those whose work it is to buy and cook food; as well as to serve in future years as a kind of record of how we cooked and ate during the Second Great War'.

She therefore included accounts of the catering practice of major institutions such as the services, the Bank of England, various hospitals and the BBC as well as recipes from restaurants and housewives. The BBC's pudding recipes, for example, derive from two different sources, because 'the staff at Broadcasting House and 200 Oxford Street will not look at' recipes used at Bush House 'where the foreign element is very strong and decidedly different things are preferred'. Compare, for example, chocolate malt sponge from the first source with potinka from the second:

Chocolate malt sponge   This very pleasant pudding calls for ½ lb flour, ¼ lb sugar and margarine, 2 ozs dried egg, 1 teaspoon vinegar, 1 dessertspoon baking powder. Chocolate spread.

Cream butter and sugar and add egg previously reconstituted. Sift in flour and baking powder, and last stir in vinegar. Mix to a soft creamy consistency and bake in sandwich tins or in a flat baking tin for 8–10 minutes. Turn out, spread with chocolate to which a little evaporated tinned milk has been added and serve. Cold, this can be used as a cake.

Potinka   Take one layer of thin pastry and line with it a baking tin. Spread with some semolina or ground rice cooked until it is creamy and flavoured with vanilla, almond, or any flavouring preferred. Cover this with another layer of thin pastry, brush well with egg mixture and sprinkle with sugar. Before baking in a good moderate oven, mark into squares. Cut whilst still hot and before serving. The pastry should be deep golden brown.[12]

From mid-1940 onwards, the belt was gradually tightened. Tea rationing was more severely felt than it would be today, and this check to the traditional working-class (or self-consciously Bennite) mug of heavily sweetened tea 'strong enough to trot a mouse on' not only began to turn many people (women especially) away from taking sugar in their tea, but also made it easier to sell the coffee extracts which in one form or another have been mass market beverages ever since. (Instant coffee powder represented by the Nescafé brand had been launched before the war but did not reappear on the British market till the 1950s. The coffee substitute of the 1940s was a bottled essence called Camp, which British, and especially Midlands, taste favoured: continentals preferred, if they could not acquire actual coffee beans, ground chicory and roasted acorns.) Coffee itself was simply not important enough to ration: in 1944, when the Americans at SHAEF indented for British supplies to help feed Europe after liberation, the amount of coffee they requested exceeded Britain's entire stocks at the time.

In July 1940 caterers were forbidden to ice cakes, even for weddings; in October, the manufacture, sale and service of cream were forbidden. In successive steps, the meat ration was reduced until by March 1941 caterers were allowed only 25 per cent of their January 1940 supply. Even this was less than it seemed, because pork and offal, originally excluded, were now included in the allowance. Sweets and chocolates were not formally rationed until July 1942, but had long been hard to obtain. In Irene Veal's words:

During the year from June 1941 to May 1942 the full meaning of the much used and discussed term 'Austerity' became apparent in the diet of the nation as a whole. The taste of the entire nation has had to be turned away, as smoothly as possible, from its conservative ways, and the meat-eating English taught to satisfy their appetites, and feed their nerves without doing violence to their palates, on foods which they have not previously eaten from choice.[13]

This may seem a slight exaggeration in view of the actual diminutions on pre-war consumption that are recorded. By January 1943, subject to minor fluctuations, the low plateau of rationing had been reached, and for adults was as shown in Table 1.

TABLE I

	Ration		Average pre-war consumption
Fresh meat	1s 2d	(equivalent to about 1 lb meat including bone)	1¾ lb
Bacon and ham	4 oz		5½ oz
Sugar	8 oz		1 lb
Cheese	3 oz	No direct comparison	12 oz (all milk solids excluding butter)
Fat	8 oz	(2 oz butter, 2 oz cooking fat, rest margarine)	10½ oz
Sweets and chocolate	3 oz		6½ oz

However, this table omits the still more severe restriction of milk and eggs, except for special categories such as children and pregnant women. Besides, the absolute reduction in food quantity was for many easier to bear than the reduction in variety, and the disappearance from the shops of most of the items that in the hands of a good cook could 'rescue' a dish based on inadequate materials: spices, anchovies, blue cheese, lemons. The points system went a long way to alleviate monotony and discontent, and also helped to prevent aimless hoarding. But opportunism in the market, husbandry of temporarily available foods, and home preservation of seasonal ones became the mark of a good manager; the nation of shopkeepers had become the nation of queue formers, and as cartoonists were quick to observe, people joining the queue often discovered that the back of it had no idea what commodity the front of it was queueing for, but cherished a touching hope that it might be worth their while.

Nothing better illustrates the difficulties of rationing schemes, alike for producers, administrators, and consumers, than the history of the Ministry of Food's attempt to control eggs.[14] Eggs are emotional, as every mother is reminded when a child declines to scrape to the bottom of the shell. Without being essential to a balanced diet, they are indispensable to almost all European cookery above the Boy Scout level, performing both as aerators and emulsifiers. Again, they represent – and certainly represented during the war – one of the dividing lines between city and countryside, where the sale of fresh eggs at the farm gate had been a traditional perquisite of the farmer's wife. The writer well remembers during the early years of the war the arrival of 'Leominster eggs' in his parents' Birmingham flat, delivered by visitors from their former home in Herefordshire. Later on, when this supply had ceased, it was a question of waiting for the annual holiday on a Welsh seaside farm to recapture the dawn-of-the-world taste of the new-laid eggs that the hens had secreted in hayloft and hedgerow. In the country, eggs were dependent on the unpredictability of the layers, but there was always hope. Similarly, everyone who could keep a few chickens in his backyard and contrive to feed them on household scraps could feel himself a countryman, even if he lived in the back streets of Oldham.

But it was this very cottage-industry feature of eggs, and the backyard backdrop to the large-scale egg-packing and importing industry, that worried the Ministry throughout the war, at least until officials were partially rescued from their predicament by a technological windfall, American spray-dried egg. The convolutions of egg control need not be pursued in detail, but for some time the Ministry made the mistake of defying the elementary economic principle that controlling the price of a commodity is unsatisfactory unless you also control its supply. Late in 1939, the Treasury sanctioned the proposed import of 1,200,000 boxes of eggs from Argentina with the revealing stipulation that a 'substantial proportion' would be made available for 'the poorer classes': at this period, the social inequalities of the previous decade had not yet been subsumed in more generalised misery. Later, Lord Woolton himself showed signs of the contrary pressures he laboured under. Fortified by his scientific advisers, he told a press conference that eggs were not regarded as essential food. But he also shared the Prime Minister's strong personal interest in eggs: 'We do want eggs and chickens as well as wheat. And they pick up at least a good part of their living.' But by 1941 the Ministry's Committee on the Distribution of Unrationed Foodstuffs was naming eggs as one of the principle causes of public complaint, and seeking to divert supplies from caterers with long purses to expectant mothers with short ones. The Committee itself had clearly been leant upon. Lord Woolton:

For a long time I withstood the appeals to ration eggs. It was, however, my practice to send people to stand in queues and listen to the conversations of the shoppers. By that means I got an unprejudiced account of the reactions to rationing. I became very disturbed to receive reports from wide sources that there were people in the queues who were agitators and who were trying to create dissatisfaction among the public, using the shortage of eggs and the wide inequalities of their distribution as a justification for complaint. I believed that this was a political agitation that emanated from a foreign source.[15]

(This was, of course, the period before the Nazi–Soviet pact was broken by Hitler's invasion of Russia, and the patriotism of the British Communist Party was more than ordinarily in doubt.)

Woolton in his turn was leant upon by Churchill: 'Amid your many successes in your difficult field, the egg distribution scheme seems to be an exception. I hear complaints from many sides, and the scarcity of eggs is palpable.'[16]

Egg rationing duly arrived, but in its zeal to stamp out the lurking possibility of an extensive black market in eggs, the Ministry had devised what came to be known as 'the twelve bird dividing line', above which small poultry owners had to register with an egg packing station as their sole outlet for sales. The press was unfriendly; moreover, it was not in a headline of his *Daily Express* but in a departmental minute that Lord Beaverbrook, as Minister of State, used the eye-catching phrase 'Small poultry owners are under the harrow'. The cut-off number was raised to fifty birds, and it gradually dawned on Whitehall that there was a difference between saying 'If you sell eggs, you must sell them to the Ministry', and saying, 'If you keep hens, you must not eat their eggs without Food Office permission.' The rueful comments recorded in Hammond's history tell their own tale of a Civil Service in more or less orderly retreat: 'We are not treating the smaller man favourably because he merits any special consideration but simply because the task of getting our hands on him is beyond our capacity', and 'by no administrative means can you ensure that a producer adheres to any ration requirement. All he needs to do is to crack a few eggs and he is past you.'

Once egg control arrived, the vast majority of consumers were wholly dependent on the Ministry's distribution, and sod's law condemned this to accidental odium right at the outset. The first allocation of controlled eggs included tens of millions supplied from the United States under Lend-Lease. There existed no 'trade channel' for this purpose, since Britain did not import American eggs before the war, and the cargo included millions of unmarked eggs that had been cold-stored since the previous December and left on the quayside in a New York summer for a week or two awaiting shipping space, without being 'candled' and repacked. On arrival in the United Kingdom they were sold under the new control structure at the same price as English new-laid, and the doubtful – or worse – eggs permanently convinced the public that the bureaucratic hold-up of home-produced supplies in packing stations was to blame. Hammond claims that there was 'no difficulty' in disposing of the rogue eggs as 'cooking eggs' at a reduced price: the reaction of cooks to this description can be imagined. Lord Woolton's memoirs later let out of the bag what had actually happened:

By the time the eggs arrived and the hatches were opened, the stench was unbearable. Extra money had to be paid to the dockers to get the eggs out of the ships . . . Public feeling apart, there remained the practical question of what to do with some millions of rotten eggs. I arranged in Liverpool to transport truck-loads of these eggs secretly from the docks to a place called Skelmersdale, where there was a disused mine; I was told that quietly – and irreverently – they were dropped down the mine.[17]

Lord Woolton wondered what future archaeologists would make of this colossal quantity of egg shells in a small community. But Skelmersdale later became a New Town for Catholic Merseyside, a suitable site perhaps for a ceremonial egg sacrifice.

Since poultry feedstuffs were considered an uneconomic use of scarce grains, the shell egg allocation for non-priority consumers remained at somewhat less than one per head per week for most of the war and its aftermath. Even so, the price was controlled, and eggs were heavily subsidised: consumers who paid 1s 4d a dozen in 1944 would have paid twice this sum in a free market, and black or grey market transactions recorded suggested that uncontrolled eggs fetched 5s 4d.

More cheerfully, however, the egg supply situation was rescued in part by the Department of Scientific and Industrial Research, which since 1940 had evolved at the Ministry of Food's request a technique for spray-drying eggs which could be adopted in American factories, and save 19/20ths of the shipping space that would have been taken up by poultry feedstuffs if the attempt had been made to produce an equivalent quantity of shell eggs in Britain. The Ministry of Food's research kitchen considered that under two ounces of dried egg powder (nominally three eggs) equalled in the cooking two shell ones, which weigh about five ounces but take up vastly more space, especially when packed for a sea voyage.[18] Dried egg, for all its want of unctuosity and its limited powers of aeration, was used for everything from omelettes to mayonnaise, though it required more patience and skill in the reconstitution than some housewives and most institutional cooks possessed. 'When you scrambled dried eggs and dropped them, they bounced,' one contemporary remembers. But this development enabled the Ministry ultimately to claim that total national consumption of 'egg solids' exceeded that before the war.

A further long shadow cast by the operations of the wartime Ministry of Food fell on the food adulteration industry, which in the straitened circumstances of the early 1940s naturally began to dream of nineteenth-century ingenuities like those recorded in 1820 by Frederic Accum, a courageous scientific chemist resident in Soho at the time.[19] True, 'death in the pot' – Accum's phrase – had long since vanished: no one in the 1940s was contaminating cheese with red lead, or custards with laurel essence, or whitening the National loaf with alum. But already in the winter of 1940–1 you could buy milk substitutes made of flour, salt, and baking powder and sold at 5s a pound (this was before 'National Dried' milk arrived on the market), onion substitutes 'containing merely water and a smell', and egg substitutes made of rice flour or cornflour, colouring matter and baking powder. (This last product had been sold even before the war, which casts further light on the Treasury's remark quoted above about shell eggs for the poorest classes.)

In food as in patent medicines, it had been (and still is) an uphill struggle to ensure that the British public was at least told on the label what it had chosen to swallow. As late as August 1941, officials were still taking the line, apropos of providing ingredients for egg substitutes, that it was not the Ministry's business to enforce the law of foods and drugs (which was based on the 1938 Act, administered by the Ministry of Health).

However, in October a Substitutes Order was made and progressively strengthened by further Orders (against some political opposition) over the ensuing three years, as the opportunities for evasion by relabelling came to light. By the end of the war, Britain had the beginnings of a system based upon the practice, generally held to be superior, of the United States Food and Drugs Administration: ready-packed foods were henceforth to be labelled with the name and address of the manufacturer or packer, the 'common or usual' name of the product, a list of the ingredients, and the minimum quantity by weight or measure, of contents present.

Thus, in January 1944, a local authority's suggestion that something should be done about a product optimistically labelled 'cream custard' led the Ministry to review custard and blancmange labels voluntarily supplied by manufacturers. As a result the trade agreed to delete any pictures or references that might mislead the buyer into supposing that these preparations (composed mainly of maize starch) contained cream or eggs.

Hammond comments:

The small group within the Ministry, headed by its Manufactured Foods Adviser, who had from 1941 worked steadily, ingeniously and unremittingly to put teeth into the 1938 Food and Drugs Act, had realised from the first the outstanding opportunity the Ministry's very existence gave them of making a permanent and long overdue step forward in food and drugs legislation. . . . When the larger measures of food control should come to an end, the Ministry's reforms in the field of standards and labelling would stand out as a solid gain, unobtrusively snatched from the years of austerity.[20]

It was not the fault of these officials that with the post-war rise of the food technologists, these very labels concealed almost as much from the ordinary consumer by their accuracy as they had earlier concealed by falsification or silence: who knew the precise taste or function of glycerine monostearate in a block of ice cream, or could define comminuted orange and guess at the amount a soft drink contained?* Accelerating technical mastery means that the battle for more informative labelling is never finally won, and Frederic Accum was merely the first, not the last, analyst to realise how complaisant the British public is about what it permits itself to eat or drink. Judging by some of the products that are unabashedly sold 'as advertised on TV', and swallowed for their colour rather than their taste, prospects for the national diet in 1984 would be markedly poorer if the Defence (Sale of Food) Regulations had not come into force forty years earlier, along with other Orders making it illegal to market any food not complying with the standards prescribed for it.

It is hard to be certain, but it is at least probable that very little,

---

* As later chapters show, the rise of food and drink technology in Britain evoked various consumer responses that were sometimes forceful enough to drag legislation in their train. Readers of the magazine *Which?* (founded along with Consumers' Association itself in 1957) were introduced in September 1968 to the complexities of soft drink terminology. Comminution, it was explained, is a process in which the entire orange is reduced to a liquid and strained, and in a product called 'orange drink' this substance must form 10 per cent by volume of the bottled liquid before dilution. Orange squash must contain 25 per cent of orange fruit juice before dilution; 'orangeade' need not contain any fruit at all. See Derek Cooper, *The Beverage Report* (1970) pp. 55–6. More recent operations of an uncontrolled market in the manufacture of sausages and other meat products, mentioned on page 143–4, reinforce the point that consumer victories in these fields are seldom permanent.

proportionately, of the nation's food stocks went astray during the war years on to the black market. It was different later on, when the East End wide boys had been demobbed from khaki anonymity, but the very modesty and innocence of people's reminiscences of the time in print and voice suggest, among other things, want of opportunity. We were also then a law-abiding people. Theodora FitzGibbon, a London bohemian who later became a professional cookery writer, made up in street-smartness for what she lacked in money at this time:

Chicken was expensive and kept 'under the counter' (a current phrase) for good customers. Technically all offal was free (off ration) but as the war progressed it was difficult to find. When I remarked to the butcher that all the animals seemed to be born without tongues, tails, hearts, kidneys, livers or balls, he winked at me, a great arm went under the counter, and he flung up a half-frozen oxtail. I had never cooked one before, but even today I can taste the thick gravy and see our grease-spattered lips as we chewed on the bones. Unrationed rabbit was the salvation for many people in a low-income group . . .

Frying was quite difficult, as lard was rationed and olive oil only obtainable at a chemist on a doctor's prescription, so sometimes we were reduced to liquid paraffin. At least we didn't suffer from constipation. Another 'filler' was pasta, which could be bought freshly made in Soho; rice disappeared as the war went on, and even in Chinese restaurants spaghetti cut to look like rice, or pearl barley, was served. [It even had a name, 'soyaghetti'. – Ed.]

And again, later: 'When the horseflesh shop opened in Chelsea Manor Street not only the dogs profited but also ourselves, for I had no scruples about making enormous horse-liver pâtés and jellied tongues . . . A rook pie one day was eagerly devoured.'[21]

Other characters who flit through the pages of this autobiography prove that the chances were better if you belonged to the London catering scene itself. Indeed, the shortages and stratagems of 1939–45 greatly accelerated the demoralisation of the continental craftsmen who cooked by the *Repertoire*, and for whom nothing but the best had been good enough, whatever the cost in materials and labour. The painter Anthony Green's grandfather, who had been sous-chef to Escoffier at the Carlton, held that cuisine came to an end in 1914. He had a friend who in 1939–45 was chef to one of the military clubs in Pall Mall. 'This man had been on the steal so efficiently for so long that his basement at home looked like Fortnum & Mason: throughout the war, he had only to reach out his hand to pluck a tin of peaches or pâté de foie gras from the shelf.'[22]

Caterers, as such, were dominated by the effect of two Ministry of

Food Orders made in the early years of the war. One was the Food (Restrictions on Meals in Establishments) Order (February 1941). This put caterers on a parity with each other and with domestic consumers for amounts of rationed goods allocated per meal served, limited the number of courses that might be served, and set for all restaurants, high, middle or low, a five shilling cost limit on meals, which tempted back into the Ritz and similar hostelries a number of distressed gentlefolk who had never expected to be invited there again.

The other regulation was the Local Authorities (Community Kitchens) and Sale of Food in Public Air Raid Shelters Order (January 1941) which made local authorities responsible for setting up community feeding centres. It was this last phrase that led to Churchill's famous minute to Lord Woolton (21 March 1941): 'I hope the term "communal feeding centres" is not going to be adopted. It is an odious expression, suggestive of Communism and the workhouse. I suggest you call them "British Restaurants". Everybody associates the word "restaurant" with a good meal, and they may as well have the name if they cannot get anything else.'[23] By May 1941 800 had been opened in 176 towns, serving hot meals for under a shilling.

These Orders may seem a choice example of British hypocrisy. To relate them to the extracts from literature of the time which close this chapter, it can hardly be pretended that there was any genuine equality of opportunity between the Ivy and the beige restaurant of Swindon, as they are described in Frances Partridge's war diary, or between the *saumoneau* at L'Ecu de France and the sausage toad which Colonel Bogus disdained. But closer inspection of the recipe for braised salmon trout reveals how little of its contents were actually rationed: not the fish, the faintly improbable crayfish, the herbs and the vegetables. The miracle would have depended on the restaurant's superior access to restricted but unrationed goods such as onions, and on its capacious cellars. Restaurants and hotels of this type learnt to cover the overheads not met by the five shilling meals by charging customers well over the odds for wine (a custom that long survived the war in almost all British catering establishments) or – a Ritz reminiscence this – making crêpes Suzette compulsory at a high premium for the liqueur employed. Game was unrationed too, when cartridges could be spared from the operations of Dad's Army, and substitutions elsewhere were ingenious.

Recipes for mock cream (often using higher concentrations of 'National Dried' milk) abound in books of the period, and what went into the Ivy's mayonnaise is on record. Mario Gallati, then its manager (later owner of the Caprice) describes in his autobiography the period when, 'quite often, we had only tripe and onions and Spam on the menu', and the best face had to be put on to the invented variations for the little food they had to serve. 'For instance, I used to make a kind of mayonnaise with flour and water put into the mixing machine with vinegar, mustard, and a bit of powdered egg. It made me shudder to serve it, but everybody took this kind of "ersatz" food very much in their stride.'[24]

A similar version – without even the dried egg – was within the reach of domestic cooks similarly equipped:

Melt 1 oz of margarine in ½ teacup milk, and when the mixture is warm put through a cream machine – the five shilling kind which many of us bought before the war, and still, I expect, possess. Stir gently and put aside to cool. In about 2 or 3 hours' time add very gently to the cream 1 teaspoon made mustard and 1 tablespoon each salad oil and vinegar. Beat well and serve. If the oil is not available, it does not greatly matter, but you could be rather more generous with the margarine when making the cream foundation.[25]

The success of Gallati, like that of many other London restaurateurs of this period, depended on relationships with moneyed and fashionable clients built up in the years before the war. Clearly it was not a time when people would visit restaurants for the food, except to save domestic rations, but they were quite prepared to spend as freely on a game of conspiratorial make-believe with their friend Mario as they would have been to pay for *filet béarnaise* and *crème Nesselrode*. As Gallati remembers, they seldom complained about anything, and the knowledge that you could still get lunch or dinner at the Ivy in interesting company, at some slight risk of a flying bomb, was a minor but indisputable prop to the morale of the upper middle classes.

As for the lower orders, the learned historian of the Industrial Revolution's most conspicuous contribution to British gastronomy must complete this account of the period:

The National Federation of Fish Friers complained of 'alarmingly small rations of the wrong kind of fat', of disastrous attempts to foist dried stockfish on the Trade, of blackout restrictions which deprived them of their most profitable hours of opening and made the appearance of a 'Frying Tonight' notice the tip for a queue to form. There were also complaints of weird fish-allocations which included yellow-bellied pollack, oily conger eel, and the dreaded coalie which went a dirty grey when exposed to the air . . . A well-known source of extra fat supplies was the black market outside every American airfield. But there was nothing the Federation could do to help the frier who bought half-a-

Fish and chips: a 1930s mobile

hundredweight of star-spangled lard, only to find that all but the top layer was bricks.[26]

Finally, if the British Home Front in the Second World War lacked poets of distinction, it did not lack diarists, humorists, and advice merchants of all kinds, and as a documentary interlude between this chapter and the next, I offer a few contrasting illustrations of How We Ate Then.

GASTRONOMY IN BEIGE

We joined a swelling stream of the citizens of Swindon, all following a series of notices marked 'British Restaurant', to a huge elephant house, where thousands of human beings were eating as we did an enormous all-beige meal, starting with beige soup thickened to the consistency of paste, followed by beige mince full of lumps and garnished with beige beans and a few beige potatoes, thin beige apple stew and a sort of skilly. Very satisfying and crushing, and calling up a vision of our future Planned World – all beige also. . . .

Lunch with Janetta at the Ivy. She was looking very pretty and unusually elegant; our lunch was smoked salmon, cold grouse, chocolate mousse and Nuits-Saint-Georges.

Frances Partridge, *A Pacifist's War* (1978).

COLONEL BOGUS AT TABLE

'Direct me,' said Colonel Bogus, 'to a typical Community Feeding Centre.'
'To a what?' asked the Cabman.
Bogus corrected himself. Of course – they had been forced to abandon that

title. The 'beastly' Mr Priestley had pointed out it suggested feeding pigs. 'To a typical British Restaurant,' he amended airily . . .

The Community Feeding Centre was established in a large and surprisingly clean hall. Outside the dining-room itself a small queue had formed . . . Bogus did not like the people in the queue, nor the announcement on a large blackboard which stood at the entrance to the Restaurant.

Being so accustomed to the softly lit magnificence of West End eating-places, the announcement *Soup and Pud 4d. Sausage Toad 6d* didn't sound very appetising.

However, the people inside were just the sort of human material Colonel Bogus considered suitable for his purpose, and accepting a plate of Sausage Toad he made his way towards the window and settled himself at a table much too small for him, opposite a man reading a paper . . .

The other man had finished up his British Restaurant meal in no time, and Colonel Bogus with a friendly gesture pushed forward his plate. 'I can't finish mine', he said, imagining that this was the sort of place where you could do this kind of thing. 'Would you like to help me out?'

The other man looked most offended. 'What – you probably dine at the Ritz and can't finish up a bit of Sausage Toad?'

Michael Barsley, *Common Man and Colonel Bogus* (1944).

A DAY IN THE WARTIME LIFE OF NATHANIEL GUBBINS

Monday Off to grocer's with ration book after sharing morning milk with Sally the Cat and offering her kipper scraps begged from a neighbour. Sally the cat, accustomed to whole kipper to herself in peace-time, sniffs disdainfully . . .

At grocer's receive seven neat little packets: 2 oz butter, 2 oz lard, ¼ lb margarine, ½ lb sugar, ¼ lb bacon (three rashers), ½ lb cheese, and 2 oz tea.

Ask grocer what about delicious Spam on points. Grocer says family has had all points rations for month. Eggs? Grocer says Uncle Nat is entitled to one egg a week if available. Egg not available . . . Meat? Oh yes, meat. Ring up butcher (also about two miles away) and ask how much meat one man is entitled to per week. Butcher says it would be about size of small chop. Oh goody. Can butcher send small chop. Can butcher do what? Can butcher *send* small chop? Why, says sarcastic butcher, nothing could be simpler. Would Uncle Nat like small chop sent in six-wheeled lorry or dropped by plane? . . . Problem now is what for lunch? Shall Uncle Nat dig potatoes from garden and fry rasher or have bread and cheese? Problem solved by fact that U.N. not very good at cooking potatoes. Eat bread and cheese and half week's butter ration . . .

Explain to Sally that Lord Woolton won't allow cats to eat anything fit for human consumption, but if piece of cheese is left on kitchen table by mistake an intelligent cat should know what to do.

Godfrey Smith (ed.) *The Best of Nathaniel Gubbins* (1978).

VEGETABLE FLAN ('WOOLTON PIE')

For the pastry:
4 oz flour
2 oz cooked sieved potato
½ teaspoon baking powder
½ teaspoon salt
1 oz margarine
cold water to mix

For the filling:
6 oz cooked chopped spinach, or
cabbage or carrots, or a good
mixture of vegetables
½ oz margarine
½ oz flour, ½ pint milk
2 teaspoons chopped parsley

Line a flan tin with the pastry. Prick it well over with a fork, and bake in a fairly hot oven from 20 to 30 minutes.

Melt the margarine, stir in the flour, and allow the two to blend together for a minute or two. Add the milk gradually and allow to come to the boil, stirring smoothly. Season, and add the chopped parsley.

Stir in the vegetables, and when the pastry is cooked turn in the mixture, and garnish with peas or grated carrot. Return to the oven for five to ten minutes, and serve very hot.

Anon. *Food Facts for the Kitchen Front* (with a foreword by Lord Woolton), *n.d.*

LE SAUMONEAU BRAISÉ COMME AU CASTEL DE NÉRAC

From A L'Ecu de France. This restaurant, famous for some of the most artistically produced cooking in London, and second to none where wines are concerned, is bestowing its artistry even upon wartime rations.

We are directed to dress with paprika a small salmon, weighing about 1½ lbs, then to braise the fish, as it lies upon a soft cushion of vegetables including carrots, onions, celery, a little thyme, bay leaves, parsley, and as much minced lean bacon as you can spare. While the fish is in the oven, baste with its own liquor and that from the vegetables, adding a little Madeira if possible, and some white Jurançon wine.

In the meantime prepare a fine mirepoix (chopped vegetables and a little bacon) and lightly cook in it a dozen freshwater crayfish; give them a taste of brandy (Armagnac, according to A L'Ecu de France, but this would not elsewhere be obtainable in these days.) Set the brandy alight, squeeze over a little essence of lemon, or in peace-time lemon-juice, and a dusting of chopped parsley. Put all in the same dish as the salmon when it is three-parts cooked, adding also some diced mushrooms and pieces of tomato. When the salmon is sufficiently cooked, take it out and drain it, then place it in the centre of the dish, the crayfish round it, and over it the 'fond', or vegetable puree in which it was cooked. In peacetime, add a fine dusting all over it of chopped truffles which have been steamed in port wine beforehand.

It is suggested by the editor that cod should be cooked in this way by the average household, following the above directions as closely as possible.

Irene Veal, *Recipes of the 1940s* (1944).

CHAPTER THREE

Yes, we have just a few bananas

Eating under Labour, 1945–51

Tommy Handley: 'What's cooking, Curly?'
Curly Kale (the chef): 'Don't ask me, sir.
It makes me ill to think of it.'   ITMA

Politically, the peaceful revolution which the British electorate accomplished or thought it had accomplished in July 1945 had been brewing for the best part of a decade, not only in suburban villas but in tents and messes and prison camps and wherever a new deal was hoped for and the old one bitterly remembered. But the frenzied parliamentary activity of the Labour government's first year – fifty-five Acts in nine months – was unaccompanied by either innovation or revival on the domestic front. For at least the first three years after the war ended in Europe, experience triumphed over hope. True, on 31 December 1946 the first shipment of bananas to reach Britain for six years – a late Christmas present from the Caribbean – was officially welcomed on the dockside by the Lord Mayor of Bristol: a generation of children's parties had had to make do with mashed turnip flavoured with banana essence. But many butchers still closed for five days in the week for want of anything much to sell. The threat that dried egg might disappear from the British market with the ending of Lend-Lease provoked the newspapers to squawks only outdone in shrillness when the Minister of Food had to announce, in July 1946, that bread was to be rationed, a step that had been avoided in both wars.*

It should not have come as a surprise, for Attlee had had to send Morrison to Washington to discuss the situation. In the first half of this

---

* However, at the height of the shipping losses in 1917, official and social pressure to economise on bread was extreme. The writer's mother-in-law, a Newnham undergraduate at the time, recalls the scales kept on High Table, and her own disposal of mouldy crusts into the Cam at dead of night.

year of general dearth Europe was short of 8 million tons of wheat, and Britain found herself responsible for helping to feed the British Zone of Germany. British India needed grain too. But Labour's flair for mishandling public relations was already becoming apparent. Britain's diversion of some of her own wheat imports to the starving people of conquered Germany – the price for American consent to shouldering the main burden – was successfully presented by the Conservative opposition as incompetence rather than generosity. The Ministry of Food itself had lost the instinctive psychologist who had kept the nation grinning and bearing it through most of the war years. Under Labour it acquired first a bluff trade union nonentity (Sir Ben Smith), then in the spring of 1946 a sensitive ideologue (John Strachey) with an insensitive bluestocking (Dr Edith Summerskill) as his junior. The department itself made matters worse by quietly subtracting two ounces a pound from the statutory weight of loaves – without remembering about the Weights and Measures Act. The ration, when it arrived, was sufficient (two large loaves a week for adults, with less for young children and more for manual workers, with one pound of flour counting three bread units as against four for a two pound loaf).

But the measure was not exactly a success. Housewives were given three weeks' notice, which they used to hoard flour. They then exercised the right they had been given to exchange bread units for points, and consumption of tinned goods shot up. This forced the Ministry first to halve the exchange value of bread units, then abolish the right of exchange altogether. In restaurants, bread was made one of the maximum number of three dishes allowed at any one meal. 'Served as bread and cheese, or as the ground floor of welsh rarebit or sardines on toast, it didn't count as a separate dish. But any customer who now demanded bread with his soup would find by the end of the meal that he had forfeited his right to a pudding.'[1] It was no wonder that by the time bread rationing was abandoned in July 1948, 750 Food Officers were dealing full-time with bread alone, and in retrospect, 'the most that could be said was that consumption had not gone up'. Politically, the chief beneficiary of bread rationing was the young Edward Heath, who reduced Labour's majority from 11,000 to 1,000 at the 'bread rationing by-election' in Bexley, and won the (redistributed) seat at the 1950 General Election.

Other rationed foods were no more generously supplied. In 1948, three years after the end of the war, the weekly ration for a man was: 13 ounces of meat, 1½ ounces of cheese, 6 ounces of butter/margarine,

1 ounce of cooking fat, 8 ounces of sugar, 2 pints of milk, and one egg. Not surprisingly, in the dire years between the end of Lend-Lease and the negotiation of Marshall Aid, the Ministry of Food's commercial officers scoured the world's markets for alternative protein at a price Britain was prepared to pay. They returned with products for which the national palate – less catholic then than it afterwards became – was not ready: whale, snoek, and barracouta (as it was called before James Bond popularised the spelling 'barracuda').

The trouble with whale was not entirely the fault of the cetacean species. As Peter Lund Simmons pointed out a century earlier, 'the flesh, which is red and looks like coarse beef' was considered 'very wholesome and nutritious' by Eskimos and Japanese, to name only two of the animal's hunters.[2] Besides, a single blue whale weighed about 90 tons, which made up for a good deal of missing Argentine beef, and since it was being killed anyway, for the sake of its blubber and skin rather than its meat, it would have been hard for conservationists to argue against its import, even if ecology had been a preoccupation of the time.

But whatever the merits of the whale as meat – and as East Anglians say of the coypu, it was really better curried in the vinegary vindaloo manner – they were efficiently disguised by the Moby Dick-like arrangements the whalers made for the preservation of the carcase on its long journey to the British table, once they had possessed themselves of the blubber. The meat also required a butcher and cook of more than ordinary competence. Perhaps Messrs Lyons had access to both, for by September 1947 they were selling 600 whale steaks a day at one London Corner House. But

I am told that out of four Norwegian dressers who prepare the meat before it ever reaches the butcher, two will prepare it so that it eats excellently and steak meat will be separated from sausage material, whereas two will make an oily mess of it . . . The better cuts, marinated half a day in a mixture of vinegar and water, do make excellent steaks. I know a City restaurant in London where for months city gents consumed the steaks in great gollops, happily convinced they were eating on the black market and spiting Mr Strachey. . . . If they had known they were not breaking the law they would have left in a huff.[3]

Less fortunate eaters remember whalemeat, in Susan Cooper's description, as 'a curious powdery-textured substance resembling a meaty biscuit with overtones of oil', and by 1950, even though the meat ration still stood at a mere shilling a week, 4,000 tons of whalemeat lay unsold on the Tyne quayside.[4]

Snoek fared little better, or indeed rather worse. The Ministry imported ten million half-pound tins from South Africa in May 1948. Many English words beginning with 'sn' convey dislike or disparagement, and snoek, sounding like some form of sea-snake, was a gift to the cartoonist in a nation that had suffered much, or thought it had, from Ministry of Food 'snoopers' attempting to uncover peculation in eggs or jiggery-pokery with pigs. Mr Strachey ventured on an introductory description of the fish: 'It is long and slender, weighing up to 18 lbs. It is good, palatable, but rather dull.' Eighteen months later, when his confidence that he could 'sell every tin at 1s 4½d' had proved misplaced, candour overtook discretion and he called it 'the dullest fish I have ever eaten' – a poor reward for the Ministry cooks who had evolved recipes like snoek *piquante* for promotional tastings presided over by Dr Summerskill:

Snoek piquante   Four spring onions, chopped; liquid from snoek; 4 tablespoons vinegar; half a can of snoek, mashed; 2 teaspoons syrup; salt to taste; half teaspoon pepper.

Cook the onions in the fish liquor and vinegar for five minutes. Add the snoek, syrup and seasoning and mix well; serve cold with salad.

Today it would be called snoek sweet and sour, but in the forties they still preferred it in French. By the summer of 1949, there were still about 4½ million tins of snoek in the warehouse or the pipeline, and reinforcements were at hand: in August of that year, 9 million similar tins of barracouta arrived from Australia and the Ministry cooks went to work again: 'Barracouta is helping out with breakfast in many homes today. This economical smoked fish, now off points, makes delicious fish cakes. These can be made overnight and re-heated . . .' But by that time, the patient British stomach had had enough, and snoek and barracouta went underground altogether until, amid the distractions of the Festival of Britain eighteen months later, a windfall quantity of tinned fish came on to the market at tenpence a tin labelled, 'selected fish food for cats and kittens'.

The worst year had been 1947: *annus horrendus*, Hugh Dalton called it. The most severe and long-lasting winter of living memory, followed by catastrophic floods, not only paralysed a country still almost wholly dependent on the mining and movement of coal; it destroyed 80,000 tons of potatoes and 70,000 acres of wheat, 32 per cent of the hill sheep and 30,000 cattle. The long hot summer that succeeded the floods brought the first great post-war sterling crisis. This was provoked in essence by the American negotiators of the American Loan Agreement of 1945, who insisted on sterling being made convertible into all other currencies a year after the agreement came into force. Within a month, $700 million slipped away from British reserves, and on 23 August the meat ration was cut, foreign travel was suspended, and the basic petrol ration abolished. The Marshall Plan, though announced in 1947, did not come into force until 1948. Unfair though it was, the Opposition's slogan 'Starve with Strachey and shiver with Shinwell' stuck all too well.

At least, however, the seas were safe again and the parcel post was getting through. This form of outdoor relief for beleaguered Britain from the rest of the Anglo-Saxon world had been permitted to a limited extent when the U-boat menace to shipping was at its height. Food parcels were all the more welcome during the hungry peace when more official forms of assistance (from America at least) had been discontinued. At the receiving end, the sense of privation bravely borne at this period is nicely conveyed in a letter written in April 1947, by a personality type now almost vanished, on behalf of a north London Congregational chapel that had been somewhat damaged in the blitz. It was addressed to church members in Highgate, Australia, who had collected gifts to send to Highgate, London:

You may like to hear details of the pleasure your gifts afforded.

It was decided to give a children's party for those who attend Children's Church. The tables looked most colourful with the various jellies, etc. and the little ones thoroughly enjoyed their party tea. They were told of your generosity and in their childish ways expressed their appreciation. It was the first party that had been possible since before the war so was an outstanding event for them.

Another way in which items were distributed was by giving some to people who live alone, as 'rations for one' leave no margin. I happen to be one of those people, and my share was a good-sized portion of cheese and fat. Both were very acceptable indeed and I was tremendously pleased and grateful to have them. The quality was really excellent. For my own special share I would say a very big 'thank you'.

The tinned meat was saved for the London Missionary Society Supper – a hitherto annual event now revived for the first time since the war. About 60 Church Members were present and you were all very much in our thoughts as we ate and enjoyed the meat your kindness had provided . . . The evening was a great inspiration.

There remains one more item to acknowledge – the soap. The toilet soap is being exchanged amongst church members for household soap which will be very much needed for cleaning the Church when the repairs are completed.[5]

It is not easy to explain why during the second half of the 1940s, after surviving all danger of serious dietary deficiency over the previous five years, Britain continued to eat as boringly as it did. The particular dips in supply, and (in semi-starved parts of Europe) peaks of demand, that followed the ending of Lend-Lease occasioned bread rationing and prolonged other shortages in Britain. But these are in themselves insufficient reasons for what seemed to middle-class people with pre-1939 memories a revolution of declining expectations. As a young historian (son of one of Attlee's ministers) put it fifteen years later:

The British people were far from starving, although a casual newspaper reader might have been forgiven for doubting the fact. The working class was better off than it had ever been, and even the middle class was better off than it felt. In strictly physical terms, more could have been squeezed out of the British people, and less given back. A Government ruthlessly determined to obtain maximum production at the minimum cost would have reduced still further the quantity of luxuries available, and met the problem of morale by giving higher and better rations to those engaged on work of national importance. Politically, however, that course was out of the question. After six years of war, the British people were in no mood for heroic sacrifices. Even as it was, 'austerity' became the subject of a violent propaganda campaign by the Conservative Press, and the greatest single cause of the Government's failure to hold its position in the 1950 elections.[6]

That *post bellum triste* feeling was a typically middle-class affliction. Most manual workers, and above all their wives, had never enjoyed abundance, let alone luxury, and the monotonous but nutritious diet of the industrial canteens that had grown up during the war represented a marked improvement whose effects began to show in the health of the population, even though – or rather because – there was little to be had from the sweetshop on the corner. It was the higher socio-economic groups that had watched their servants disappear into those factories and canteens, never to return, and had spent the war years learning at the worst of times how to shop and cook and keep their families tolerably fed. Various influences contributed to a coarsening of the national palate, if that is not too high-faluting a notion. These included a forced contraction of choice and of the opportunity to make comparisons between different brands or strains of the same product, the persistent and often lazy-minded substitution of materials in cookery books and newspaper articles, the climate created by years of official advice to 'make do and mend', and the unpopularity, indeed suspect patriotism until the declining days of the Labour Government, of anyone who complained about not obtaining the quality of goods or the courtesy of service that he or she had been brought up to expect. The phrase 'Don't you know there's a war on?' lasted several years after the war, only half in jest.

In the Ministry of Food itself all was not well. Under the direction of Ministers who lacked Lord Woolton's skill at fireside chats, the permanent officials took the bit between their teeth:

The Ministry of Food prosecuted a greengrocer for selling a few extra pounds of potatoes, while admitting that they were frostbitten and would be thrown away if not cooked at once. The Ministry clamped down on a farmer's wife who served the Ministry snooper with Devonshire cream for his tea. A shopkeeper was fined £5 for selling home-made sweets that contained his own ration of sugar. Ludicrous penalties were imposed on farmers who had not kept strictly to the letter of licences to slaughter pigs; in one case, the permitted building was used, the authorised butcher employed, but the job had to be done the day before it was permitted; in another case the butcher and the timing coincided, but the pig met its end in the wrong building.[7]

National emergency could no longer enforce national discipline and a certain equality in misery. In 1947 there were 30,000 prosecutions for what amounted to minor black market offences and breaches of the food regulations: it was the period in which it was important to 'know a man who can get hold of' farm eggs, or chickens, or chocolates, or who enjoyed access to some grocer's unclaimed rations of butter and cheese. Arrangements of this kind were so informal that it seems unlikely that the 30,000 represented even a tenth of the number of offences that took place: for the fixers, or spivs as they came to be called, it was the 1940s equivalent of parking fines. 'Gifts of sausages' were among the persuaders mentioned at the Lynskey Tribunal, which in 1948 entertained a nation and brought down the Parliamentary Secretary to the Board of Trade.

They must have been rather unusual sausages, because by this time the British sausage was in a poor way. Food scientists had begun the war in an obscurity from which Lord Woolton had rescued them. By the end, they were in sight of the brave new world that could synthesise margarine from coal and meat paste from yeasts (as the Germans had already done before hostilities ended). But scientific nutrition was still relatively new as an instrument of national policy, and it was too early for scientists to realise that if the war had been won by measuring the protein, carbohydrate and vitamin content of food, economic success in peacetime would have something to do with scientific assessment of its taste. Magnus Pyke, who had been Principal Scientific Officer (Nutrition) in the wartime Ministry of Food, could still write in 1952:

The food scientist unfortunately has very little scientific to say about taste. . . .
When the British Ministry of Food issued its Statutory Instrument No. 1509 of
1948 declaring that the minimum meat content of luncheon sausage, breakfast
sausage, meat galantine and polony might not be less than 30 per cent., whereas
before the 1939 war a meat content of 80 per cent had not been uncommon, they
overlooked the fact that when the meat content of sausages is depressed lower
than 20 per cent., the flavour of meat falls below the threshold of taste altogether
and the manufacturer might just as well make his sausages with no meat at all.[8]

Politically, after 1945, the country was divided between people who
were more or less preoccupied with making the new world work, in so
far as external circumstances allowed, and a smaller if more vocal body
of people who expressed their fears that the old world had gone for ever
in a mixture of contempt and envy for the new-found independence of
servants-become-masters. These were not years in which connoisseurship or pernicketiness about food could be safely expressed outside
small circles of like-minded people in a local Wine and Food Society.
Even when reconstruction was far advanced in Europe, and the riches of
continental markets again drew the covetous gaze of British visitors
denied access to them for the best part of ten years, the £25 a head travel
allowance was all the foreign exchange the Exchequer could spare for
tourism. This effectively curbed people's exploration of unfamiliar
tastes when the napkin was tied round their necks in the agreeable little
restaurants of Florence or Rouen or Bruges.

It was in these days that the essential fragility of the grand hotel
tradition in Britain betrayed itself. It had never been genuinely indigenous. This meant that when prime materials and exacting customers
were withdrawn during the war years, it reverted to type. After the war,
Tom Laughton (brother of Charles the actor, who also paid close
attention to his food) returned to Scarborough to revive his family's
hotel, the Royal:

The war had left behind depressed kitchen conditions. The use of packet soups
and gravy browning was accepted; meat was boned, roasted and then allowed to
go cold so that it could be cut paper-thin on a meat-slicer to be warmed up and
served with ersatz gravy. The chefs had got used to these abominable practices
which were easy for them and, in those days of scarcity, accepted by the
customers. The chefs resisted my efforts to revert to the sound classical methods
of pre-war days. Eventually, I had to take over control, write the menus, follow

them up day by day in the kitchens, and check the quality of the kitchen output in the food services at the start of every lunch and dinner.[9]

Not many British hotels of the type had owner-managers like this. Laughton had been one of the Army's Command Catering Advisers and was later invited to perform similar services for British Rail. ('Talking to the chef of the Caledonian Hotel, Edinburgh, in his kitchens, I asked him where his smoked salmon came from and he told me that he smoked it himself. I asked him diffidently if he would tell me his method. "Certainly", he said, "I would tell you anything. You are the only director who has ever visited my kitchens." ')[10]

Far more typical of British provincial 'inns' of the period (*c.* 1950) was the one served by Nicolas Freeling, a classically trained French chef who was on his way to becoming a novelist instead:

A nice little place, called the Bull or the Bear or whatever, which had had a panelled coffee room for twenty persons in 1900, and a kitchen where a fat honest country woman made pigeon pie and suet roly poly. By my time it had a restaurant for forty, a choice of table d'hôte menus in imitation French, a 'carte' with twenty items to order, a wine list of undrinkable pretentiousness, and an 'American Bar'.

The manager would be the son of the house, who spent his days in the bar being cheery with the local notabilities.

He came to me every morning with his pleasant brainless features arranged into artificial severity, and a list of complaints about my misdeeds. What had happened to old Colonel Withers' grilled tomato? I must use margarine and not butter. Customers did not like garlic; and so on . . . If I suggested plain English food it was too expensive and the customers disliked it. If I made genuine French food, like a cassoulet, it was even worse, at once plain and exotic, to their mind the worst combination. They wanted decorative flashy dishes like chicken Maryland – a single-handed cook's nightmare. If I pleaded for a small menu I got knowing smiles, to show that they saw through my little game. When for economy's sake I suggested cheap things, paupiettes of veal or braised beef, I would be told that customers did not want 'cheap meat'. I saw no way out.[11]

The portrait – an accurate one, of which faithful copies survive up and down the land to this day – is of a country which had forgotten almost everything it had ever known about food beyond the basic domestic level.

On the other hand, by 1950 several different revolutions were beginning to germinate, in both domestic and professional catering. In this year, with an election looming, controls began to be lifted. In January milk was de-rationed (though cream was still hard to find except within

Pub scene by Susanne Einzig

range of the farm gate). In May, hotels and restaurants were set free
from the five-shilling limit on the cost of meals and the sumptuary
restrictions on the number of courses that could be served. Butcher's
meat was still short, but as Raymond Postgate put it in the seminal
magazine article that launched his 'Good Food Club', that was all:

There is, and there has been for a long time, plenty of chickens, poultry, rabbits,
geese, game, salmon, sole, cod, herring and all kinds of fish: and of vegetables
when they are in season; and of green cheeses and Camemberts and so forth . . .
We have been extremely patient. But now the last excuses have ceased to be
valid. Food is ill-cooked in hotels and restaurants, or it is insufficient, or it is
badly and rudely served up – or all three. The pretence that this is due to
Ministry of Food regulations will not do any more.[12]

While more far-reaching changes in the British diet than the return of
green cheese were pending, it was inevitable that as the supply of food
began to improve, it should not be the new generation but the old one
that moved with most alacrity to take advantage of it. It would have been
a slower process altogether if the post-1940 generation of young people
had been left to discover for themselves from half-forgotten cookery

books how to roast a large joint, exploit the harvest of a good fishmonger's slab, or put a soufflé together. (The books themselves, like many others not then thought worth collecting, often vanished into wartime drives for paper 'salvage'.) Early in the 1950s, however, two individuals came to symbolise – much to their own surprise – the richness and variety of what was again permissible to eat. They were a social historian of notoriously leftist views, and a diplomatic wife of scholarly tastes who had spent most of the war in the Middle East.

The first, or at least the loudest, public salvo came from Raymond Postgate, in an earlier issue of the *Leader Magazine* (23 April 1949). The article, whose comments on whalemeat have already been cited, was headed 'Society for the Prevention of Cruelty to Food' – 'I am founding it as a result of the horrifying things that I have myself seen in restaurants.' The significance of Postgate, at the time and subsequently, was that he was not a food writer, but a historian, novelist and political journalist of established reputation. Born in 1896, he was the son of a well-known classical scholar, and kept up his own Latin and Greek at this level all his life, publishing distinguished translations and editions of the *Pervigilium Veneris* and the *Agamemnon* of Aeschylus. But in 1916, while still at Oxford, he quarrelled comprehensively with his father by becoming a conscientious objector and was spat at in the High by the Town Clerk (though befriended by Gilbert Murray). Postgate remained on the far left of the Labour Party throughout the twenties and thirties, married George Lansbury's daughter Daisy, and later collaborated with his sister Margaret's husband, G. D. H. Cole, on *The Common People 1746–1946*. He wrote prolifically throughout his life, notably about Wilkes and other aspects of the eighteenth century, with a sideline in novels and thrillers, of which *Verdict of Twelve* was the most compelling and widely sold example. The connoisseurship with which the public came to associate him in the last twenty years of his life had more to do with wine than food. His love of the grape was an inheritance, perhaps, from his donnish origins, and it is easy to imagine how this shy, peppery, rubicund man would have developed had he remained in academic life. Instead, he paid for his own claret and burgundy out of a Grub Street income – 'a good judge of cheap wine', the benign André Simon once unkindly called him – and in 1951 published *The Plain Man's Guide to Wine*, which coincided with the rise of a popular taste and deservedly went through many editions, including a revision by John Arlott.

Postgate – the 'Public Stomach Number One', who had to insist that the OBE granted him by the Wilson government was in recognition of his work as a labour historian, not as a restaurant critic – owed his status as a food commentator largely to his circle of friends. Before 1939 he founded a dining club, called the Half Hundred, with Philip Harben, later to become famous as post-war television's first chef. Harben was at the time running the kitchen at the Isobar, in the basement of Wells Coates's then avant-garde flats in Lawn Road, Hampstead. Half Hundred members took it in turns to introduce the food and drink at club dinners, and a characteristic utterance survives from Postgate's programme for a meal (20 June 1939) devised to accompany the burgundies he had chosen:

I am thinking of a centre piece consisting of a real full grown piece of mutton, such as old and enraged clubmen keep for themselves. This has nothing whatever to do with lamb, an insipid food that has to be made palatable by sauces, garlic, stuffing, etc. But nowadays people breed small joints for small families and to get a decent-sized joint with the real taste of mutton is very rare. Most people don't know what it is.[13]

Early in 1949 Postgate was approached by Stephen Potter, a family friend and fellow member of one of London's better-fed clubs, the Savile. Potter was the author of *Gamesmanship*, *Lifemanship* and other guides to survival in the post-war world. He was also editing the middlebrow *Leader Magazine* for the Hulton Press. Potter suggested a series of articles on British catering. In his piece on his notional Society for the Prevention of Cruelty to Food (the Good Food Club was not yet born) Postgate looked back over the London restaurants of his working lifetime and the emblematic sauce bottles that stood on their tables:

They were provided on the justified assumption that you would want to hide completely the taste of what you would be offered. Sodden, sour, slimy, sloppy, stale or saccharined – one of these six things (or all) it certainly would be, whether it was fish, flesh, vegetable or sweet. It would also be over-cooked; it might be reheated. If the place was English, it would be called a teashop or caffy; if foreign it would be called a restaurant or caffy. In the second case it would be dirtier, but the food *might* have some taste.[14]

However, even after this it was more than a year before Postgate realised that he stood with a ball in front of an open goal, and only had to kick it through. The Good Food Club, launched with a membership form in the *Leader* issue of 20 May 1950, was not explicitly founded on memories of Florence White's pre-war *Good Food Register* (though

Postgate had probably been aware of it at the time).* Instead he cited French models such as the guide of the Club des Sans-Club:

It is no good simply nagging. It does no good; and in any case English law does not allow you to tell unkind truths about hotels and cafes, unless you are very rich and don't care about libel actions. The only useful action is, not to start on the unending task of condemning sin, but to reward merit. We must help those who do try; and soon they will be joined by others. There are few things more discouraging than to go on, week after week, offering good cooking and service, and never to have it recognised. They don't do things that way in France. . . . Virtue is rewarded, and vice punished; and that not through the action of a Ministry or some well-meaning bureaucrat but by the unceasing, unresting commentaries of ordinary men and women. Innkeepers are kept on their toes, for they do not know what meek customer may be watching them on behalf of the Society. They only know that if he says he is an agent of the Society, he is a fraud; for that is forbidden.

To a remarkable extent, the principles and practice of the club and of *The Good Food Guide* (whose first edition, compiled out of *Leader* readers' recommendations, was first published the following year) sprang full-formed from Postgate's head at the outset:

The five questions we ask are these: 'Is the cooking good and ample? Is the price reasonable? Is the drink good and ample? Is *its* price right? Did you find the service courteous and adequate?' Regretfully, we must add that we cannot accept recommendations from caterers. They are, after all, interested parties. And when we publish our register in book form (as we shall when it reaches adequate size) we shall not accept any advertising in it from hotels and restaurants. The objects are:
1. To raise the standard of cooking in Britain, and to keep prices reasonable; 2. To encourage the drinking of good wine and the proper care of beer; 3. To earn foreign currency by improving British hospitality and by offering overseas guidance, not official puffs; 4. To reward enterprise and courtesy; 5. To do all ourselves a bit of good, in due course, by publishing an annual which will make our holidays, travels and evenings out enjoyable.

Twenty-two individual recommendations accompanied this article, signed by Graham Hutton, Honor Balfour, Naomi Mitchison and others. They ranged from The Ox on the Roof in Chelsea, 'a gay little restaurant where the owners, Ruby and Alfred, personally serve you with snails', to a country pub where the manageress 'who is the sister of Violet Loraine knows all there is to know about wines'. Not one of the

* My former colleague Catherine Mant, who possesses the only copy of the *Register* I have ever seen, showed it to Postgate once, and says he expressed no curiosity about it.

twenty-two places survives in *The Good Food Guide* at the time of writing (1982), though the next list published included an inn whose distinction proved more durable, Gerard Harris's Bell Inn at Aston Clinton, Buckinghamshire. The owner of this 'characterful old pub', as the first edition of the *Guide* described it, was like so many of his kind in the post-war years not a caterer by profession, but a solicitor, whose passion was fine wine – 'and wine is used in cooking, too', breathed Postgate's entry respectfully before listing the kitchen's specialities: 'hot lobster in madeira and cream sauce, poached salmon with red wine sauce and red caviare, Maryland fried chicken.' The inn remained in the hands of the same family and, with a short gap, in *The Good Food Guide*. But few of its early customers dissented from the book's judgement that its cooking and individuality declined as its fame, size and expense grew. This too became a common symptom as the *Guide*'s circle of influence widened. However, at this early stage the Bell is a useful illustration of the way the *Guide*, and the places it contained, spread by word of mouth among what might be described as the *England, Their England* circuit. Michael Meyer, the translator of Ibsen, recorded for the *Guide*'s historians Hope Chenhalls and Neil Rhind how he came to 'devil' for Postgate on later editions of the book:

I first heard of the *Guide* when playing a game of cricket at Great Missenden for the BBC Bushmen; other members of the team included Hugh Carleton-Greene, Patrick Gordon-Walker, and R. J. Yeatman, co-author of *1066 And All That*. After the game Hugh Greene suggested we ate at the Bell, Aston Clinton, and when I asked how he came to know of such an excellent place, he told me it was recommended in the GFG. I joined the Savile in September 1950 and one day in the club Raymond said to me, 'Would you be willing for £50 to help us along?' and I agreed.

By this time, the first edition of the Guide (1951) was in print and Cassell sold 5,000 copies (about a tenth of its current annual circulation). There were over 500 entries, from Aberdeen ('a foreign visitor wanted to congratulate the chef but feared that it would only be taken as Latin extravagance') to Wembley ('The chef is a Spaniard, trained in Paris, and his speciality is a whole beefsteak braised "bordelaise"'). All were based on the recommendations which interested readers had sent to the *Leader*, and when Hulton abruptly closed that magazine, to *Lilliput*.

Lilliput continued the series (but botched the organisation of report collation, with near-disastrous results). Postgate's preface to the edition

– the first in a series of *Crockford*-like biennial discussions of the state of British public eating – explained the principles and practice of the Good Food Club, but also contained several passages which cast light on the assumptions of the time among educated people about the best ways to obtain satisfaction when forced or inclined to eat away from home in the British Isles:

We have no worse materials than the French have; indeed, in some cases our materials are undeniably tastier – as, for example, strawberries, tomatoes, apples, asparagus, and (when we have it) Lowland beef and mountain mutton . . .

British cooking – so far as it has adapted itself at all to realities – is commonly intended for a country where the meal-time drinks are not wine but beer, tea, coffee, and even cocoa; and tea and coffee, through propaganda and fiscal favouritism, have been edging beer out. This means that the French pattern of good lunches and dinners – the 'wine' meals – is not the basic British pattern, outside London, anyway. Breakfast and tea – in the north the remarkably good meal called 'high tea' – are the meals on which the British have spent some thought; these are the meals more likely to be good. At breakfast you may hope for a real kipper (that is, one which is smoked and not painted), grilled herrings, oatmealed herrings, genuine porridge, kidneys and bacon, real marmalade (but avoid the sausages); things that you will not get easily in other countries. At tea you may get good cakes and bannocks; at 'high tea' you may get most of the breakfast dishes (except porridge) and in the North black puddings, white puddings and faggots, too, which can be a great deal better than the tasteless, overcooked, imitation-French 'late dinner' served in a cold, half-empty hotel . . .

If you are in a strange town, without any guidance from a friend or an entry in this list, always prefer a clean and brisk-looking public house. You are more likely to find there than in teashops a survival of the older English tradition of solid eating. In both cases the cooking may well be, at the best, unimaginative, but in a pub, at least, you are not expected to peck like a sparrow. . . .

The first picture that anyone has of British cooking, outside the home, is of dullness and incompetence; and of British service it is of ineptness or downright surliness. There is no sense in pretending that there are not places of which that impression is just. But this list makes it clear that there are literally hundreds of places of which it is totally untrue. There are so many inns in the countryside at which one will be offered venison, hare, game, trout, salmon from the river, and so on, admirably prepared. There are so many people who are proud and delighted to be cooks and innkeepers, and will show their pleasure at the appreciation of any discriminating customers. There are even – though this is not France and cannot be – really individual dishes that one is anxious to taste, such as lobsters in whisky, roast cygnet, salmon in cider, and ormers. If it were possible, or proper, to print the letters received from innkeepers, many readers would be very astonished at the goodwill and anxiety that is already going into British catering.[16]

These passages, although based on more grassroots evidence than had ever previously been collected together, now also sound expressive of 'the world we have lost'. Postgate was an eighteenth-century man in more than one sense; not Francophobe, but fiercely English in his tastes and affections. He would not seriously have expected to encounter roast cygnet very often on his travels, but would have been puzzled by an England that lost its taste for herring even when herring could still be caught, and that allowed agribusinessmen to destroy the hedgerows which sheltered the hares. At the same time, he had a demotic touch and experience that were denied, for instance to André Simon. Simon, the French historian of the English wine trade, had become the symbol of gourmandise in his adopted country through his presidency of the Wine and Food Society, and his output of books and articles was prolific to the point of blatant pot-boiling. A peasant at heart, as he was the first to acknowledge, Simon was treated by his monied but in those days small circle of British – and American – wine-lovers with deferential respect, as the lovable representative of a gastronomic culture whose superiority was universally conceded. Postgate shared many of the same tastes, but stood on his own country's literary and historical ground, as writers such as Morton Shand and Edward Spencer had done before him in the same connection, and fought for a popular hearing with all his considerable gifts as a pamphleteer.

At this point, with the first edition published, the history of Postgate's *Guide* can be left to mature for a while. The second spring of the British post-war culinary revival was equally sudden and unlikely in its appearance: a decorous little book in brown cloth from a small and select literary publisher (John Lehmann), with pen and ink decorations by John Minton. It was called *A Book of Mediterranean Food*, and the author, Elizabeth David, was quite unknown, except to readers of *Harper's Bazaar*, whose editor, Anne Scott-James, had printed some of her recipes. Quotation here from the first *GFG* is justified by the scarcity of all the editions of the early 1950s: bibliographically, the book was unusual in instructing its readers to throw it away when its currency was over. *Mediterranean Food*, and the six books that have followed it at increasingly long intervals, have remained in print with negligible gaps for an entire generation: it is highly probable that there is a paperback

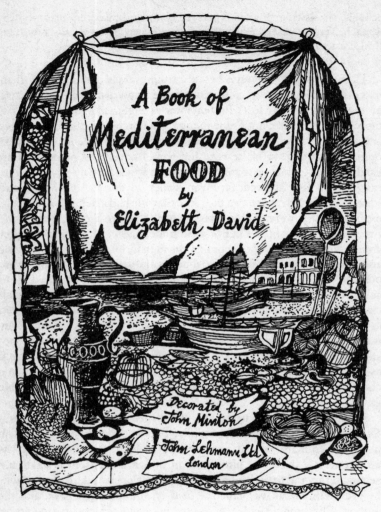

John Minton's original title page

copy of at least one of the series in any household to which the present work penetrates.

In personal ways, Mrs David's background could hardly have been more English: descended directly from a Victorian Home Secretary (Viscount Ridley) and a Conservative MP for Eastbourne, educated at an ill-fed English girls' school, married for a while to a British diplomat. She tried both painting and acting before turning in her late thirties to cooking and writing. She had behind her two formative experiences: several months living in Paris with an exceptionally greedy *famille bourgeoise*; and a spell on a Greek island followed by war years in Cairo, running the Embassy library and exchanging ideas in the kitchen with her Sudanese cook. But numerous women of her generation had similar advantages. It was the literary curiosity and obsessional accuracy of a born writer and researcher that brought her books to life and made them work. It is true, as Katharine Whitehorn has said, that *A Book of Mediterranean Food* presented people with the *kind* of food they might wish to cook, not with conventional, much-measured recipes. This is exactly why its post-war British readers fell upon it with delight while the literalist American cooking public, wanting for nothing, left it to the ecstasies of professional reviewers. After all, the very first page contains the sentence 'anyone who has lived for long in Greece will be familiar with the sound of air gruesomely whistling through sheep's lungs frying in oil'.

At the same time, people who have cooked from Mrs David's recipes often testify that although they often seem economical in compass, they almost always yield the heart of the matter to anyone prepared to read attentively and imaginatively. She seldom tells you anything unnecessary for the matter in hand; equally seldom – unlike even the most graceful and admired of her English contemporaries and successors – does she leave out the tiny detail that makes all the difference. Read, for instance, her recipe for eggs en cocotte in her second book, *French Country Cooking* (1951).[17] It is for this reason, as well as the sheer variety of content, that the most influential and admired of all post-war British chefs, George Perry-Smith of the Hole in the Wall in Bath, honourably told an editor who asked him for recipes that he could not supply any because almost everything he did was derived from Elizabeth David.[18]

The appearance of these two books in quick succession was followed in 1954 by *Italian Food*, a more substantial work whose research can be supplemented but not supplanted. It confirmed her reputation at this crucial time of birth and rebirth in British consumer society. The first book itself could not have appeared at a better moment: indeed, as the author interestingly observed, 'so odd has the system of export and import become that the ingredients of many Mediterranean dishes are not only easier to come by in London than the materials of plain English cooking but sometimes more plentiful than they are abroad'.[19] Her philosophy – it does not seem too grand a word – of cooking and entertaining is most succinctly and vividly put in the second book, *French Country Cooking*, the precursor of the more compendious and scholarly *French Provincial Cooking* (1960):

Rationing, the disappearance of servants, and the bad and expensive meals served in restaurants, have led Englishwomen to take a far greater interest in food than was formerly considered polite; . . . personal supervision of the kitchen garden induces a less indifferent attitude to the fate of spring vegetables; those who have churned their own butter, fed their chickens and geese, cherished their fruit trees, skinned and cleaned their own hares, are in no mood to see their efforts wasted . . .

Even more than long hours in the kitchen, fine meals require ingenious organisation and experience which is a pleasure to acquire. A highly developed shopping sense is important, so is some knowledge of the construction of a menu with a view to the food in season, the manner of cooking, the texture and colour of the dishes to be served in relation to each other . . .

Some sensible person once remarked that you spend the whole of your life either in your bed or your shoes. Having done the best you can by shoes and bed, devote all the time and resources at your disposal to the building up of a fine kitchen. It will be, as it should be, the most comforting and comfortable room in the house . . .

If every kitchen contained a bottle each of red wine, white wine and inexpensive port for cooking, hundreds of store cupboards could be swept clean for ever of the cluttering debris of commercial sauce bottles and all synthetic aids to flavouring.[20]

Mrs David glosses the last sentence with an extract from *Lady Bountiful's Legacy* (1868), listing the nauseous methods by which the Victorians manufactured such popular synthetics as pineapple rum and oil of bitter almonds, and she goes on to wonder 'how artificial flavourings are concocted nowadays'. As for the kitchen as 'the most comforting and comfortable room in the house', such a notion must have astonished many British architects of the period. 'It is important to plan the kitchen well so that you need spend as little time in it as possible – as I am sure my women readers will agree!', writes the author of *Good House Design*, adding: 'The sink is undoubtedly the focal point of the room.'[21]

The 'kitchen sink' school of British post-war painters, as John Bratby and others were labelled, may have taken this remark too seriously. But in the 1950s, the arrival of detergents, stainless steel sinks, and Formica surfaces altered the perspective of housewives, even if the new artefacts lacked the visual interest of porcelain and bars of soap, and had to be set off by *marmites* and *mandolines* borrowed from the French bourgeois kitchen.

Changes in food and drink were less sudden. After this glimpse of the emergent bottle-and-*daube* culture, sketched by Postgate and David for their middle-class readers, it is necessary to be reminded how many tastes and patterns still lay in the future for the mass of the population. Wartime memories were also still fresh. For years after the foundation of *The Good Food Guide*, the highest praise of restaurants in Postgate's postbag was time and again that 'helpings were generous' and that there was 'more than I could eat'. Again, a 16- to 21-year-old in 1950 was unlikely to have a mother who shopped in a supermarket; unlikely to have consumed a fish-finger, a hamburger, a frozen pea, a glass of wine or a mug of instant coffee; and certain not to have been given Sugar Frosties for breakfast, wrapped sliced Mother's Pride with soft margarine for lunch, and for dinner, spaghetti with texturised vegetable protein in the bolognese, followed by Instant Whip.

On the other hand, he might have expected to be familiar with other tastes that would now count as unusual, if not exactly exotic: oatmeal porridge cooked overnight, dripping toast, tripe and onions, bubble and squeak, corned beef hash, apple suet pudding, Pontefract cakes, black treacle and junket. The reader must decide for himself or herself which of these generations has the advantage.

CHAPTER FOUR
Back to normal or nearly

The public went beef-mad in 1954.   Devon landlord quoted in *The Good Food Guide*, 1955–6.

Greater and ever-increasing softness and luxuriousness of modern life. Rise in the standard of physical courage, improvement in health & physique, continuous supersession of athletic records.
Qy. how to reconcile?   George Orwell (notebook, 17 April 1949), *Collected Essays, Journalism and Letters*, Vol. IV.

The pattern of British food consumption and taste since war-time rationing began to be felt in 1940 has so far been divided into two periods: one in which the national diet rapidly contracted in quality and scope (though not in overall nutritional value); and another, beginning in 1948–49, when it began to expand again. The process of expansion seemed slow at the time. The writer remembers at this period asking the best grocer in Chesterfield, a provincial town of substance, for long-grain rice and receiving the reply, 'Oh sir, we haven't seen that since before the war.' In some respects, as we have seen, 1947 was tighter than 1945. But the pace quickened, and by 1955, the food world with which we are familiar in the 1980s was already present in embryo. Other points of transition in the 1960s and 1970s may be easier for later writers to identify. For instance when he came to add a post-1945 chapter to the revised edition (1979) of his *Plenty and Want* (1966), John Burnett found himself writing after the British economy had suffered serious inflation combined with recession, though before world forces allied to Conservative government had depressed living standards and pushed unemployment to levels that in some parts of the country approached the level experienced between the wars. Part of Burnett's table of domestic food consumption, compiled from the bulletins of the National Food Survey, is therefore reproduced here (Table 2) with an additional column for the latest (1981) figures. The years 1950 and 1980, both

TABLE 2: Estimates of average household food consumption and expenditure 1950–81

	Consumption (ounces per person per week)			
	1950	1960	1974	1981
Liquid milk (pints)	4.78	4.84	4.74	4.01
Other milk (equiv. pints)	0.43	0.31	0.35	0.42
Cheese	2.54	3.04	3.74	3.89
Butter	4.56	5.68	5.61	3.69
Margarine	3.94	3.66	2.60	4.11
Lard and compound cooking fat	3.11	2.63	1.82	1.80
Eggs (number)	3.46	4.36	4.09	3.68
Preserves (inc. syrup, treacle)	6.30	3.21	2.47	2.08
Sugar	10.13	17.76	13.03	11.08
Beef and veal	8.06	8.74	7.41	6.96
Mutton and lamb	5.43	6.63	4.11	4.25
Pork	0.30	2.02	3.20	3.82
Bacon and ham (inc. cooked)	4.52	5.32	4.18	5.17
Poultry	0.35	1.68	5.18	7.30
Sausages	4.01	3.52	3.50	3.41
Other meat products	7.82	7.98	7.57	6.84
Fish, fresh and processed	6.18	4.69	2.76	2.81
Canned fish	0.44	0.95	0.60	0.69
Frozen fish and fish products	n.k.	0.29	0.96	1.42
Fresh green vegetables	13.81	15.34	12.70	11.98
Other fresh vegetables	11.38	9.13	10.20	11.83
Tomatoes, fresh	4.78	4.75	3.74	3.92
Frozen vegetables	n.k.	0.63	2.66	4.88
Canned vegetables	4.55	6.21	7.28	8.00
Potatoes (excl. processed)	62.04	56.14	45.66	38.91
Fruit, fresh	14.41	18.16	17.79	19.97
Canned fruit	3.68	6.84	4.90	2.61
Flour	7.25	6.76	5.30	5.96
White bread	50.91	36.63	28.24	21.85
Brown bread (inc. wholewheat and wholemeal)	2.55	3.35	2.64	5.56
Other bread	4.29	5.49	2.62	3.84
Buns, biscuits, cakes	10.37	11.98	10.08	9.16
Breakfast cereals	1.40	1.80	2.88	3.53
Tea	2.16	2.80	2.24	1.98
Coffee (inc. instant)	0.21	0.39	0.51	0.52
Soups	1.31	2.10	3.46	3.10

In 1950, rationing was still in force, though less severe than it had been. In 1960, the Macmillan government had just been re-elected on its 'affluent society' platform. In 1974, recession was beginning to take effect, and 1981 closes the period this book covers.

relatively constrained though for different reasons and in different degrees, embrace intervening decades which were commonly perceived as affluent. These thirty years were certainly marked by a popular assumption – correct or not – that in real terms, British levels of income, both monetary and 'social', were tending to cluster more closely, avoiding the extremes of wealth and poverty alike.

In interpreting the table, it is important to realise that even though rationing was still in force in 1950, the national diet was already in measurable respects (that is, 10 per cent in protein and 4 per cent in energy value) better than it had been in 1939. Even from the 1950 baseline, pork, poultry and breakfast cereals were the only major items on this domestic shopping list whose consumption more than doubled in the following twenty-five years, and a proportion of these gains were at the expense of other nutritionally comparable items: 'red' meat, fish, oatmeal. Statistics for the period of comparison unfortunately do not allow one to see how far the striking and progressive reduction in the consumption of white bread and potatoes can be set off against increases for pulses, rice, and pasta. But the effect of working wives and of more sedentary employment in the working population as a whole can be perceived in these figures. So can more recent preoccupations with fresh or 'healthy' foods, though the effect here is marginal, and the recent lead margarine has secured from butter (a 'war' more than adequately reflected in advertising campaigns) probably has more to do with price and quality changes than with cholesterol *angst*.

From 1954 onwards, people were free to eat as much as they wanted of anything they could pay for. This restored freedom, coupled with a decisive increase in real disposable income, put the onus for any inadequacy of supply and choice, in food as in other consumables, on to the market mechanisms which are controlled by capitalists small and (increasingly) great. It is therefore no coincidence that from this point onwards, advertising campaigns, cookery literature, immigration, foreign travel, and the ebbs and flows of fashion could make their effects felt quickly and directly. Most people's food choices remained conservative, but they were no longer, as they had once been, almost entirely predetermined by family, neighbourhood, and social class. In turn, the rise of British scientific and market-oriented research into new food products, and into techniques of processing and distribution, is also traced to the mid-1950s by historically-minded practitioners in these fields.

In 1955, too, a new Food and Drugs Act arrived on the statute book, nearly 100 years after its predecessor, the Act for Preventing the Adulteration of Articles of Food and Drink (1860). The central provision is clear enough: 'If a person sells to the prejudice of the purchaser any food or drug which is not of the nature or not of the substance or not of the quality of the food or drug demanded by the purchaser he shall . . . be guilty of an offence' (para. 2). Control of the grosser forms of adulteration had long been established in Britain. The thalidomide episode, and the accidental distribution of poisoned grain in the American Mid-West a few years ago, prevent one saying with absolute certainty that there could never be a British counterpart to the adulterated rape seed oil which killed or maimed 20,000 Spaniards in 1981, but a disaster on this scale must be accounted unlikely. At the same time, the lists of additives and preservatives permitted by the Food Additives and Contaminants Committee have grown rapidly during the subsequent twenty-five years of food chemistry, and some of those at first permitted – cyclamates for example – subsequently had to be withdrawn on suspicion, however faint, of noxious effects.

As often with British legislation of this type, much depends on court interpretation of what an ordinary purchaser expects to get for his money; and also on codes of practice worked out previously between the responsible ministry and the trades concerned. For instance, a coconut biscuit must contain coconut 'in a readily recognisable quantity' but a wine biscuit indicates the use of the biscuit, not its ingredients. The ordinary purchaser might well have been bemused by the Fish and Meat Spreadable Products Regulations 1968, under which 'salmon spread' had to contain at least 70 per cent of salmon, while in 'salmon paste' the 70 per cent fish content could be made up of only 25 per cent of salmon, and 45 per cent anonymous fish. 'Smoked salmon paste', to earn the name, needed only 10 per cent of smoked salmon. It proved harder and harder for regulations to keep up with the technology. Among the ingredients specified by weight under the Labelling of Food Regulations (1970), water did not have to be mentioned – an exclusion that was found extremely useful when scientists found a way to obtain more weight for a given amount of meat protein by artificially 'moistening' chicken, ham, and other meats with the aid of polyphosphates. The disquiet of those awkward individuals who insist on reading the small print on labels – and wish there were more – remains unallayed.

However, in 1955 life was simpler, and there was certainly less small print to read. Consumers' Association campaigned from the start for more informative labelling on a wide range of goods, but was not founded until 1957. The Trade Descriptions Act was not passed until 1968. In the 1955–56 edition of *The Good Food Guide* Raymond Postgate felt obliged to call his readers' attention in his Preface to two practices which, he suggested, 'they should now begin to treat as intolerable':

1. The provision of any synthetic white greasy material as 'cream'. When a 'cream substitute' is used, this should be clearly stated on the menu.
2. The provision of margarine instead of butter, or of a mixture of margarine and butter.

Time as well as legislation dealt with the former nuisance: actual cream became a relatively cheap way of making cold puddings look alluring, especially when devices appeared that could 'extend' it with milk or air, though more recently, the concept of 'mock cream' has reappeared in the guise of 'non-dairy whitener'. The second nuisance is more obstinate, partly because butter remains markedly more expensive than margarine, partly because certain margarines are now difficult to distinguish from certain butters,[1] and partly because British customers are so unexacting: it is a brave man or woman who inquires what is being spread on his or her bread in London sandwich bars.

The *Guide*, by now in its fifth edition, was still growing, and carried almost 1,000 entries – 400 pages in the pocket-sized edition that Cassell published at 5s (25p). Reprehensible practices of the kind just described were clearly not adopted in a Kensington *restaurant intime* called the Marquee, which made its debut in this edition. The *patron* was a migrant from Budapest called Egon Ronay, a caterer who shortly afterwards turned gamekeeper by issuing restaurant, hotel, pub and café guides of his own over a period – to date – of a quarter of a century. His Marquee offered 'several specialities cooked with a really Parisian touch, such as kidneys in port (7s 6d)'; also Ch. Langoa Barton '47 for 18s. At this time a chef of a more humdrum kind, responsible perhaps for a canteen or hospital kitchen, was paid less then £400 p.a., and the *grande bouffe* of the late Fifties and early Sixties was just beginning to swell. Many young people of the kind who, ten years later, would have been wolfing tagliatelle in the Terrazza or its cheaper Soho competitors were in 1955 still to be found in coffee bars, 'practised in eking out a cup of espresso for an hour and a half'.[2] These places, normally run by Italian caterers, multiplied in London and a few other cities on the strength of the machine that had been invented by Achille Gaggia in 1946, and been imported into Britain along with the Vespas, Lambrettas, and Olivetti typewriters which demonstrated so effectively to the tired British the resilience and ingenuity of post-war Italy. The Gaggia delivered, for the first time in England since coffee houses of a much earlier period, drinkable coffee in a public place – places, moreover, whose Festival of Britain colours, false ceilings, potted plants, and engaging flimsiness encouraged the young to believe that austerity had been banished at last. As Malcolm Bradbury put it:

The spirit of postwar materialism was just beginning to take off, and you could get Dundee cake, chocolate off ration, and washing machines. You could also go into that daring continental innovation, the espresso bar, order a cup of froth, and immediately find a crowd of your peers – the new welfare state young, the lower middle class or working class young men who had been pushed upward by the Butler Education Act, done grammar school and university, and were now all writing theses or novels.[3]

The coffee bars vanished as suddenly as they arrived, though not before Max Adrian had learnt how to reproduce the hiss and gargle of the Gaggia on stage at the Comedy Theatre, in a sketch that was still going strong on Not the Nine O'Clock News twenty-five years later.[4] The fundamental problem was economic: the contemporaries of Malcolm Bradbury and David Lodge did indeed stay a long time talking much and spending little at these expensive West End addresses; Italian caterers on their way up realised that there was more money to be made out of real food and a drinks licence. But there was a technical reason too. There were far more espresso machines installed in London than there were ever Italian engineers to maintain them. Typically, operators ran them until they seized up with their own sludge: British coffee returned to its weak norm or succumbed to the instant substitute, and restaurateurs found it easier to amuse their customers with hour-glass Cona devices (also popularised in the early Fifties). Critical consumers were left reflecting – and reflected again when cafetières arrived in the late 1970s – that a fool-proof or economy-proof coffee-making device has yet to be invented, and may never be, since the British market is the only one that stands in need of it.

By time measurements less tangible than coffee spoons, 1955 seems distant enough. It is not just that restaurant customers and food buyers, single or married (but seldom cohabiting), were the neatly suited, buttoned-down, pre-Suez generation for whom jeans and the Beatles both lay in the future. British food was still recognisably British, because immigrants from what was later called the New Commonwealth had not yet taken it in hand. Government statistics were still colour-blind at this time, so figures are hard to come by, but it is indicative that in the same edition of *The Good Food Guide* – which was at the time and long remained the only publication to take oriental restaurants seriously – there were nine in London but only four outside, led by Nazir Uddin's Bombay in Manchester where 'two people, first introduced to Indian food here, lost their last bus home because of their excitement; another, never before defeated, was unable to finish all her mushroom biriani'. At this time, there were as many Poles and Hungarians cooking in *Guide* restaurant kitchens as there were Indians and Chinese, although interestingly, far more English country inns then offered curries of a more or less convincing Anglo-Indian kind than do so now that British India is a fainter memory and curry fanciers have access to the real thing.

In 1955 or thereabouts, the Britishness of British food had no sooner been restored than it came under attack from the diversity created by plenty. This revolution was not led by restaurateurs – who were fully occupied with the beefsteak boom and, in Soho, with a developing appetite for scampi and risotto. The running – appropriately enough in a nation of shopkeepers – was made first by the retail food business. Most forms of food shopping had scarcely changed since the 1930s, and indeed since multiple retailing had lined up behind Sir Thomas Lipton half a century earlier still. But in the mid-1950s, with comparative suddenness, three separate forces projected British food shops and their customers' habits into a new age, not so much by responding to dietary demand as by creating it.

The first stimulus was the removal of rationing and controls. This automatically multiplied the number of 'lines' that an old-fashioned grocer felt obliged to stock if he hoped to satisfy his customers (many of whom at this period still expected to buy on credit). Labour costs, in the long period of full employment that had arrived with rearmament and the Korean war, propelled him towards self-service systems. However, not only small individual grocers, but also the big multiples such as Home & Colonial, lacked the frontages, the square-footage, and perhaps the managerial vision to take the necessary leap forward into American-style supermarkets, and the opportunity went to firms and individuals better equipped to take it: Sainsbury's (which went public in 1973), Tesco, Waitrose and the rest, joined later by a bulk frozen food specialist, Bejam. These food-based stores were joined by Marks & Spencer and other chain-stores diversifying into food from garments and other preoccupations. Competition was intense, and pressure to abolish retail price maintenance was on other grounds becoming irresistible, though it might have been resisted longer by the Conservative Party, which was in power throughout this period, had not Edward Heath, nicknamed 'Grocer' for his pains, pushed abolition of RPM through during the run-up to the 1964 election, over some muttering from his colleagues. Competition, moreover, slowly began to take quality into account as well as price. In 1955, Marks & Spencer was still a down-market garment store from which debs and blue-stockings condescended to buy their knickers – but little else. Twenty years later, they were buying French wine and Israeli avocados there too.

The second force was a new medium of advertising: commercial television. This, like the growth of supermarkets, got off to a slow start. Even after a Conservative government had bowed to a powerful supporters' lobby and passed the Television Act (1954), several backers had bitten their fingernails to the quick or withdrawn their stake altogether before the measure proved, as the Canadian media mogul Roy Thomson had prophesied, 'a licence to print money'. It needed an un-English type of vision to perceive that television advertising was ideally matched to the correspondingly visual display of supermarket shelves, where weight-for-price, assessable quality, and point-of-sale advice became secondary considerations in the housewife's mind, once a trigger in the brain had been pulled by a half-remembered package and a half-heard jingle. So touching was shoppers' faith in the magical powers of the box that it was often sufficient to label a product 'as advertised on television', as though the Radio Doctor (Charles Hill) had personally recommended it from his new base in Television House.

James P. Johnston suggests that without television advertising, Maxwell House instant coffee – an imitation of an imitation – could hardly have snatched 20 per cent of the instant coffee market from Nescafé (which had been launched before the war, but had then been promptly rendered virtually unobtainable).[5] The concomitant price and coupon war between these brands helped to make coffee – of a kind – a classless drink, which it had never previously been, though 'real' coffee remained the boast or stigma of a more conscious minority.

The third force, without which the other two must have been much less effective, was the real-term rise in disposable incomes that enabled Harold Macmillan, in the run-up to the 1959 election, to say without fear of contradiction that 'most of our people know they have never had it so good', and Rab Butler, his lieutenant, to promise a doubled standard of living in the next twenty-five years (by 1984, that was). There was an obvious link between steadily rising affluence of this kind and patronage of restaurants for evening pleasure rather than mid-day utility, though as the catering trade later discovered to its cost, habits of this kind proved easy to discard when times turned bad again. The effect of affluence on home consumption and food shopping was equally marked, but more patchy and unpredictable in its effects. The consumption of bread and potatoes declined, and that of chicken (which had become as cheap as any other meat) rose. The sales of breakfast cereals and frozen vegetables expanded hugely as housewives took advantages of their employment opportunities. But there was no conspicuous switch or trade-up from one foodstuff to another more expensive one. It was in beverages that volatile shifts in allegiance turned a nation of tea drinkers into coffee addicts, and later, introduced the mass public to wine. But beer sales held up quite well too, mainly because it became more respectable for women to drink it, both at home and in the pub, and a national average consumption of six bottles of wine a year left plenty of room for the next generation of wine marketers.

Nor did British folk choose, as the French to some extent did in similar circumstances, to increase their actual expenditure on food painlessly by allotting to it something near to a constant proportion of their income as their prosperity grew. Instead, they allowed the proportion to fall steadily – from 33 per cent in 1954 to 25 per cent in 1975 – and inequalities between the consumption of different class and income groups centred on goods and services of other kinds. In 1975, 'the richest households spent £5.89 p.w. a head on food, the poorest, including many old age pensioners, £4.30'. Wealth still affects the dietary pattern significantly, but it is not solely for economic reasons that 'the poor eat 56 per cent less fruit than the rich, 31 per cent less fresh meat, 28 per cent less cheese, 26 per cent less milk and 19 per cent less fresh green vegetables, but consume 57 per cent more potatoes, 33 per cent more cereal products and 32 per cent more sugar'.[6] Working men chose grease guns and power drills rather than butter; their wives chose time-saving 'convenience foods' – at first fish fingers and peas, latterly whole dinners – to buy time for paid work that would in turn buy them further labour-saving devices in the home, or an annual holiday (packaged like the peas, but still a holiday).

Lobster and caviare were not on the agenda, even when people were invited by the Gallup Poll to name their dream dinners: in this context, the only significant *food* change between 1947 and 1973 was the substitution of prawn cocktail for tomato soup and steak for chicken in the meal desired. By 1982, 'Black Forest' and other gateaux were edging ice cream out of top place in caterers' menus; the mass market meal choice thus neatly encapsulated was calculated to make a caterer rub his hands and a food critic wince. It is not difficult to provide – and take short-cuts with – the stereotyped things that content so many. (But it has to be remembered that in Britain under 4 per cent of household income is spent on meals outside the home, compared with over 20 per cent spent on food for domestic consumption. Restaurant and hotel dining room expenditure, substantial though it is in certain sections of the community, mainly affects heads of households, and by being charged to business expenses, often bypasses the domestic economy. Even the dream meal, for 364 days in the year, remains a dream for most of the people whom Gallup invites to give it expression. Were it eaten more frequently, the menu might read more adventurously.)

Also in 1955, research was being conducted for the second 'Crawford' report,[7] a sequel to *The People's Food*, a similar survey published twenty years previously. The difference between the two sets of findings, such as it was, is of less interest than the difference which would surely be shown if – as is devoutly to be wished – a similar survey were now to be conducted again. The enquiry reports what a representative nationwide sample of 4,457 people ate, summer and winter, and the times of day at which they ate it. At this period, not only the Marketing Division of W. S. Crawford Ltd but British social science as a whole was proud of its recently-acquired ability to count heads effectively, and almost reluctant to make deeper probes that might upset the figures. The report is marred by the questions no one thought of asking, and by the answers no one thought of questioning, as well as by the patronising commentary that links the tables. For instance, after remarking that few adults in any class eat their principal evening meal after 7 p.m., summer or winter, because 'the majority of people live near their work' and finish around 5 p.m., the author continues: 'Time may then be taken for a look round the garden and a glass of sherry and a moment with the children on the one hand, or for the manual worker a change, shave and general clean-up. Either way, they are "ready, willing and able" by 6 p.m.'[8]

However, it may be fortunate that the survey was conducted at the very moment that the information it contained, and the social assumption of its interpreters, were both about to go out of date. The twitchiness about class at this period of galloping social change is understandable; it was in 1955, too, that Nancy Mitford was telling *Encounter* readers that 'dinner' was non-U for 'luncheon' and 'sweet' non-U for 'pudding'.[9] The Crawford survey showed that even 'upper' class women were almost equally divided on the former point: one wonders how reliable the interviewers' social categories were, and how many well brought-up respondents rebuked them for saying 'lunch' for 'luncheon'. At this date a two-thirds majority of all regions, ages and social classes also called their evening meal 'tea' or 'high tea' rather than 'dinner' or (a tiny sub-section) 'supper'.

A similar majority had started eating it by half past six. Even in the trivial matter of nomenclature, changes were in train. Dinner, according to the OED in 1898, was already a meal being eaten, 'by the professional and fashionable classes', usually in the evening. But as early as 1950, a character in Barbara Pym's novel *Some Tame Gazelle* (1950) says pertinently of a meal at the vicarage, 'We had supper . . . well, dinner really, because there was soup, though I *think* it was tinned.' John Silverlight, quoting this in his *Observer* 'Words' column, envisages 'a barrister sitting down with his wife in the evening to soup and a roast with vegetables (cooked by her); cheese and fruit; modest wine; coffee. Dinner or supper? . . . My guess is that, unless there were formally invited guests, it would have been supper.'

Two different pressures can be identified behind this shift in middle-class language: on the one hand to find a word that does not have either the social or the temporal ambiguities of 'dinner'; on the other, to find an everyday domestic substitute for 'dinner' that would express fashionable informality and not be confused – if a friend were invited to share the meal – with the overtones of 'dinner-party'. (The Crawford survey uses the term 'late supper' to describe the snack meal that about three-quarters of the population take between their early evening meal and going to bed.) It is still possible, in accepting invitations to British homes in different regions or milieus, to be offered either much more or much less food than the guest is expecting.

It is certainly useful to be reminded that in 1955, six out of every ten men were eating their mid-day meal at home; that two-thirds of homes had potatoes mid-day, but only on Sunday did a similar proportion offer green vegetables or salads as well; that while main dishes varied at mid-week meals, for Sunday dinner over half the population had either roast beef or roast lamb, with no other main dish – not even pork or poultry – mustering more than 6 per cent of choices; that omelettes were statistically negligible at any meal in any class; and that the middle and upper classes, especially in the south, consumed more custard than their social inferiors did. Milk puddings were still the most popular sweet.

But the anachronistic limitations of Crawford's research design are shown by the detailed enumeration of possible food options, which fails to distinguish between tinned and frozen vegetables or fish, includes 'shellfish (oysters etc)' but not fish fingers, finds room for boiled mutton but lacks separate headings for chicken and other poultry, mentions pasta and rice but not lentils and beans, and disregards chocolate and chocolate-based sweets as a food. Throughout, 'beer, wines and spirits' are treated as the same answer, with cider omitted altogether. Cream and tinned milk, both less popular than custard, are similarly combined.

Both at mid-day and in the evening a clear majority of those who drank anything at all with their meals drank tea. Coffee achieved 10 per cent at mid-day, 5 per cent in the evening, and 'beer/wines/spirits' reached 3 per cent at most. The negative information from this section of the enquiry is more striking than the positive: roughly a quarter of the sample at mid-day, and up to an eighth in the evening, claimed to drink nothing at all with their meals, not even water. This may go some way to explain the 'wetness' of British vernacular cooking, in which not only do flavours have to be intensified by bottled sauces, but natural juices have to be extended by artificially compounded liquids. Perhaps Bisto gravy and Bird's custard ought to be reclassified in social surveys as drinks rather than foods.

'In the Torture Chamber' by Norman Mansbridge

PART TWO
Themes – why we eat as we do

CHAPTER FIVE
The melting pot new-flavoured
The rise of immigrant cuisines

The most important activity in human life is eating. As any community progresses, its diet is the most salient guide to its refinement.
A. H. Sharar (1860–1926) *Lucknow: the last phase of an oriental culture.* Translated by E. S. Harcourt and Fakhir Hussain, 1975.

Good cooking does not depend on whether the dish is large or small, expensive or economical. If one has the art, then a piece of celery or salted cabbage can be made into a marvellous delicacy; whereas if one has not the art, not all the greatest delicacies and rarities of land, sea or sky are of any avail. *Yuan Mei, Eighteenth Century Chinese Poet.* Translated by Arthur Waley, 1956.

Chicken's blood porridge. Soyed pig's bowel. Items on a Cantonese restaurant menu, Soho, 1982.

Putrefied mucous discharge of an animal's guts. Chinese description of strong cheese, to E. N. and Marja L. Anderson.

The collision of food worlds in Britain over the past generation can be expressed either as triumph or tragedy. On the one hand, it opened literally insular British cooks and eaters to the influences and materials of at least three major culinary civilisations: Chinese, Indian, and Middle Eastern. Nothing like it had happened since the mediaeval world discovered the spice routes. On the other hand, it yielded a squalid harvest of mutual contempt between native and newcomer: urban legends of cat-bones in the curry and full-grown Alsatians in the fridge; court histories of loutish bilkers, decaying ducks, and VAT transgressions. Perhaps it can be safely said that cross-fertilisation is permanent, while some of the misunderstandings are at least capable of being softened with time.

There has not yet been very much time. We have already seen that by

1955, the British diet had completed its post-war recovery and the contemporary food scene was beginning to take shape. But, in the present connection, only beginning. In the mid-1950s, the predominant styles of cooking, and the staple foodstuffs on which they were based, were British to the last chip, whether the meal was being eaten at home or away, and indeed whether the menu was couched in English or the French of Stratford-atte-Bow. Outside the specialist restaurants and restaurant districts of London, with a few individualists elsewhere – for instance, Maurice Ithurbure, a pupil of Escoffier who practised at Chez Maurice in Eastbourne – most serious restaurant menus depended on plainly cooked meat, with a few 'continental' decorations for the adventurous. The cookery book and the restaurant markets were almost entirely distinct. The former belonged to women who behaved – and were expected to behave – with extreme diffidence in restaurants. The latter belonged to men who did not profess to know anything about cooking. (Raymond Postgate himself referred most technical questions to his friend Philip Harben. Other male correspondents of early *Good Food Guides* knew what they liked but had not the faintest idea of how to achieve it.)

A typical entry in *The Good Food Guide 1955* said of The Warwick Arms in Warwick: 'The chef here makes a very good Indian curry, and some noteworthy simple Italian dishes such as spaghetti and ravioli. Otherwise the cooking is good standard English – roast beef, fillet and minute steaks, jugged hare . . . Adequate omelets.' The chef concerned need not have been British by birth. In most branches of the catering trade, Italians, Poles and Swiss were already among the nationalities well represented. But outside London, the concept of an entire restaurant devoted to a non-European, or even a European, 'ethnic' style was almost wholly unfamiliar. In the same year, the *Guide* included single examples of Chinese places in Brighton, Liverpool and Manchester, a single Indian in Manchester, and a single Greek in Nottingham, and that was all. The London pages carried two Chinese, seven Indian (including one Burmese) and four Greek or Turkish. Italians were more firmly established, and not only in London. Edinburgh's seaside district – called Portobello – boasted several family cafés (Demarco, Di Rollo) whose ice cream drew customers from all over the city.

It was not that 'exotic' materials could not be found in Britain – by the determined – at this date. It was thought worth remark in the trade press that Gennoni's restaurant in Plymouth was selling half a hundredweight of spaghetti weekly, and a greengrocer's advertisement promised rare fruit and vegetables that would 'transform ordinary menus into master-pieces of culinary art: courgettes, fennel, curly endives, artichokes, au-bergines, capsicums, honeydew melons, grapes, mandarins, passion fruit, dessert dates and fresh litchees (*sic*)'. But it was with an air of wonder-ment that *Guide* readers found such things at a Welsh inn reached by obeying the following directions: 'Go out through Swiss Cottage on to the A5, turn left when you cross the Menai Bridge and keep left till you come to the waterfront opposite Caernarvon.' When the weary traveller disembarked from his Riley or Hillman, Mrs Anne Hinchcliffe-Davies's dinner menu at the Mermaid Inn in Foel Ferry was apt to offer 'hors d'oeuvres aux pimentos à l'orientale; ham braised in white wine with Hungarian stuffed tomatoes, peas, beans and potatoes Anna; and Chinese chow-chow mousse, sponge kisses with strawberries and cream mandarins in orange curaçao, or raspberries in kirsch and Melba sauce. This cost 10/6.' Anglesey, alas, has seen nothing like it since.

However, the tastes and capabilities of a few isolated individuals were about to be overtaken by the provision made by and for whole popula-tions. In the mid-1950s, immigrants who had arrived during the employ-ment boom of the previous ten years from China and Hong Kong, the Indian sub-continent, and the Caribbean were still a relatively un-noticeable minority. They were confined to particular districts – seldom the most savoury districts – of particular cities. Pre-war immigration of a different kind had been similarly localised, but more readily absorbed. If instead of taking the A5 to Anglesey from Swiss Cottage you took a short walk along the Finchley Road from 'Schweizer Hauschen' you could hear most Middle European languages – plus Yiddish, of course – and eat Austrian patisserie at the Dorice, whose Silesian baker had learnt his craft in a British internment camp in 1940.

Those 50,000 Jewish refugees allowed into Britain from Europe during the 1930s left their mark on the diet of Hendon, Finchley and Hampstead as well as on most of the arts and sciences. The cafe and restaurant trade has always been one of the first flights of independence for an immigrant who possesses little capital and no knowledge of his host country's language. Food is an international system of communica-tion, the return on investment at market in the morning arrives the same evening, and no wages have to be paid to the housebound family. In similar ways, over a much longer period, anglicised Italian cafés had become integral to the London street scene, and Chinese restaurants, even more primitive, had established themselves round the docks with which Chinese seamen had become familiar: Limehouse, Liverpool, Cardiff. At this period in Liverpool, when domestic necessity compelled a week's cafe eating, it was possible to pick a different, equally mediocre Chinese place every night within a quarter of a mile of Great St George's.

Liverpool, too, had a coloured population of long standing, just beginning to expand rapidly in the district which the world now knows as Toxteth, notably the patch – locally known as the Jungle – round Upper Parliament Street and the Rialto cinema that was. But it was to be many years before either officials or academics thought it worthwhile not merely to collect housing and employment statistics but to study in detail the particular circumstances, origins, needs, qualifications and desires of particular immigrant populations. Public opinion itself naturally reacted to the newcomers' colour, which was visible, rather than to their culture, which seemed inaccessible. Even specialists in race relations were often reluctant to confront the implications of differences that among Chinese, for instance, seemed to produce disciplined children and rapid capital accumulation via laundries and restaurants, and among West Indians, conscientious industrial work but unruly youth (when outside the home), hardly any small businesses, and no restaurants (though a sufficiency of drinking clubs). It simply did not occur to Anglo-Saxons, prisoners of their own culture, that the complex of attitudes and behaviour and opportunity which make up a diet and a food culture could be a clue to anything else. More than a decade later, the nutritional sociologist John McKenzie expressed to me his own surprise that 'race relations studies have not looked at food much, even though it generates so much emotion'. His own studies in Notting Hill (scene in 1958 of the first British disturbance that could be called a race riot) suggested that although public restaurants were not part of Caribbean food ways, West Indian immigrants were at pains to keep their own nutritional culture intact:

'You would expect West Indians to accept our own food patterns more rapidly than, say, Pakistanis. But in fact they are very slow to do so. Even after five years residence the main meal in a British West Indian household still consists of West Indian dishes.'[1] This in turn explained the quick appearance of yams, red snapper and other Caribbean favourites in London markets serving West Indian districts.

Table 3 sets out the proportionate pace and extent of the penetration of Britain by different immigrant populations in the 1950s and early 1960s. The versatile chef of the Warwick Arms, *c.* 1955, has been noted.

TABLE 3: Commonwealth natives in England and Wales by place of birth 1951–1966, excluding children of UK-born parents born in India and Pakistan.

	1951	*1961*	*1971*
Indian	30,000	81,400	282,680
Pakistani	5,000	24,900	134,620
Caribbean	15,300	171,800	304,070
African			
(including Asians)	9,500	30,400	156,290
Cypriot and Maltese	24,700	66,600	107,140
Hong Kong and Malaysian	12,000	29,900	55,200

Here is a later traveller's account of the difference the ensuing twenty years made to the same locality:

There are restaurants and delicatessens in a dozen national styles. Yams and tortillas, cabanos and cracowska, grappa and pitta bread can be found with ease. So, for that matter, can local rabbit, hare, pheasant and trout. All this may seem commonplace to those who live in more obviously cosmopolitan places, but I can assure them that it is not the normal state of affairs in medium-sized English provincial towns; and to someone like me, who comes from a town where they have only just heard about green peppers, it makes Leamington seem like London and New York rolled into one compact sample-sized city. Equally, as I was brought up in a town with only one cafe, the existence of *five* bistros and *five* Indian restaurants – as well as upwards of 50 other eating places – seems to suggest a level of luxury and extravagance to tempt the fate of Sodom and Gomorrah.[2]

However, the older-established north Italians, reinforced by newer arrivals from south of Rome, remained the most pervasive external influence upon British food habits, even without counting as Italian the operations of Charles (later Lord) Forte, whose financial acumen consolidated his success in giving the British mass public what it was prepared to swallow in milk bars and motorway cafés. By 1970 he was in a position to take over Trust Houses, a stolidly British chain of hotels, and start to build a large international hotel empire whose formidable profitability silenced most critics of his food, service, wine and industrial relations. In 1965 the largest pasta factory in Europe was opened in St Alban's (a Roman colony from way back) and for a generation now, mothers at home and teenagers on the town have used first spaghetti bolognese, later frozen pizzas, to meet the daily quest for something filling, quick, and cheap, however denatured the actual taste.

'Zuppa Inglese' (extract) by Posy Simmonds

Italianisation at this level ran concurrently with the superior *trattorie* –
owned by Mario and Franco, and designed by Apicella in white tile, like
Jimmy Porter's university – that excited fashionable London during the
1960s, after the eclipse of the coffee bars. But even this striking importa-
tion of Mezzogiorno light and noise only represented the organic growth
of an influence that had begun to shape London catering well before
1900. The Census of 1911 already records the presence of 1,600 Italian
nationals as waiters, 900 as chefs, and 1,000 as labourers in hotels and
restaurants in the United Kingdom. There were also 1,200 domestic
servants, 1,400 bakers and confectioners, and 500 café or restaurant
owners. Their prime source of origin was and partly remains a comparatively small district of the Emilian Apennines, which Robin Palmer
disguises in his fieldwork under the name of Abbazzia:[3] 'In 1973 I traced
184 Abbazzini households in London; 93 of them were associated with a
private business. All but eight of these were cafés, snack-bars or restaurants.'

In Emilia, Palmer comments, the outside observer is struck by
people's intense desire for economic independence, and also by the
region's capacity to produce and consume foodstuffs:

Emilians spend more on food than the average Italian. Abbazzini traditionally
make their own wine and cure their own ham and salami; in the autumn the
women gather mushrooms and the men are avid hunters. In London, Abbazzini
also make their own wine with grapes bought in street markets; some purchase
pigs in the countryside and form salami-making cooperatives; whole families go
on mushrooming expeditions in the New Forest; and the men rent 'shoots' in
Cambridgeshire or Surrey (p. 250).

This talent for transferring a 'rich' ethnic food culture to a new
habitat is relevant to the success of any immigrant cuisine. But the
Italian 'Abbazzini' were overtaken, outside London at least, during the
1960s, and if the criterion for culinary influence were limited to restaurant penetration, there would be no doubt about which nationality
has held the post-war lead. Brendan Bracken once said that if you set
down two Poles in the middle of the Sahara they would promptly start a
newspaper. Do the same to two Hong Kong Chinese and within days
there would be a restaurant, offering unmentionable parts of the camel
in savoury disguises. The Chinese restaurant trade began to take off in
Britain (outside the traditional localities) in the mid-Fifties, and the
boom continued without intermission until the early Seventies, when it
was curtailed by political and economic pressures which lie outside the

scope of this book. However, by that time the rice-bowl revolution in Britain had come to stay. (Indian restaurants were less widespread, but similarly successful where they congregated.)

There is no need to accept James L. Watson's own suggestion that the boom was directly attributable to the British 'changing their eating habits and developing a taste for foreign cuisine, most notably Indian and Chinese'.[4] The taste for Indian cooking had existed in Britain since the eighteenth century, indeed in a sense since the beginning of the spice trade. The taste for Chinese cooking had to be acquired, with cheapness as the most obvious stimulant to the appetite. (It was clearly not learnt from foreign travel, as is too glibly assumed in other contexts.) It would have been a brave Cantonese restaurateur who in 1955 set up a smart restaurant in an affluent suburb and waited for customers. That day was to arrive, but not yet. However, it did not take the immigrants from Hong Kong and the New Territories long to realise that in Britain's resolutely declining economy there were better prospects for chefs and waiters, as service industry workers, than for engineers and electronic specialists. Even the catering boom slackened off in the early 1970s, and by this time increasingly draconian immigration laws had made it harder to obtain work permits for chefs. The introduction of VAT – a tax which most Chinese restaurateurs resented and one or two fell foul of – further encouraged customers to switch from restaurants to more economical take-aways and fish and chip shops, which require fewer staff and are not subject to VAT.

In the past decade, the main thrust of Chinese restaurant expansion has shifted, taking advantage of EEC passport regulations, to West Germany and Scandinavia – good choices, for both financial and culinary reasons. But smaller British towns are still being colonised for the first time. For instance, a few doors away from my 'second home' in Dorset, the second oriental worker to take up residence in the town (the first was a Ugandan Asian carpenter) started and has managed to sustain a take-away unpromisingly (to Dorset ears) called Yuk Wah, which means 'Up China'. While fitting out the premises, a local builder's labourer found an ancient bird's nest and put it in the window, with a placard advertising 'bird's nest soup here soon'. The joke did not long survive the owner's arrival next morning: perhaps it went down in someone's records as an instance of racial harassment.

By 1970, the number of UK Chinese catering businesses of all kinds had levelled out at about 4,000. Already, according to research for Smethurst's National Catering Enquiry five years earlier, 31 per cent of

those who ate out regularly or occasionally had visited Chinese restaurants (in Liverpool 48 per cent). The other national figures given
were for Indian restaurants (8 per cent), Italian (5 per cent), French or
'French style' (5 per cent) and German or other (2 per cent). Only in
London and Cardiff did the figure for visitors to Indian restaurants rise
above 10 per cent. In *The Good Food Guide 1963–4* (the book was then
biennial) eight Chinese and six Indian or Malaysian restaurants were
listed in London out of a total of 164 that satisfied the examiners; in Egon
Ronay's 1964 guide, there were 15 Chinese and 10 Indian places in
London out of 270 listed. Outside London, the *GFG* listed eight
Chinese and four Indians; Ronay's attention to oriental restaurants did
not extend beyond the capital.

Most of these were small family businesses, angled towards what
their owners conceived to be European taste: lurid sweet and sour pork,
inauthentic chop suey and chow mein. Only in the 1970s did shadow
Hong Kongs emerge in south Soho and central Manchester, with
different restaurants and 'lineages', often bearing familiar Hong Kong
names. These places competed with each other vigorously for chefs,
and for the patronage not just of white customers but of other Chinese
catering workers, who make weekly trips from their suburban take-
aways to shop, gossip, and find out what's cooking in the centre. This
gregariousness is characteristic of the south Chinese: it takes at least two
to make either a meal or a gambling session, and menus and meal
structures are ill-adapted to solitary diners. Nor can life have been easy
for the first lonely settlers in locations where livings could be made.
Convinced of their own cultural superiority to white devils, and slow to
learn the language until taught by their own children, most adult
caterers had few educational resources to fall back on. In Hong Kong a
catering career begins, as it once did in France, from the age of twelve
upwards, with years of carrying coal and tending the spit until the chef
decides that a youngster has looked and listened long enough to be
allowed to chop a spring onion. He is then embarked on a craft apprenticeship of a rigour undreamt of in British catering colleges. Indeed, as
E. N. and Marja L. Anderson point out, in Hong Kong cooking and
eating is not an alternative to culture and education; in its technical
accomplishment and imaginative innovation it is itself a medium of
communication: 'Many a non-Chinese has come away from a meal
cursing the "inscrutable" Chinese for saying nothing but bland, polite
phrases, when the meal itself was the message, one perfectly clear to a
Chinese. In short, food management is critical to all harmony – in one's

own body, in one's social life, and in one's interaction with the world.'[5]

Until the late 1960s, there was little regional differentiation between one style of Chinese or Indian cooking and another in Britain. The Anglo-Chinese mainstream had always been the styles associated with Canton, Hong Kong and Shanghai (based on fast steaming or stir-frying of finely chopped, very fresh vegetables, fish and pork, with rice or noodles the staple, and oil the medium). Nothing but a long sea voyage separated these waterfronts from those of Liverpool, London and Cardiff, and the family connections established by shipboard service survived both the cold war and the age of the aeroplane. To a remarkable extent, Chinese catering families can be traced to particular villages in the New Territories, just as Bengali ones can be traced to the north-east of what is now Bangladesh, where whole villages once monopolised cooking and galley work in the British Merchant Navy.[6]

However, to the British all these sub-groups remained simply 'Chinese' and 'Indian' until immigration populations rose to the point where the pool of customers made it possible for regional colours to be reassumed. Coincidentally, at this time in Britain and in Europe too the rise of regional consciousness of all kinds began to affect the work of cookery writers and tourist guide editors alike. This in turn affected the level of awareness at which other nations as well as our own were perceived. In the case of Chinese cooking in Britain, this process of differentiation, begun by the (Cantonese) Friends group of restaurants in east London, was materially assisted by a talented Pekinese chef who objected to the ritual self-criticism imposed upon him by the Chinese chargé d'affaires in London. In 1966 this chef, Mr Kuo, migrated to the more sympathetic environment of Willesden High Road, in what *The Good Food Guide* later described as 'the most important cultural defection since Nureyev'. From then on, it was possible for British eaters to distinguish between the wheat-based menus of north China and the rice-based restaurants of the coastal south (a distinction made even easier by the introduction of *dim-sum* – snacks steamed in baskets – into Cantonese places and by the set 'banquet' meals, almost invariably including crisp-fried duck with pancakes and *hoi-sin* sauce, which Mr Kuo and his Pekinese followers preferred). Other distinctions followed, for instance between the eclectic, enormous repertoire of Hong Kong style, and the more specialised Szechuan school, which is hotly spiced with chilli and Szechuan pepper (*fagara*), at least until London customers mute a chef's taste.

Somewhat later, a similar diversity began to appear among Indo-Pakistani restaurants. With few exceptions, such as the Tamil cuisine at the India Club in the Aldwych, such places relied on Bengali cooks and Pakistani (Bangladeshi) Muslim owners. Since British Army and administrative experience of India had centred on the meat-eating Muslim north, this suited the market, and although there were still plenty of majors (retd.) who prided themselves on the 'heat' of the curries they could swallow without sending themselves up in flames, customers of tenderer years or sex were better pleased with the mild pilaus, sweet dhansaks and creamy khormas of north Indian cuisine. Late in the 1960s, *tandoors* – clay ovens – for dry-roasting of yoghourt-marinated and spiced chicken began to be imported. Apart from providing for British taste more rice and less of the various Indian pulses and breads – *nans*, *chapatis*, *parathas* – this type of cooking, whether in cheap student places or in elaborately 'Moghul' settings, continues to dominate 'Indian' restaurants all the way from Newcastle to north Soho. (Geographically, by the way, an unspoken comity agreement seemed to operate whereby the Chinese took the north-west of England and the south of Soho, while the Pakistanis took the north-east coast and north Soho.)

But during the 1970s, several other cuisines of the Indian subcontinent and its Indonesian neighbours emerged in London, notably on sites near the main railway stations. Minor examples include Nepalese and Goanese: a Gurkha restaurant turned up, predictably, in Aldershot, and it gratifies the culinary geographer to trace the effects of religion and colonisation in the spiced Goan sausage called *chourisam*, inherited from Portuguese *chorizo*, and in the roast sucking pig Goans eat on Christmas Day: by 1981 a popular book on Indian cooking distributed by Marks & Spencer included three recipes described as Goan.[7]

Much more influential, partly because by British standards conspicuously cheap, are the 'chat houses' and 'sweet centres' opened in the late 1970s by vegetarian Hindus, originally from Gujerat. It was not commercial opportunism that precipitated this migration, but Britain's reluctant acceptance earlier in the decade of East African Asians with British passports, when the black rulers of Uganda and Kenya threatened to make them stateless refugees. Their concentration in small businesses in London and Manchester (eight pages of Patels are to be found in the 1981 London telephone directory) suggests that the restaurateurs and confectioners among them would have prospered from the patronage of their own countrymen even if the service they offered had been less well adapted to the manners and economic circumstances of the time. Sharad Patel of the Diwana Bhel Puri Houses near Euston and Paddington must have been surprised himself by the glove-like fit achieved between what Gujerati food culture was used to providing and what the shifting street culture of the metropolis found it wanted: ingeniously compounded and spiced food, mainly based on pulses, that cost little and could be eaten casually and quickly (in 1982 he was planning to open a Paris branch). Sweet centres of similar origin are also beginning to appeal to the notoriously sweet British tooth: as the Lucknow gourmet A. H. Sharar observed over fifty years ago (and he was a Muslim): 'Taking all things into consideration, Hindu confectioners are on the whole much better and more popular than Muslim, and the people who really appreciate sweets are the Hindus. Possibly because Muslims are meat-eaters, they prefer food containing salt. Hindus on the other hand prefer a sweet taste.'[8]

This is certainly true of the Gujeratis, who may have been the Hindu chefs Sharar actually encountered in north and central India. The Tamil cooking of the south, as yet found only in relatively few restaurants in London, is more sour and savoury, with lemon or coconut rice, *dosai* (crisp pancakes with coconut chutney) and fiery *rasam* and *sambars* among the most characteristic dishes.

The most recent Far-Eastern cuisine to establish itself in London (and Oxford) was the south-east Asian, embracing Malaysia and Singapore, Thailand and Indonesia. (The Vietnamese normally gravitate to France, for linguistic reasons, and more recently to New York.) Singapore functions in relation to this vast, fertile quarter rather as Hong Kong does for China: an entrepot where trades, tastes, languages and cultures mingle and interact: one of the world's great street scenes. But throughout the region certain ingredients are held in common: rice, of course, and also, under different names, *blachan*, derived from shellfish that have been salted, dried, pounded and rotted – a very ancient taste in all senses, for it is the nearest modern equivalent to the Roman *garum*, specified in the recipes of Apicius. Lemon grass and *laos* are other flavourings, peanut and coconut are included in many dishes, along with chillies, garlic, ginger and soy. A wide variety of fruit and vegetables, decoratively used, accompany beef, lamb and pork as well as fresh and dried fish. Rosemary Brissenden points out that in the climate of religious syncretism that pervades south-east Asia, the prohibitions characteristic of Indian diets are seldom strictly applied.[9]

As the names of the more elaborate Indonesian restaurants in London suggested – Bali, Mata Hari – this style at first belonged more to international tourism (and doubtless to Singapore financial houses) than to genuine ethnicity. However, by the mid-seventies, the large south-east Asian student population in London had begun to generate cheaper, more authentic restaurants (the original Rasa Sayang, Melati, and in Oxford Munchy Munchy) which made it possible to feel that the style was here to stay, even if the majority of their Indonesian customers are temporary rather than permanent residents in Britain. Less arrogant than Chinese, less segregated than most Indians, and more economical of expensive protein than Japanese or Koreans, south-east Asian caterers can fairly regard their future in London as secure, and would probably do well in any British university city that also has a busy trade in conventions and tourists.

Japanese cuisine is a closed circuit to most British people (Americans, originally because of the Japanese community long established in California, are often better informed). The style was slow to arrive in London after 1945, probably because of doubts about how it would be received, for there were already by the 1960s enough Japanese businessmen suffering the City of London's restaurants in polite silence for a serious Japanese restaurant to be a safe investment. The Hiroko, opened in the West End in 1967, was soon followed by others. But everything about expense-account Japanese restaurants suggests that Europeans are hardly expected to flock to their tatami rooms except as guests. Many places keep their regulars' opened bottles of whisky – Suntory for patriots, Dimple Haig for snobs – against their return.

Japanese facility with the English language, though it has improved considerably in recent years, at first seldom penetrated to waitress level. Similarly, British businessmen in Tokyo seldom have time, inclination or encouragement to explore Japanese cooking outside their stereotyped westernised hotels, and British tourism to Japan is negligible. Even if cultural factors of this kind are discounted, there has been little to promote mutual understanding between Japanese and English tastes. A civilisation that demands copious helpings of meat and potatoes, lumpishly presented and followed by rich puddings, has little to say at table to a civilisation that traditionally demands refined, almost self-consciously economical meals based on fish, soy, and rice, takes no interest in a sweet course, and affects a style of presentation that makes every dish not merely into 'a picture' but into a recondite set of aesthetic references. Only the pickle jar – when allowance is made for the difference between suimono and piccalilli – stands at the divide between the two cuisines, indispensable to both.

Even fish, which might have been thought a natural bond between two islands rich in marine resources, divides as much as it unites: fish and chips on the one hand and *tempura* on the other have little in common but the technique of deep-frying, and *sashimi* – slices of fish served raw with a dip – seldom appeals to British palates and sensibilities. Shizuo Tsuji, director and inspiration of the 2,500-student hotel school in Osaka that bears his name, and author of the best book available in English on his country's cooking, recalls sending a colleague to Billingsgate fish market to buy something for the raw fish course, when they were both in London and needed to serve a Japanese dinner to guests: 'He came back horrified, saying the fish looked listless and wan – as if they had all just come out of hospital. The only thing he could find that was at all lively was the crayfish. He made us an excellent sashimi dish out of that.'[10]

In her typically discerning foreword to Tsuji's book, the American writer and cook M. F. K. Fisher stresses the contrast between the high art of Japanese cuisine at this level, 'evocative of seasonal changes, or of one's childhood, or of a storm at sea', and the utilitarian, denatured Chinese, Indian, Italian – and American – fast food on which contemporary urban Japanese live for nine-tenths of the time. The beauty of simple, popular, cheap and quick *udon-soba* (soup-noodle) houses has almost gone, along with the domestic architecture and woodblock prints of the old Tokyo, and the Japanese predicament is nearer to that of the British than we realise from the stylised London Japanese restaurants. As Tsuji puts it:

Japan must be the only country in the world where the everyday fare is such a hodgepodge, and whose people know so little about their own traditional cuisine that they do not try to preserve its authenticity. *Tempura soba* – buckwheat noodles with deep-fried prawns – has been a popular favourite for years. But now these large shrimp are so scarce they are an exorbitant luxury. The dish would be perfectly authentic made with the still plentiful small shrimp, but no, the Japanese are such slaves to form – to the mere appearance of the dish, with the large decorative tails prominently displayed – that they would rather use large shrimp imported frozen all the way from Africa than be true to the traditional spirit of our cuisine. They have forgotten the very essence of *tempura* – the quick, light deep-frying of *very* fresh seafood.[11]

In this perspective, Japanese cuisine in the twentieth century has undergone the same kind of crisis that nearly destroyed English cooking during our own industrial revolution. Paradoxically, western cuisines, or at least their most sensitive practitioners, have begun to respond in Japanese ways to their developing awareness that the years of uncritical consumption and mechanisation may be numbered; that they too have to learn, as the Japanese have always instinctively known, how to make much of little. Michel Guérard, the apostle of *cuisine minceur*, acknowledges his debt to the years he spent in Tokyo. M. F. K. Fisher again:

> The long-time association between the refinements of French and Chinese cooking seems to have shifted to one that is more applicable to our current life-style, so that we now think easily in terms of French and Japanese similarities. We want to make less seem like more ... In a Japanese rather than a Chinese way we shun many starches, fats, sugar.[12]

The influence of the Near and Middle East on British eating habits has taken a quite different form. By far the most richly differentiated cuisine of the region (culturally speaking) is the one whose chief elements are shared among Turks, Syrians, Lebanese, Persians, Egyptians, Armenians and other nations between Mesopotamia and the Nile; and this spread in Britain with the help of Claudia Roden's *A Book of Middle Eastern Food* (1968; Penguin 1970). This book tipped middle-class taste in its own direction somewhat as Elizabeth David's books had done fifteen years previously, by bringing to life not just food but the history and predilections of an entire society.

At the same period or somewhat earlier, a cruder but more popular eastern Mediterranean influence on British eating was communicated entirely by restaurants and, latterly, take-aways. The source of this influence was primarily Cyprus. Graeco-Turkish cuisine from this source had been established in the West End of London for generations. The social distance between a *relais routier* and Le Gavroche is scarcely greater than that between a provincial kebaberie and (in its best days) John Stais's White Tower restaurant in Percy Street, north Soho, with its menu descriptions written by Daniel George, and personally devised specialities such as roast duck stuffed with bulgar wheat. Some of Manchester's Armenian cooking also achieved recondite excellence. But on the whole, Cypriot chefs are markedly conservative in their repertoire. This probably helped rather than hindered the cheap places which acquired a large new market in the 1960s and 1970s, and there was a further forced expansion of the Greek Cypriot restaurant trade after the Cyprus civil war of 1974. This sent thousands of dispossessed Greek Cypriots to London without a penny to their names. On a smaller scale, the political polarisation of Turkey itself may have had similar effects, though pure Turkish – and, for that matter, pure Greek – restaurants in Britain are uncommon. (Both in Britain and in Cyprus, Greek Cypriots outnumber Turkish by about five to one.)

The particular impact of the Cypriots on British foodways has been twofold (threefold, if one includes their impact in London on the efficient but tradition-bound greengrocery trade). Their pattern of settlement in London was centred on Islington and Camden, spreading outward to points north, notably Haringey. During the 1960s the best of their small restaurants and cafés were 'discovered' by Britons anxious to recapture the relaxing pleasures of meze and bouzouki music which they had enjoyed under warm skies in the eastern Mediterranean. By the mid-1970s the Cypriot community in Britain – about 50,000 at the 1971 Census – had more than doubled. British restaurant-goers enjoyed the atmosphere of genuine or spurious jollity they created, and felt comfortable with the predictable, easily memorised menu. Like the Cantonese, Cypriots also realised that elements in their menus were admirably suited to take-aways and street-eating on traditional Turkish lines. Indeed, with centrally baked pitta bread and baklava, and equally standardised hummus and taramosalata, there was very little for the café-owner to do but tend the butane grill and look amiable enough to convince his customers that neither these short cuts, nor consumption in Upper Street, Islington on a wet November night, would affect the Mediterranean taste.

Chinese, Indo-Pakistani, Italian, and Turco-Greek caterers are now the *gros légumes* of foreign catering in Britain, controlling between 80 and 90 per cent of the market for what used to be called 'continental' but are now more nearly 'global' meals out. The British mass market has forced on all four genres various compromises of technique and taste, or economies of time and money which amount to the same thing: the tandoori chicken is dyed, not marinated; the taramosalata is flavoured with smoked roe rather than made of it; the Pekin duck is not Pekin duck because it is deep-fried not roasted; and if you want your spaghetti *al dente* (as I was once advised in an Italian restaurant) 'it will take a little longer, sir'. Cantonese restaurateurs are virtually the only immigrants who do anything like justice to the extent of their own repertoire: there is but one Italian chef in Britain (Franco Taruschio at the Walnut Tree Inn near Abergavenny) whose style is as various, imaginative and self-critical as the cuisine described in Elizabeth David's *Italian Food*; and although the repertoire of Greek cooking both on Cyprus and the mainland is by comparison severely limited, it is odd that a London food critic who holidays in the region should look in vain on her return for such relatively common dishes as *spanokopitta*, *kokoretsi*, *saganaki*, fish *plaki* and *pastitsio*.[13]

Besides these heavyweights in the league, French cooking is a middle-to-upper-class minority taste (chiefly on the score of expense and exclusiveness), even if places are included in this category whose Frenchness goes no further than a name on the lintel and words on the menu. But many other foreign styles are accessible to Britons and visitors to Britain, in Greater London at least. They are listed in Table 4 partly out of respect for the cuisines these restaurants however inadequately represent, and partly because any typology of immigrant cuisines ought to embrace as many as possible, however small the communities responsible. (Few other cities in the world can match London's diversity in this respect, and it has always been puzzling how little the British Tourist Authority has made of it in advertising abroad what Britain has to offer her foreign visitors. Americans and Frenchmen, for example, often express pleasure in Indian restaurants, which have only in recent years begun to penetrate their own countries. French knowledge of oriental spices is often rudimentary.

In an international city on the scale of London, people are free to exploit this diversity by choosing what to eat and where, and by making comparisons, in restaurant settings that are part of the messages conveyed by the food itself. For this reason, restaurants are indispensable to any attempt to isolate types and groupings among immigrant cuisines. Recipes cannot convey it all at home, however versatile the cook and assiduous the book collector, and very few people, even professional anthropologists, can be familiar with the food cultures of more than a small proportion of the world's peoples, as expressed by meals prepared and eaten within the family at both ordinary and festive occasions. An arena where numerous cuisines from different parts of the globe meet and compete in public, importing their own characteristic foodstuffs and making substitutions from what is available locally, and drawing customers from a common pool of 'floating eaters', is a new phenomenon of the twentieth century. The more neutral the complexion of the host culture, the more discernible the colours introduced by an immigrant cuisine. For instance, French bourgeois cooks have put up strong resistance to both exotic and technological change, while the more complaisant British have been and are singularly receptive to external influences upon the foods (and even more the drinks) which

TABLE 4: The London pages of *The Good Food Guide 1982* listed half a dozen places that could fairly be called British, and forty-two places where the cooking was French in style, even if the chef was British. Other nationalities or styles were:

Afghan	1	Italian	16
American	4	Japanese	3
Chinese: Canton	9	Jewish	3
Pekin	8	Korean	1
Szechuan	1	Lebanese	1
Cypriot (Greek		Portuguese	2
or Turkish)	12	Singapore/Malaysia	1
German	1	Spanish	4
Hungarian	1	Swedish	1
Indo-Pakistani:		Thai	1
Bengali	4		
Gujerati	2		
Tamil	2		
E African Asian	1		

In the same book, about half these nationalities are also represented elsewhere in the British Isles, and about a dozen more have been represented in, or nominated to, the Guide at some point in the past ten years, including: North African, West African, Armenian, Brazilian, Canadian, Danish, Mexican, Norwegian, Polish, Russian, Swiss, Vietnamese, West Indian, Yugoslavian.

The list is indicative, not comprehensive.

they consume. This in spite of the conservatism the British profess with such conviction when alterations are suggested to one of their 'birthright' dishes, and in spite of the technical ignorance that reduces almost all British kitchen processes at popular level to roasting, boiling and frying.

Reverse influences are equally possible or probable: an immigrant cuisine, uprooted from its natural habitat to a colder, wetter climate, encounters there the technological eating of a denatured late-industrial society, and it has to be unusually well armoured against change and corruption if it is to remain recognisably the same into the second or third generation. Obviously, social rather than culinary factors are likely to be decisive in this respect, nor is it a question of the vulnerability of the primitive: no cuisine gets as far as Victoria or Heathrow that has not already proved its ability to survive literacy, a money economy, and at least early-modern kitchen technology. (In a few instances, the technology may even be imported with the cuisine, in the shape of simple implements that are found superior to Europe's own for certain purposes: the wok arrived with the Cantonese, the tandoor with the Bengalis, the barbecue with the Americans.)

Almost any cuisine can follow the flag, as it were. Immigrants in a foreign city, whether dispossessed Austrian Jews in the 1930s, or rich Japanese and Kuwaitis in the 1970s, need meeting places in London where they can talk to each other in their own languages and not have to mind the host country's manners. They hanker after dishes that their womenfolk may be too busy to bother with while they are scratching a living or raising a family under difficult circumstances. (Asian and Middle Eastern forms of purdah for women help to keep culinary cultures intact, but do not help to provide meeting places.) 'Colonising' cuisines of this kind are seldom conscious of an 'audience' beyond their own community, though when an audience eventually arrives it is gladly accepted in most cases, not just for economic reasons but because its presence can be taken as a token of acceptance and respect. (However, among the foreign restaurants where the native Briton most often feels something of an intruder are the ones which have least to worry about economically, because they are supported by oil sheikhs or Japanese bankers.)

Certain cuisines can also drag the flag behind them. A nation whose food culture is rich and powerful enough can despatch its chefs and restaurateurs to gather abroad a better living than they could make at home. The early colonists then repatriate a substantial proportion of their earnings, and send urgent messages for reinforcements, until – as happened in Britain in 1968 – the host country itself anxiously pulls up the drawbridge. Chinese cooking in Britain is the principal example of this process. Immigrants from Hong Kong are numerically much less important than West Indians and Indo-Pakistanis, but a very high proportion work in the catering trades. Their strength – and their weakness – has been social cohesion and cultural assurance, and, coupled with language difficulties in the first generation, this virtually ruled out real communication between immigrant and host. This factor is even stronger with the Japanese, who often express not just surprise but something akin to alarm and displeasure when *geijin* invade their food-ways by demanding esoteric dishes and foodstuffs. 'You velly brave man,' I was once told by a Japanese restaurant manager, gold teeth flashing, after one such order, probably involving jellyfish, or raw sea urchin. In a French or Chinese restaurant curiosity of this kind is treated much more matter-of-factly, though Chinese restaurateurs have learnt to inquire whether a person who orders chicken blood or tripe knows and likes what he is going to get.

The sincerest compliment one country can pay to another is to borrow its diet and imitate its cooking. The occasion may be a defeat or it may be a victory (leaving aside longer-term colonisation and intermarriage, as in Portuguese Goa). The most famous example is Brillat-Savarin's commentary on the years after Waterloo, when the British conquerors not only ate copiously while they were billeted in Paris but took the taste home afterwards and looked round for French chefs to recreate it for them. The British were not too proud to borrow curry from their subject peoples in India, though interestingly, that influence was at its peak in the years before sahibs were joined by memsahibs. Military and ICS wives imposed the Victorian proprieties (French influence and all) on their husbands' Indian servants, who had previously had it all their own way. As 'Wyvern' (Col. Kenney-Herbert) put it in his *Culinary Jottings for Madras* (1878): 'Our dinners of today would indeed astonish our Anglo-Indian forefathers. Quality has superseded quantity, and the molten curries and florid oriental compositions of the olden times – so fearfully and wonderfully made – have been gradually banished from our tables.'[14] The cooks on Indian hill stations returned the compliment by continuing to prepare brown Windsor soup long after the British had gone for ever, as though it were an elixir of successful imperialism.

But it has to be admitted that British cuisine as such is a weak power, globally speaking. British colonists in distant lands have often clung to their diet faithfully (the Falklanders, as sheep farmers, had little alternative) but they have seldom persuaded foreigners to adopt it, even in countries with suitable climates. Likewise, the export success of high-prestige British foodstuffs – Stilton, marmalade, kippers, Christmas pudding – is disappointing both in variety and geographical spread, considering how easy it should have been to establish the taste for them through the imperial distribution network, and the political prestige Britain enjoyed on the continent of Europe.

What follows is a very tentative attempt to construct a model for comparing the distinguishing characteristics of some of the different immigrant cuisines found in Britain. The basic material differences in the foodstuffs they favour and the staples (both starch and protein) on which they depend will be tolerably familiar to most readers. Their social functioning in the midst of indigenous British food-ways is less apparent to casual restaurant visitors. But it is crucial to the different rates at which immigrant cuisines in Britain may be expected to evolve and cross-fertilise, both with each other and with native British styles. A recent stimulus to this attempt has been the anthropologist Jack Goody's discussion in his *Cuisine, Cooking and Class* (1982) of culinary differentiation and hierarchy in Eurasian cuisines, *vis-à-vis* the relatively undifferentiated cuisines of food cultures in his own professional field (Africa south of the Sahara). The practical significance of work of this kind should not be underestimated. For instance, restaurant critics and others have often noted the failure of black cultures (whether African or West Indian) to help themselves to economic self-sufficiency and cultural assimilation in Britain by opening restaurants and food shops whose appeal to their own people would gradually extend to the public at large. This deficiency has sometimes been attributed to a general want of entrepreneurial, capital-forming skills, or merely to material poverty at an earlier period of their history. Poverty as such in a country or a people might be thought almost as likely to stimulate culinary skills as it is to stifle them, unless it included a serious shortage of fuel – and even fuel economy, as it happens, has not been a brake on Chinese and Indians. The curious air – at once self-conscious and desultory – that pervades the few African and Caribbean restaurants that exist or have ever existed in London should rather send inquirers looking for deeper causes in social organisation and perhaps role division between the sexes. Factors of this kind have not yet worked their way out of Africa-based cultures (if indeed they ever will, or should). For instance, in the tribes studied by Goody, no male chef class has evolved, because even in a chief's house the cook is also the sexual partner.

Any attempt to classify such diverse social institutions as foreign restaurants with contrasting styles of cooking and ethnic origin must be highly speculative and arbitrary. But there do seem to be certain characteristics which immigrant cuisines and food cultures possess less or more of; and the categories themselves may be easier to think about if they are anchored to actual styles which can be found and with pleasure examined in the streets of London.

1. The first question to ask is the extent of *differentiation* in each cuisine, first on its home ground, and second in its adopted country. I owe this concept of differentiation to Goody (see further discussions on pages 167–9). Differentiation within a people's cooking may arise from hierarchical divisions (with rich man and poor man, noble and

peasant, eating different foodstuffs, or the same foodstuffs differently prepared); from regional variety in produce, recipes, or both; from the allocation of different foods to different ages or sexes; and so on. A balance has to be struck if such variable factors are to be used to measure differentiation, bearing in mind, for instance, that in France children eat grown-ups' food and in America grown-ups eat children's food; that Italian food is differentiated by region and Indian food additionally by religion and caste. It must also be borne in mind that the differentiation that a cuisine exhibits on its own home ground may not survive export to this country: Mediterranean styles seem to be more vulnerable than oriental ones to British stunting and stereotyping.

2. The second variable is *propensity to evolve*. Here again, different types of influence have to be considered in different cases. For instance, American market-place cuisine evolves, but not necessarily in directions dictated by culinary logic and economical supply, as it did when Chicago was built on the hog. There are exceptions: Californian cooking responds to the state's copious production of exotic fruit and vegetables. But American food culture now responds more readily to new, often deliberately created appetites and life-styles that originate outside the catering trade altogether. America also tends to iron out or put its own gloss on imported food cultures, unless they are as deeply rooted as Jewish in New York or Chinese in San Francisco. The marketing man proposes and the chef disposes: in the phrase 'TV dinner', television is the master, dinner the slave.

Chinese cooking is also evolutionary, but in a different sense. Marketing considerations are normally missing. A Hong Kong meal (this is sometimes also said about the Lyonnais) is a statement to which customers are secondary. The cuisine of the leading Chinese creators evolves on a day-to-day basis without ever being written down.

Antitheses of both these styles are the Cypriot, which barely evolves at all, and the Japanese, which is class-stereotyped in business communities abroad, but on its own ground is classically subtle and various, capable of evolution within certain limits.

3. *Imitability*, the third variable, is usually a function of the printed word. In America, and more recently in Britain, television and video demonstrations of different culinary techniques and styles arouse the interest of cooks who seldom read or use printed recipes. But their ultimate effect – as Delia Smith, Madhur Jaffrey and other popularisers discovered to their profit – is to multiply sales of books, which are easier to

consult while a meal is actually being prepared. An entire cuisine can leap from obscurity to ready imitability with the publication of the right reference book, as happened with Claudia Roden's *A Book of Middle Eastern Food* when the Penguin edition appeared. Chinese cuisine, a bigger subject and a more demanding technique, has publicists and annotators but no expositor in Britain worthy of the richness of the subject and the complexity of the materials and techniques involved. India has lately been better served.

4. *Accessibility* to strangers, the fourth question to be raised, is a factor more cultural than culinary. Physiologically, man is an adaptable animal, and what he eats somewhere could in principle be eaten almost anywhere. But psychological, historical, religious and tribal factors often count for more. The Chinese have actual physical difficulty in digesting unprocessed milk, and cheese. But the British are not less affected by psychological problems in contemplating the flesh of dogs and horses. And apart from the food itself, accessibility of the social kind is a factor of great concern to British customers contemplating a visit to a strange nationality's restaurants and expecting – it is our most American trait – to be received with warmth and cordiality, even if we suspect that the cordiality is thinly veneered. Yet here too there are contradictions. No one would call a Japanese restaurant – even one as individual and sympathetic as Ajimura in Covent Garden – stylistically accessible. Yet Japanese *politesse* is impeccable.

Again, Greek and to a lesser extent Turkish restaurants are popular with Britons at various social levels, but the underlying structure of Cypriot family life is carefully held back, and the jovial interaction between customer and restaurateur takes place at a very superficial level. This is also the case in Italian restaurants, where waiters often seem to have been trained to do the job as a substitute for thinking about it. In Chinese restaurants waiters are often rude, offhand, and deliberately uncomprehending until they have been shown reason – by patience and curiosity rather than abuse – to behave differently. Yet, as in French places of a similar character, professionalism can be depended upon by people who know enough to insist upon it.

Ambitious British cuisine itself is singularly *in*accessible by this criterion, short of an invitation to private homes or a club in St James's, for the few urban restaurants that find it worthwhile to specialise in British cooking are usually served by foreign nationals who understand neither the language nor the food culture they are trying to represent.

(In recent years the Tate Gallery Restaurant's well-trained British female staff have been an honourable exception to this rule.) At popular level, as in pubs and fish and chip shops, British style is socially more accessible, but – again with honourable exceptions – the food less so. Malt vinegar, kept-hot chips, cardboard pies and frozen fish coated with thick batter are not tastes widely shared among the world's peoples.

5. Finally, *vulnerability*, the fifth variable, can also be viewed two ways. From the standpoint of a community relations specialist, rapid assimilation of an immigrant culture – and by extension, its cuisine – to the (British) host culture is theoretically desirable. But only social scientists with defective tastebuds actually think on lines like these, and anyway, even in this field other experts would now argue that in a fundamentally hostile social environment, an immigrant people that keeps its cuisine intact from British flavour-blur and similarly insidious forms of social syncretism enjoys a better prognosis, communally speaking, than one that has let its historical identity go: it is a question of human dignity. However, most immigrant cuisines have now been lodged in Britain long enough for the symptoms of resistance or surrender to be recognisable. Italians almost always surrender, not for want of quality in the ingredients or of skill in their treatment, but for want of self-criticism and out of an excessive desire to please. Americans, likewise, taste the customers, not the ingredients. Talented Frenchmen and Chinese know better, but often succumb to the commercial temptation presented by customers who *don't* know better and who can safely be fobbed off with something that sounds right, however it tastes. In the kitchen, pride protects the Japanese, religion the Jews and the Hindus, competition the Cantonese and habit the Cypriots. Put the British in a similar situation and their cuisine, in its turn, might be protected against the influence of its host culture by the familiar combination lately identified as the Falklands factor: instinctive patriotism combined with resolute ignorance.

CHAPTER SIX
Tastes of Britain

The age of choice

Street provisions consist of cooked or prepared victuals, which may be divided into solids, pastry, confectionery, and drinkables.

The solids, according to street estimation, consist of hot-eels, pickled whelks, oysters, sheep's trotters, pea-soup, fried fish, ham-sandwiches, hot green peas, kidney puddings, boiled meat puddings, beef, mutton, kidney, and eel pies, and baked potatoes. In each of these provisions the street poor find a mid-day or midnight meal.

The pastry and confectionery which tempt the street eaters are tarts of rhubarb, currant, gooseberry, cherry, apple, damson, cranberry, and (so called) mince pies; plum dough and plum cake; lard, currant, almond and many other varieties of cakes, as well as of tarts; ginger-bread-nuts and heart-cakes; Chelsea buns; muffins and crumpets; 'sweet stuff' includes the several kinds of rocks, sticks, lozenges, candies and hard-bakes; and, lastly, the more novel and aristocratic luxury of street-ices; and strawberry cream, at 1d a glass (in Greenwich Park).

The drinkables are tea, coffee, and cocoa; ginger-beer, lemonade, Persian sherbet, and some highly-coloured beverages which have no specific name, but are introduced to the public as 'cooling' drinks; hot elder cordial or wine; peppermint water; curds and whey; water (as at Hampstead); rice milk; and milk in the parks. Henry Mayhew, *London Labour and the London Poor* (1851).

Most of the world's great dishes were created by people who could not read or write. Rupert Croft-Cooke in *English Cooking* (1960).

When the heir to the throne bought a mango and a tin of baked beans at a fund-raising event in Brixton, the Court Page jester in *The Times* devised recipes to help the Princess of Wales make dinner out of them when her husband came home. The intention was absurd, but on another occasion the same paper's diarist reported the existence of people who spread their kippers with marmalade, and eat Yorkshire pudding with scampi. A cloud of unknowing hangs over dietary habits and choices, when reduced to the particular and the individual. There is so much that surveys and averages and marketing campaigns conceal, given the anarchy of choice in the consumer society of the past twenty-five years, and one person's choices may be a closed book to another's. I have often been asked, in a vegetable market or a fishmonger's, what I am going to do with the food I have just bought, when I get it home.

The impact of immigrants, immigrant cuisines, and associated produce from abroad was discussed in the previous chapter. There is no such thematic unity about the concurrent episodes in the evolution of indigenous British taste, which I have clustered together in this chapter. If there is any unifying factor, it can only be the concept of choice, theoretically unlimited but in practice severely constrained, in the myriad individual diets that add up to national trends in consumption.

We have already seen that in Britain during the mid-1950s, certain dietary trends that later became apparent were either being predicted, or being observed at an early stage of growth. Frozen vegetables and instant coffee are examples of products whose dissemination was likely to be rapid because they were in effect inter-war innovations delayed by the break of the 1940s. The cheap battery chicken multiplied exceedingly, as soon as new breeding and rearing methods made it cheaper than other meat, because the British market had long cherished a desire for 'white meat' which could not be satisfied while poultry remained relatively expensive. (Even British tripe is rendered white, at the expense of taste, texture, and everything else that other nations consider desirable in tripe: Chinese restaurants have to process their own.) Fish fingers not only provided busy mothers with instant meals: they solved at a stroke the widespread juvenile distrust of fish as a source of skin and bones, both disagreeable, and enabled a child to pick at a little rather than be overfaced. (The sweetened crumb coating of the product is also a minor example of doing ill by stealth in food manufacturing.) Breakfast cereals subverted the British cooked breakfast not because they were actually preferred to bacon and eggs – still a holiday or weekend treat for millions who survive their working days on cornflakes – but because they saved women in employment the time their mothers had had to spend over the porridge saucepan and the frying pan. Extensive provision of industrial canteen lunches – a legacy of the war years – and more recently, the tendency to take late evening snacks in front of the television probably also contributed to the devaluation of cooked breakfasts.

As for the predictions current in the mid-1950s, in science and technology several years normally elapse between idea or hypothesis and product development, and are in turn followed – if the product is a new food for human consumption – by protracted user trials and marketing procedures. It was therefore possible for science correspondents to announce the approach of man-made protein long before TVP arrived in packets on the supermarket shelf. But social behaviour is harder to predict. The British diet has its old reliables, from Worcestershire sauce and its associated label to the Mars bar, which has kept in uncannily precise step with inflation for half a century. But the quarter-century between 1955 and 1980 has also been notable for the wide range of edibles and potables which the British have in some sense found for themselves, without either inheriting them from grandmother's store cupboard or being browbeaten into purchase by a television advertisement. Even in 1982 the sudden popularity of (mostly inferior) wine in boxes was capable of taking its promoters by surprise. More generally, it would have been difficult to predict in 1955 many of the choices, actions and reactions that characterise the food world of the 1980s. For instance:

1. The rise of vegetarianism and 'health' or 'whole' food.
2. The emergence of food and cooking as a fashionable pastime for the intelligentsia.
3. The rise of the dietary guru and his or her doppelganger, the anorexic or bulimic patient.
4. The persistence and in some contexts revival of regional variation in tastes.
5. The sudden and continuing revolution in British drinking habits, female as well as male.

The whole notion of an individual eater or drinker's freedom of choice – within the limits of his pocket – has been set in a different light by two contrasting developments of the period we are exploring: on the one hand rationalisations and amalgamations in the basic industries of food and drink, such as brewing and baking, and in the retail outlets they serve; and on the other, the rise of semi-amateur protest movements, as Davids to the Goliaths of United Biscuits, Rank Hovis McDougall, Allied Breweries, and Trusthouse Forte.

In theory, a supermarket or hypermarket, like a comprehensive school, presents maximum choice, with 6,000 'lines' displayed on shelves, compared with perhaps 600 in a well-stocked corner grocery store. But just as a comprehensive school, because of traits inherent in its clients, may develop a culture that constricts both quality *and* diversity, so it is in the output of a big manfacturer or the stock of a supermarket chain. While apparent choice of products has widened, choice within a particular range of foodstuffs may narrow, because the sheer size of the market precludes extremes of taste and favours the common (not necessarily the lowest common) denominator. 'We usually eat what we like, provided we can get it and can afford it,' wrote J. C. McKenzie and John Yudkin in 1964, expressing general satisfaction as nutritionists with the wider choice made possible by improvements in food preservation and transport. But already they felt obliged to add: 'Unexpected restrictions in availability are beginning to be seen in the wealthier countries, with the growth of super-markets and their tendency to reduce the number of brands of particular foods which they offer.'[1]

Subsequent developments – notably in baking and brewing – further sharpened questioning about the amount of choice a consumer enjoys if all the brands offered him vary little in substance, taste, quality, and price. As often in Britain, spontaneous consumer resistance movements matched or surpassed the role of media-based professionals in noticing and objecting to the subtraction of true variety and flavour from foods and drinks on the British market. Inevitably, such movements usually represented a small but vocal minority rather than the silent majority that eats anything put in front of it. The Good Food Club of 1950 was followed in 1970 by the Campaign for Real Ale (CAMRA). The influence of both bodies far outran the circulation of the annual guides they published (well under six figures in both cases) and the number of real or notional members enrolled in any one year. As pressure groups they attracted individuals prepared to do their homework on the issues involved. They were seldom successfully contradicted or sued by the commercial interests they criticised, and as controversialists they stayed lively enough to keep the media interested in them. Alongside sectional-interest campaigns of this kind, whether focussed on bread, beer, ice cream, apples, or catering techniques, a quieter, larger movement of dissent from mass-market foodways could often be detected, even among people who pushed their supermarket trolleys along with the rest. By the 1980s, for instance, Radio Four's weekly Food Programme, covering a range of topics which BBC administrators had declined to take seriously until late in the 1970s, enjoyed an attentive audience of nearly half a million.

Man owes his survival as a species as much to his omnivoracity as to any other feature of his make-up. But he seldom pines for a foodstuff that neither he nor anyone in his circle or ancestry has tasted. Anyone who seeks to introduce a novelty, whether genuine or spurious, to people who are already able to satisfy their appetites from the safely familiar is taking a considerable commercial or social risk. When Erin Foods – an agricultural and marketing corporation in Ireland heavily supported by the government of the day – joined forces with Heinz for an early plunge into accelerated freeze-dried vegetables, the ensuing commercial debacle was pleasantly called by one commentator 'the Greek tragedy of the grocery trade'. Much of the interest in the changing food habits of the British generation immediately past lies in the attempt to isolate what constitutes actual changes of *taste*, collective or individual, from what can be attributed to other types of influence or manipulation. Is it an evolution of taste, or foreign travel combined with the steady drip of comment in *The Good Food Guide* and other publications, that has persuaded British folk in a certain sector of society to eat their beef and lamb pinker and their vegetables firmer than any previous generation of the same milieu would have contemplated?*

Clues to the process of action and reaction that affects food choice can sometimes be found in the dietary confessionals of individuals. My wife, in adolescence, was virtually force-fed lobster mayonnaise for a fortnight in La Baule by a French family she was staying with on an exchange, and she took twenty years to recover a taste for either component (a period, alas, in which the price of lobster rose well ahead of inflation). In my own early childhood I was indecently fond of rice pudding, and woe betided my parents if they took me to a café that did not offer it (in those days, most did). By the time I went to boarding school, sweet rice disgusted me and for the most part still does, while savoury rice became one of the first dishes I learnt to cook. Jane

---

* Research commissioned by the Meat Promotion Executive (*British Beef Gets a Roasting*, 1981) suggests that a taste for rare beef is confined to about ten per cent of the population in all ages and social classes. Compare Samuel Pepys's revulsion three centuries ago (*Diary*, vol. 8, p. 483): '. . . It was an odd strange thing to observe of Mr Andrews about a fancy he hath to raw meat, that he eats it with no pleasure unless the blood run about his chops; which it did now, by a leg of mutton that was not above half-boiled; but, it seems, at home all his meat is dressed so; and beef and all, and eats it so at nights also.'

Grigson's testimony is worth quoting in a parallel context, not least for the relevant-irrelevant conclusion:

All our childhood, my sister and I were carefully shielded from the horrors which my mother had had to eat at the same age. This meant that rice, sago and tapioca pudding hit us with full institutional force when we were sent to boarding school in wartime (shielding children from the realities of life often ends disastrously). For 25 years the thought of milk puddings made me queasy. Then, a while ago, an American friend made us eat 'quick' tapioca – it was delicious. And not long afterwards, passing through Normandy, we saw some puddings with a rich dark skin on top, in a pastry-cook's shop in Isigny. . . . Three conclusions – a rice pudding must be flavoured with a vanilla pod or cinnamon stick, it must be cooked long and slowly, it must be eaten with plenty of double cream. Like so many other English dishes, it has been wrecked by meanness and lack of thought.[2]

Appetites, repugnances and conversion experiences can be collective as well as individual. It may be that the British are collectively about to undergo (perhaps through a combination of immigrant and literary influences) a conversion away from the horror of fungi (other than mushrooms). For centuries this has been a dietary oddity that noticeably distinguishes us not just from the French, Germans and Italians but from Swedes and Russians too.* Who is to say that other primal national fears and disgusts – for instance, tiny birds, and the meat of dogs and horses – may not disappear one day, powerful though they are among folk who may simultaneously express surprise that a primitive people on the point of starvation will reject the unfamiliar grain offered them by famine relief workers. The anthropologist Jack Goody tells the story of the frosty reception he got from equally hungry British colleagues in a German prison-of-war camp when he merely asked to use the communal utensils for cooking a cat, after a taste (in ignorance) of the same dish in another camp had convinced him that between cat and rabbit there was no great gustatory gulf fixed.[3] Perhaps the same is true of coypu, which I have eaten, and other rodents, which I have not. The British often seem almost as inhibited about eating their pests as their pets. Neither pigeon nor rabbit (since myxomatosis, usually imported)

* In William King's *A Journey to London* (1698) the author pretends to be a Frenchman – parodying Sorbière's *Relation d'un Voyage en Angleterre* – on a visit to the vegetable markets. 'I desired to know what Mushrooms they had. I found but few, at which I was surpris'd, for I have all my Life been very Curious and inquisitive about this kind of Plant, but I was absolutely astonish'd to find, that as for Champignons, and Moriglio's, they were as great strangers to 'em as if they had been bred in Japan.' (King was hardly to know that the Japanese too were besotted with 'this kind of plant'.)

are as popular as their relative cheapness and freedom from fat suggests they should be, and coypu is seldom eaten even in East Anglia, where it is endemic. Ironically – since like whale in the 1940s, it is best curried hot and sour – it would be a suitable dish to be offered in Indian restaurants, but one can imagine the outcry if it were. Kangaroo meat is another shock-horror product that has been recently noted, though it would surely go down well with that other Australian export, Kanga Rouge.

Enough has been said to remind us that human diet is more a matter of conditioned responses than of economic exploitation of the animal kingdom. At the same time, the old saying that what the eye does not see, the heart does not grieve over can be extended from the notoriously unhygienic conditions of many British cafés and restaurants to the British eating public's resolute refusal to make visual and imaginative connections between what is consumed and the source of it in field, slaughterhouse, pot, and even plate. (In many restaurants, the light too is more romantic than practical for the minority who are curious about what they are actually eating.)

However, minority tastes in food have been rapidly increasing in size. Up until 1939, and indeed up until the 1960s, the complex of attitudes and foodstuffs clustered round the various sects of the vegetarian and health food movements was statistically insignificant. In 1941, vegetarians had to wait upon Lord Woolton in person to secure their supplies of cheese in exchange for meat coupons, though he told them that he had been 'worrying a good deal about the vegetarians and sometimes lay awake at night thinking about them'.[4] In 1950 the Vegetarian Society had no more than twenty-eight affiliated local societies although according to the Society's annual report, 'the recent comparatively small supplies of flesh foods – a condition likely to persist for some years – gave vegetarians a very favourable opportunity to put before the public the advantages of a non-flesh dietary'.

There have always been certain sub-cultures in Britain – prisons, schools, army camps – where it has been similarly advisable to eat cheese rather than risk the cooking. For similar reasons, it is often wiser to demand vegetarian food on airlines, especially oriental ones. However, since the free market in 'flesh food' returned to Britain it has been clear that shortages converted fewer people to vegetarianism than abundance does, especially when abundance of meat is coupled with vague apprehensions about its wholesomeness. In some quarters, there can also be discerned a new-found sense of solidarity with that large proportion of the earth's surface where most people have little choice but to obtain their essential protein from vegetable sources. An ideological connotation to British vegetarianism is nothing new, remembering George Orwell's scathing characterisation of sandal-wearing, fruit-juice drinking appeasers in the 1930s. But the more self-interested 'health food' movement, which during the 1960s grew from 100 shops to 800 nationwide, espoused no particular ideology and certainly made some people a great deal of money. By the 1980s, 1,200 such shops were taking £80m. a year.

The distinction between vegetarianism and health food is fine: as one source puts it: 'Although almost all health food restaurants are vegetarian, not all vegetarian restaurants serve health food. It is possible to eat a very nasty synthetic meal without any animal products in it.'[5] However, there were plenty of people in the new generation who were interested not only in health, hygiene and ideological purity but in food and cooking as such. Enterprises such as Cranks – note the belated admission of self-mockery to the vegetarian canon – found a ready market in cathedral cities and country towns as well as in the metropolis. Lighter, spicier successors were later founded under oriental influence. Moreover, both movements, the old and the new, shared the intensity of their distastes, and there can be no doubt that it was not only, or even mainly, cruelty to or exploitation of animals for food that fuelled missionary fervour. Brash scientism and insensitive display in the food trades had sown fear and disgust in a growing, vocal, and – in the long run most important – youthful minority.

Nicholas Tomalin's *Sunday Times* article on 'The Natural Goodness Business'[6] made it clear that in spite of appearances, health food was no stranger to (human) nature red in tooth and claw: its chief entrepreneur sold his interest for £1 million to Booker McConnell, best known for the refinement of their sugar. A similar sum was being spent annually by customers on a Swiss-made elixir called Bio-Strath – suggesting, according to the Consumers' Association whose magazine *Which?* reviewed the stated contents, that some people still believed in fairies.[7] The editor of *Organic Gardening and Farming* estimated that half the food sold in Britain as 'organic' did not deserve the label, which was no surprise in a country where every other garden shed contains enough pesticide to poison the whole parish. Tomalin concluded that 'people go to health food stores partly to buy rather expensive ordinary food and partly to buy hope and innocence in a sullied, dangerous technological world'.

However, his critics pointed out that by concentrating on the quackery that often blinks up from the medicinal shelves of health food (later 'whole food') shops, he had missed what had persuaded Booker McConnell and later Cadbury-Schweppes to join the movement rather than try to beat it. Up and down the land, individual shops of this kind had become the only places in their localities where basic foodstuffs from sea salt and coffee beans to cream cheese and stone-ground flour could be obtained. Supporters of such shops did not necessarily subscribe to any system of vegetarian belief, and went to supermarkets for their bulk groceries. Other changes in retailing had at once simplified and expanded food-shopping for city-dwellers, but done little for smaller towns, where supermarkets are usually too small or unimaginatively managed to be efficient. Very few such shops are like the one Robert Moore describes in Peterhead, on the east coast of Scotland:

The manager was a graduate and an incomer who had married into Peterhead ... He adopted a policy of supplying whatever the customer wanted. He contacted the first English-speaking member of each incoming group of foreigners to find out what they needed. Thus by mid-1977 his store had a vast array of pastas, pâtés, exotic seafood, hams, sausages, cheeses and biscuits from virtually every country in Europe ... This policy brought new customers in and as a result the manager had been able to expand other parts of his business; his malt whisky stock had risen from 4 to 40 varieties and his wines from 6 to 250, and people were coming from as far as Aberdeen to shop in the store. Local people were gradually trying some of the more unusual foreign foods partly because they were on the shelves and partly because they recognised food from their foreign holidays.[8]

All this time, too, the market in vegetables as such was changing and its standards rising. Not only the free European market in fruit and vegetables, but air-freight from Third World countries in a wide spread of latitudes and longitudes, came close to eliminating the seasons on the tables of British vegetarians. (Sometimes, it is argued, this is at the expense of living standards in producer countries which sacrifice their best agricultural land to the cash crops favoured by agribusiness). It became easier to buy kiwi fruit or mangoes in suburban greengrocers all the year round than to find a good traditional strain of British tomato, apple or pea in the months appropriate to them, and recondite British natives such as seakale and samphire are seldom seen outside their localities. At the same time, many people realised for the first time that vegetables they had always cooked could also be eaten raw in salad. 'In March, I found nine salad stuffs in various shades of green and red at the greengrocer's nearest this Fleet Street office,' wrote one culinary journalist recently, registering protest at the British obsession with the drear combination of lettuce and tomato.[9] A list of the different fruits and vegetables sold by a first-rate London greengrocer during the course of a year would match quite closely the contents list of Jane Grigson's *Vegetable Book* (1978) and *Fruit Book* (1982). It would be a very different story in Scotland, for in London and the south-east, people have for centuries been relatively more concerned to obtain variety in fruit and vegetables. The frenzied activity in thousands of private gardens today ('How are your peppers, John?' 'Not bad, but you should see my mange-touts') is still but a pale reflection of what was achieved in the eighteenth century by the gardeners of great houses under glass and against the warm brick walls of their kitchen gardens.[10]

By 1980, the profession of vegetarianism no longer sounded like the equivalent of wearing sackcloth and ashes. Even in restaurants, vegetarians and vegetable lovers are now punished less severely in Britain than they are in carnivorous France, where the vegetables grown and sold in markets are usually superior, but where leguminous appetites and feelings are less well understood. Philip O'Connor's observation is apposite: 'If the English eat sentimentally, even anthropomorphically, the French eat cruelly, showing their teeth more, tasting dreadfully in contrast to our faithful and superstitious swallowing.'[11]

In 1981 *The Good Food Guide* joined the greens revolution by distinguishing in its pages twenty-eight restaurants whose vegetables it was prepared to recommend, and the editor suggested that 'ideally, no vegetable is worth eating unless it is cooked well and interestingly enough to be presented as a separate course'. Most people still find that it takes more time and trouble to produce in English style a vegetarian meal as palatable as one based on meat or fish. But this drawback is accepted more cheerfully by a middle-class generation that enjoys its kitchens and its Magimixes, and has easy access to recipes drawn from east of Suez. However, no doubt Jill Tweedie spoke for thousands of fully-occupied liberal feminists when she wondered in the *Guardian* 'what veggies to serve with the veggies' in a houseful of coarse and hungry adolescents.

The vegetarian Alan Long's prophecy that 'by AD 2000 Britain will be a predominantly vegetarian society' seems unduly optimistic (or pessimistic, according to one's point of view). Even in India, Gandhi's diet is by no means universally preferred, and in Britain, Churchill's remark on Stafford Cripps's vegetarian dinner is affectionately remembered: 'Are you about to eat that or have you just finished?' It is possible to convert away from vegetarianism as well as towards it, and after a few years' residence in this country numerous emancipated members of traditionally vegetarian religions and cultures have found themselves enjoying chicken tikka and lamb dopiaza. We live in a land whose hill farms support sheep and little else, and whose coasts are rich in fish (an ambivalent item in the vegetarian canon, called 'sea vegetable' in at least one Indian language). It seems rather more probable that vegetarianism will become and remain, like marriage and the priesthood, a vocation easier than it once was both to take up and to put down, according to age and socio-economic status; and that other 'ecological' minorities, not necessarily vegetarian, will become conscious of separation from the relatively mindless mass consumption of increasingly adulterated meat products. These minorities are likely to include people who have absorbed from various foreign cultures a less squeamish, more rustic attitude to the meat and fish on which the British diet has traditionally been based.

Even here there are marked regional differences. The Scots, for instance, will have little to do with offal, unless it is safely enclosed in a haggis and offset by earnest jocularity. This makes them for once polar opposites of the French, for whom the liver – the very emblem of carnality – assumes a double importance:

The closest thing to liver worship still in business is the reverent sorrow with which the French regard their beloved *foie* . . . That these same French viciously funnel great quantities of grain into the stomachs of their geese in order to fatten the livers for pâté de foie gras, I consider simply a regrettable transference of their own hepatic anxiety onto their poultry.[12]

At the modish end of Anglo-Saxon society, a strong stomach for life and death has become fashionable, and besides, it improves the taste. Food writers may have led the vogue (since about 1970) for pink, even carmine, lamb *à la française*, but they found a sympathetic audience, in the south at least. Richard Olney's discussion of rabbit-butchering is symptomatic: 'Cut off the head and split it in two symmetrically (it will add flavour, and many people enjoy nibbling at the cheeks and the brains).'[13] A professional caterer reported in the mid-1970s that a decade previously, 'when I was inquiring about having a trout tank installed, the suppliers very strongly advised against having it in view, as the customers didn't like it'.[14] Now, they are into the theatre of cruelty: bread and circuses combined.

Compared with France, regionalism in the production of specialities and in the palate for distinctive local foods is not pronounced in Britain. It would be surprising if it were, given the other centripetal tendencies in British language and culture over the centuries. The survival – lately revival – of local and regional consciousness in gastronomic guises is slenderly supported outside the ranks of tourist boards and cookery writers, bloater freaks and tripe fanciers. However, two strands of behaviour and differentiation are worth exploring.

The first is the minor variation, of which individuals are barely conscious, in regional patterns of mass choice and taste. These are noticed by market researchers and manufacturers who distribute nationally; they are obliged to notice which products leave the shelves and which ones linger there. Some of these variations are marked enough for it to be plausibly supposed that a genetic as well as a cultural or historical element enters into them. If it is permissible to talk of a 'Celtic fringe' in terms of political allegiances, which shift violently only at periods of national crisis, it is much more tempting to find hereditary explanations for gustatory preferences at the grassroot level where changes may be imperceptible from one generation to the next. Dorothy Hartley's romantic-historical characterisation of the different food habits that successive invaders of Britain brought to the national diet between AD 500 and 1500 has its counterpart in the twentieth century geographical variations catalogued by D. Elliston Allen.[15] According to him, these began to reappear, or be noticed commercially, when the superficial uniformities of Britain's national press (more accurately, a London press) gave way to the more sophisticated regional breakdowns of market research required by advertisers in the different commercial television areas. Allen's interpretations of his data are often pleasantly fanciful: 'an almost Grundyish distaste for innards ... a masochistic aim to chastise the palate rather than to soothe and caress it'. (Scotland).

This approach has its weaknesses. For instance, Allen attributes the Scottish salty palate to a preferred culinary technique (stewing and boiling) but traces other food customs to the Auld Alliance with France that preceded the Calvinist revolution in the seventeenth century. But the French also own to the salty palate (Roux brothers' chefs have often inflicted it on their customers in London) without sharing the Scottish sweet tooth: do these similarities and differences belong to nature or nurture, climate or history? Allen's more extended comments on this topic occur in his acerbic chapter on Midlanders:

Though the centre of the diet appears drab and monotonous, as if Midlanders scarcely noticed what they ate, the edges are excitingly pungent. Pickled onions, pickled cabbage and pickled walnuts are all great Midland favourites; and their acidity – at least in the Black Country – is reported to be twice as high as is customary in London ... It would appear that it is sharpness, irrespective of whether this is sweet or sour, that is aimed at first and foremost ... Whether this springs from hereditary biochemistry or from mere conditioning and upbringing or, as is most probable, from an inextricable fusion of the two, it is quite impossible to be sure. We do know, however, from study of identical twins living apart, that the degree of taste sensitivity is, at base at least, an inherited characteristic; and it is tempting to suggest that this distinctive, sour-biased palate of the Midlanders, so different from that of most of the rest of Britain and so suspiciously similar to that of Mediterranean peoples, may be one more part of their peculiar racial legacy ...

This is not a region that dedicates itself to 'Good Cooking'. Even before the war Birmingham, out of all the major British cities, showed the least interest in cookery books. There is less home-baking than almost anywhere; and even cakes are not very often made from packet-mixes, but bought from shops. Ready-made foods, equally, are rarely condemned for lacking in flavour, for most food here is sadly undertasted: flavour is something poured on later, out of a bottle. Kitchen skills, altogether, are at a discount, illustrated by the lowest interest in methods of preparing and serving vegetables.[16]

The difficulty, again, lies in deciding which factors are relevant or associated and which are not. Is the sour-biased palate a symptom or a cause of the Midland food habits described? Should it be traced, instead, to the availability or non-availability of certain foodstuffs at a period when limitations of transport and uncertain preservation denied dwellers in the region the kind of flexibility which they are now free, but disinclined, to express? Coffee essence and sterilised or evaporated milk are among other tastes that survived longer in this region than elsewhere. (The many Indians who have settled in the region will have reaffirmed that taste for 'cooked' milk.) Gluts of fruit and vegetables in the market garden country south-west of Birmingham, and inexhaustible vinegar from the Staffordshire maltsters, would make pickling as natural a solution to an economic problem as cider and clotted cream were to other seasonal gluts in the West country. To-day, tourists and food critics normally prefer the alcoholic creaminess of West Country meals to the typical Midlands alternation of bland convenience foods with convulsive shocks from the sauce bottle. But the sympathetic will realise that once tastes of either kind are established in a region, for whatever reasons, mother's knee transmission of culinary skills and habits makes them endure from generation to generation.

Environment diet is so marked that where a countryman is forced to move he usually takes his taste with him; so a cook can trace the invasions of foreigners by changes in the preparation of food. The basic materials cannot change, but the different recipes, the different herbs, the like or mistrust of certain local fungi or shellfish, these things are the cook's own 'history book'.[17]

The second aspect of regionalism in food – the revival of particularly British foodstuffs and dishes in published recipes and articles – must be in part associated with similar upsurges of local patriotism, sentiment or self-confidence that in the past twenty years have made regional accents – or at least, *some* regional accents – acceptable in national broadcasting. Broadcasting too is itself a direct influence, through the appetite of regional television and local radio producers for appropriate feature material. For instance, Derek Cooper's 1975 BBC 2 series on 'the taste of Britain' was concerned less with actual recipes than with photo-genic rural crafts and craftsmen who produced, on large or small scale, specialities in which it was possible for a local community to take a certain pride, whether or not samphire or elvers actually figured on local tables from one year's end to the next. The title of this series was itself derived from the slogan under which Lester Borley, then a Scottish Tourist Board official, had previously sought to attract English visitors to the region, or rather nation, for which he was re-sponsible.

For the smaller circle that is open to influence from the written word, rescue archaeology on British dishes and primary products in some danger of extinction was begun, as we have seen, by Florence White in the 1930s and was extended after the break by a remarkable post-war generation of learned cooks. Dorothy Hartley, Elizabeth David, Jane Grigson and (for fish) Alan Davidson are the names most likely to be remembered, and others hardly less energetic can be found in the bibliography on p. 199. Rupert Croft-Cooke's *English Cooking* (1960), a worthy heir to P. Morton Shand's *A Book of Food* in the 1920s, was written elegantly and defensively at a time when continental influence was at its fashionable peak in middle-class kitchens, and makes a useful benchmark for the subsequent resurgence of British culinary sensibil-ity. Guide books, directories and monographs of other kinds also sought to despatch the newly mobile, weekending, car-owning democracy in search of oysters in Orford, crayfish in the Cotswolds, black puddings in

Bury, rum butter in Cumbria, and cheeses everywhere from Chewton Mendip to Swaledale.

David and Richard Mabey's *In Search of Food* (primarily about markets), Susan Campbell's *Good Food Shops*, Patrick Rance the cheese factor's definitive account of the decline and revival of *The Great British Cheese*, and the culinary conventions organised at Oxford by Alan Davidson, who also publishes the periodical *Petits Propos Culinaires*, all suggest that a tide has been turned.

Besides, ever since Postgate's first *Good Food Guide* saluted 'lobster in whisky, and ormers', successive annual editions have seldom failed to mention any British regional restaurant or dish that actually lived up to the claims made for it. In the Preface to the 1977 edition, the present writer wondered why a country that could afford the National Theatre did not see fit to act as impresario to a national restaurant in London where foreign visitors could obtain, properly cooked, the British dishes known and unknown which they normally seek in vain on holidays and business trips. However, the difficulties are not negligible: among them, quality control (the English Tourist Board's 'Taste of England' listings exhibit all the deficiencies of self-nomination by restaurants wishing to be included); the technical unsuitability of many characteristic British dishes for delivery under restaurant conditions (even the Tate Gallery Restaurant's brave attempts to recreate Hindle wakes, Elizabeth Cromwell's grand sallet and other early English receipts foundered on this rock); and above all, no doubt, the British political community's inability to take national food seriously except when complaining about the enormous subsidy misapplied to the House of Commons dining room.

TASTE IN DRINK

Although this book is mainly concerned with cooking and eating in the past four decades, it would be eccentric to take no account of British drinking in this period, just as a meal is incomplete for most (but not all) people without a glass or a cup at hand.* It is worth noting that fundamental shifts in taste often affect drink long before they affect

* The findings of the 1958 Crawford survey on this point have already been mentioned (67–9). They suggested that about a quarter of the population drink nothing – not even water – with their mid-day meal; and not far short of a tenth drink nothing with their evening meal either. With both sexes, at both meal-times, and on all days of the week, tea beat all other drinks together by margins of between two and twelve to one. (Warren, *op. cit.*, pp. 75, 123). An updated version would doubtless reveal many changes, but it is less clear what they would be.

food. The reasons may be psychological rather than sociological. With all novelties designed to be swallowed, the marketer's or the mother's problem is to get the first sip or mouthful past the lips: repeat orders are less of a worry. It may feel easier as well as cheaper to order a strange drink in a pub – or to sip someone else's – than it is to ask for mouthfuls from someone else's plate (though this too is a practice much more common in middle-class circles than it was a generation ago, and not only among affectionate couples and wary restaurant inspectors). It is certainly easier in domestic circumstances to offer a choice of tea, coffee or chocolate, or various bottles of this and that, than it is to take the risk of investing time and money in cooking unfamiliar foods which half the family may dislike.

But no one could call a nation conservative in its tastes which in the past twenty years has gone so far to adopt coffee rather than tea as its favourite beverage from dawn to dusk, has consumed by the million gallon soft drinks of which its parents had never heard, has alternately delighted and infuriated the brewers by opening its throat to lager and recovering a taste for real ale, and has increased its consumption of a socially inaccessible foreign drink – wine – by over 250 per cent, admittedly in the context of a marked general increase in alcohol sales. In 1980, the British and their foreign visitors bought 1,440 million gallons of beer (270 pints per head, an increase of 40 per cent on 1960 figures), 100 million gallons of wine (15 pints per head, an increase of 250 per cent), and 38 million proof gallons of spirits (six pints a head, an increase of 135 per cent). There is a neat balance between the number of people employed in the manufacture, distribution and sale of alcoholic drinks and the number thought to be physically or psychologically dependent on them: 700,000 in both cases.

Working men and women earn the price of these pints or nips (especially the nips) in something under half the time it took 20 years ago, so the dependence is less surprising than successive governments' reluctance to restore the fiscal balance. Like children at school, we have had to be persuaded to drink more milk, ironically by advertisements whose phrasing has sometimes aggrieved schoolteachers hoping for better orthographic models on public hoardings than 'drinka pinta milka day' and 'milk's gotta lotta bottle'. Cocoa, the drink of the 1940s in battleship and bedsitter alike, is seldom seen, though chocolate and Horlicks both survive. Even British water has not been spared the bottle and the advertising campaign, which again is hardly surprising since in many parts of the country, notably the over-populated south east, tap water has such a second-hand or chlorinated taste that it is hardly fit to make a cup of tea with, let alone consume neat. Sales of Perrier, Evian, Malvern, Highland Spring and the rest reached 5 million gallons in 1981, and even the Abbey National Building Society began to market in bottle the water it draws from an artesian well underneath its premises at the notional home of Sherlock Holmes, 221b Baker Street. It is literally the soberest of reflections, as you cup your hands under the rocky lip of a Lakeland mountain stream and joke about the residual peril of liver fluke, that even in one of the world's most liberally watered countries access to water of such character and freshness remains a traveller's privilege rather than a stay-at-home's right.

The role of taste as such must not be exaggerated in assessing the movements of alcohol consumption and expenditure. Economic and wider social factors may weigh more heavily. For instance, in 1960 it took a male manual worker on average earnings 23 minutes to earn the price of a pint of beer and six hours to earn a bottle of spirits. For the same result, in 1980 he only had to work twelve minutes for the beer and two hours for the gin. As a result, when British entry to EEC began to depress the price of table wine somewhat against the price of beer and cider on the home market, people in work who had money to spare for inessentials were more prepared to help mop up the Community's wine lake. At the time of writing, roughly speaking, £1.60 buys a couple of pints of beer in a pub, a bottle of cheap wine or a couple of quarts of cider to drink at home, or four fares on the London Underground from Charing Cross to Piccadilly Circus. It is interesting to note that these are all relativities which the government of the day, as principal source of taxation and subsidy alike, is empowered to alter if it chooses.

Restaurants, in Britain (and now to an even greater extent in France) normally load on to their wine prices food costs and profit margins which they dare not charge the eater directly. But even here the relative changes are equally striking. In 1951, a bottle of claret in a restaurant normally cost about twice the price of a set meal at the same place (most Spanish and North African wine imported at this period was only fit for mulling and has to be left out of the reckoning). In 1961 the wine still cost more than the meal, but not much more: say 15s. (75p) against 10s (50p). In 1971 it was quite possible to find London restaurants where the set lunch cost more than the basic claret (both about £1.50). By 1981 the ratio of 1951 had actually been reversed here and there. In London's Le Chef, for example, a restaurant well regarded for two decades, a southern French wine cost £2.30, the set lunch £5.75. The chief reasons for this reversal were, on the food side, the steepling price of kitchen and dining room labour, and the gradual phasing out of Britain's historic cheap food policy; and on the wine side, the arrival of well vinified, keenly priced wines from regions and countries able to compete with the British market's traditional sources of supply. Other contributory factors included a developing popular awareness, through travel and the media, of what wine cost a shopper to buy both in French and in British supermarkets; and the adoption by a few sensible restaurateurs and hoteliers of a policy of small profits and quick returns. A restaurant mark-up of at least 100 per cent on retail prices remained common, and in theory subsidised other services. But by the 1980s only famously brazen restaurateurs in Britain, most of them French, saw fit to mark up their wines by 200 per cent or more. This had been common form in the 1950s.

In the circumstances, given the upper middle-class image of wine and the plebeian or rustic connotations of ale, it is more surprising than it seemed at the time that the first successful consumer revolt in the realm of food and drink since the Good Food Club was firmly anchored to the saloon bar. As on the previous occasion, a chance conjunction of individuals was responsible. Three of the four men – at that date, it still had to be men – who founded the Campaign for Real Ale in 1971 were journalists, and Manchester ones at that, relatively free of the tendencies to embourgeoisement that afflict their colleagues in Fleet Street. Paradoxically, they were on holiday in Ireland – where there is no real ale to speak of – when they became emotional enough, probably on Guinness, to decide that it was worth trying to launch a campaign to save British beer, whose taste was vanishing almost as fast as the character of the pubs which sold it.

The immediate causes were at once financial and technological. The brewery mergers of the previous decade or so had left six large firms or conglomerates in charge of half Britain's pubs (under the tied house system) and over 80 per cent of beer production. Scores of independent breweries and brands of beer had disappeared. With these amalgamations, tenancy arrangements were often altered to increase central control over house policy and style, and pubs were being modernised in a heavy-handed, pre-conservationist manner. This normally entailed ripping out the traditional beer engines and handles that deliver cask-conditioned, sedimented beer by pump or gravity feed delivery systems. Women – to whom in principle CAMRA had no objection – were encouraged to join their menfolk in the saloon for sweet tipples as sham as the decoration. And in the south – less so in the north, and hardly at all in Scotland – the natural advantages that pubs possessed as distribution points for snacks and informal food were at last beginning to be exploited by breweries and individual publicans alike.

Technically, it had become possible to produce and install in pub cellars beer containers that were more or less publican-proof. With the sediment of spent yeast cells filtered away, a top blanket of carbon dioxide gas protected the beer from spoilage and helped give the drawn pint the frothy 'head' popular with many customers. The brewers invested heavily in machinery and promotion for this new product, keg beer, only to find that it did not taste to a critical palate as beer should, although it was being sold at a slightly higher price than ordinary bitter. This all made a natural target for a populist, sometimes unfair, but well-briefed campaign. By the mid-1970s (the peak of its influence) CAMRA had 28,000 members, a monthly newspaper, a small pub company, and an annual guide to real ale pubs. *The Good Food Guide* and Egon Ronay also thought it worthwhile to cover pub food, largely because inflation was making hotel and restaurant meals too dear for the salariat, but also because of social changes that were taking much of the formality out of British eating in public places.

In 1976 CAMRA further irritated the brewers by publishing the 'original gravities' of the beers sold by the pubs which the *Good Beer Guide* included, and in 1977 it received some official support from the Price Commission's report on the industry. From this the public learnt that the big six charged higher prices than their rivals but made smaller proportionate profits. Ten years after it was launched CAMRA could pat its collective paunch and claim that on tiny resources it had reversed what seemed at the time a trend scarcely worth the effort of resisting. In 1981, more than half of the nation's pubs were selling real ale as CAMRA defined it – the Good Food Club would have been happy indeed if as much could be claimed for restaurants and food – and not only small independent breweries, but home-brewing pubs too, were flourishing again.

However, not even CAMRA's articulate spokesmen and local branches could bend public taste in directions it did not want to go. Feminine or continental taste – perhaps the two tastes reacting upon each other – was also steering the British drinker towards lager, an even lighter, gassier, and in British versions more insipid drink than keg beer. Perhaps it is unfair to expect British brewers to be any better at brewing lager than Belgium or Czechoslovakia might be at matching the ale brewed by Adnam, Gale, Wadworth, Fuller, Young, and many others. At the time of writing, it is an even guess which of all these trends will gain or lose ground in Britain's daily distribution of – in 1981 – 5.3 million foaming pints.

CHAPTER SEVEN
But what did it *really* taste like?

If English wine expert Michael Broadbent can list seven closely printed columns of descriptive terms for the fermented juice of a few varieties of one fruit, why are our food writers, whose subject is inexhaustible, at a loss for words?   John Allemang in *Epicure* (Toronto) May–June 1981.

The first taste or smell was like rotting hay, but this gave way to a very powerful rose taste, like super-essence of lychee. About the *longest* taste I've ever had.   European wine-lover on the Chinese spirit Mui Kwe Lu.

Harrogate Sparkle is freshly brisk, with a touch of stimulating impatience, though perhaps a little thin and nervous. It is much less bland and assured than Sparkling Ashbourne (Derbyshire) which is more full-bodied and flat in its personal manner.   Dennis Barker in the *Guardian* on mineral waters, 23 January 1982.

The clarty smell of cold mutton . . . boeuf bourguignonne with the texture of compressed string and the flavour of unploughed fields . . . (fish) made into a poultice with the texture of an Irish bog . . . a silky fish soup poised between clarity and gravity . . . a sour grey sauce tasting of uncooked wine and stale packet parmesan, and a gateau tasting mainly of cheap fat and instant coffee   Food descriptions noted from reports to *The Good Food Guide* and other sources.

Badly tuned chords bring to mind the effect of undercooked rhubarb on the incisor teeth . . . Two bars of music died away like the yolk of a fried egg when speared with a fork . . . The Chef's lemon soufflé had all the lightness of a Wagner piano concerto or a Brahms operetta.
Perceptions of food in terms of music or music in terms of food, solicited by the author from members of a summer school.

There exists in the vocabulary of words used with Cheddar cheeses a term known as *fightback*. This might be described as indicating the manner in which the cheese presses against the thumb when the pressure is released. The quality is also believed to be distinct from body or firmness.   Roland Harper, *Human Senses in Action* (1972).

Talking of Pleasure, this moment I was writing with one hand, and with the other holding to my Mouth a Nectarine – good god how fine. It went down soft pulpy, slushy, oozy – all its delicious embonpoint melted down my throat like a large beatified Strawberry. I shall certainly breed.   John Keats, letter to Charles Dilke, 22 September 1819.

It is quite possible to write a book about food, even a substantial cookery book, without paying the least attention to how food tastes, smells, or feels. Go into a good bookshop, take down a few volumes from the glossier end of the cookery section, or the dowdier end of home economics, and see. It is equally possible, to judge by results, to perform as the chef of a grand London hotel without tasting a single dish during the day, except the one you choose for your own supper when the last customer has gone home. However, it is not possible to edit a serious restaurant guide for twelve years and write a million words or more about other people's meals without trying to convey what it was in the constituents of these meals that made them succeed or fail. Furthermore, the spread of scientific and commercial interest in flavour description and analysis all share a common point of departure, in the first half of the 1950s.

In digesting inquiries of this kind, the casual reader and eater may well feel cast in the role of Molière's M. Jourdain, who was surprised to learn that what he talked was prose. Food, like music, can occupy either foreground or background: it is possible to enjoy Radio Three without attending too closely to the tonal difference between Mr X's pianism and Mme Y's. At the same time, most of us at one time or other, and especially during childhood, have been so vividly impressed by a taste or smell that we have longed years afterwards to have it recreated for us; and we are all increasingly dependent for our daily bread, butter and jam on decisions made for us by growers and manufacturers who may, or may not, refer their products to 'hedonic assessment' or similar judgement by professional or randomly selected tasting panels. If this had been common practice twenty years ago there might have been fewer complaints in the intervening period that tomatoes no longer tasted like tomatoes; and Michel Bourdin, chef of the Connaught Hotel, might not have needed to sum up (in 1981) the shortcomings of the entire native poultry industry by wishing that British cooks would refuse to buy 'this soft, uninteresting meat'.

However, we have now moved a little beyond the period when, as my former colleague Catherine Mant reminds me, not merely the food industry but the consumer movement's magazine *Which?* itself could publish a feature comparing different samples of cheese without taking any account whatsoever of their taste. At the same time, the attitude of mind that made such an approach possible is still embedded within British culture, including the professions of nutrition and home economics. If what follows assists this strain of philistinism to work its way out, all the better for our export and tourist trades. But it is only necessary to read the Sunday paper magazines to realise that the time is happily past when one was obliged to be defensive about owning to an interest in the problems that arise when different foods have to be described, and minute variations detected and expressed. The market researcher Mark Abrams has labelled as follows the progressive changes in British attitudes to foods in the half-century up to 1955:

Phase I	Phase II	Phase III
(animal)	(chemical)	(psychological)
Warming	Protective	Pleasurable
Fattening	Nutritious	Soothing
Filling		Eases tension

It is easy to see the relationship between 'deep structures' of this kind, and the directions which scientific research, commercial advertisement and marketing, and consumer taste have since taken. Dr Roland Harper, the food scientist to whom I owe this reference, has himself summed up in this way the range of issues with which his discipline is concerned:

Flavours consist of a complex sensory pattern, mostly determined by odour and taste, but also influenced by sight and touch . . . One big step towards scientific understanding of flavour consists in separating important variables . . . A clear distinction must be made between information which is aesthetically neutral, and statements which express likes and dislikes, or preferences.

I became interested in the descriptive terms about 1950, when food was still rationed in Britain and food quality, including its flavour, was hardly significant. Now there is a lot of interest in the study of flavour, within which a proper balance has to be maintained between the analysis of flavours into their chemical constituents and the specification of flavours in sensory (descriptive) terms. Modern micro-analytical techniques such as gas-chromatography provide a means of identifying many of the chemicals, but to the chemical data must be added information about the sensitivity of the perceiving individual, the particular qualities perceived and how these interact.

Much of this still needs to be formalised, but the creative flavourist (and the perfumer) is able to work in the light of his own personal experience. Systematic studies of taste and smell in man have been rather sporadic and, although techniques for measuring and controlling the stimuli have improved from the early 1960s onwards, the number of human studies remains small. A better understanding of the language of flavour and its use represents an important aim in the study of taste and odour perception.[1]

Taste research is in fact one of the relatively few areas of precise inquiry where scientific-numerical and critical-verbal approaches can be regarded, at least by the outside observer, as convergent rather than divergent. True, prickles have been felt on both sides during encounters between professional wine-tasters using the arcane or flowery language of their trade, and scientific proponents of statistically-ordered 'multi-variate analysis'. (One Californian from the latter discipline likes to amuse her academic audiences by projecting a lecture slide of 'a wine with a nose'.) But it is a form of crude economic determinism that limits assessment of a food grown or manufactured to its physical properties, even where these can be completely known, without taking account of its resonance in the mind and senses of the consumer. Since 31 December 1982 there has been a British Standard (BS 5929) method for sensory analysis of food.

TASTE AND THE SCIENTISTS

Scientifically, the term 'sensory quality' is the phrase now used to embrace tastes, aromas and textures in food and drink. (Most that the layman thinks of as taste is in fact aroma. The tastebuds in isolation – between 4,000 and 10,000 of them in man – pick up sweet, acid, salt, bitter, hot [including curry-hot] and cold, and little else.) The problem that all three branches of sensory quality present in different degrees is replication and measurement. Exactly what makes one vintage of a famous wine differ from another in the estimation of a taster, or today's batch of butcher's sausages differ from tomorrow's, is one of the material world's last areas of magic, even when the variations admit obvious physical explanations ('rain at the vintage' . . . 'more pepper, less sage'). The magic remains, not only because even advanced forms of gas chromatography and mass spectrometry cannot identify all the trace elements that may contribute crucially to the combination of aromas in even the simplest food, but because no machine can repro-duce even the dullest of human noses and palates. Perhaps, too, scientists tend to recoil before age-old philosophical problems such as 'can I feel another's pain/gratification?' and 'can an apple be said to have a taste independent of the taster?' However, taste scientists in various parts of the world over the past quarter-century have taken constructive steps towards the solution of at least a few of these difficulties, partly out of sheer intellectual curiosity, and partly because more people are now prepared to pay them to do so. They are no longer dependent, as were the first investigators who set out to measure crunch and firmness, on a pair of false teeth attached to a crank and a dial. Already, too, Drs. George Dodd and Krishna Persaud of the University of Warwick have described in *Nature* their electronic nose, coupled to a computer, which can recognise over twenty smells.

To explore 'the definition, measurement and control of sensory quality in foods and beverages' (to borrow the title of the Bristol conference on this topic in 1982), you have to assemble and balance information from different sources: chemical analysis, statistical tabulation of consumer reactions, and the descriptions or comparative ratings of panellists who have been trained to recognise at least a significant proportion of what are reckoned to be 17,000 odorous chemicals. Until recently the normal procedure was to assemble 'flavour profiles' for the product under examination, from the comments of tasters skilled or unskilled, prompted or unprompted. (This technique was mainly devised and practised in America during the 1940s and 1950s, when much concern was voiced about the quantities of virtually flavourless food thrown away by GIs in various parts of the globe.) In the 1980s, advanced mathematical statistical and computer techniques ('multi-variate analysis') are being used to relate the chemical analyses of sensory quality to the choices expressed by tasters when they tick their 'hedonic scales', and the stated or even unstated reasons for these choices. For instance, to take an example from the paper presented to the Bristol conference by Drs. A. A. Williams and O. G. Tucknott of the Long Ashton Agricultural Research Station, the aromas associated by tasters with Cox's Orange Pippin apples are 'scented', 'estery', and 'spicy', with a dried leaves component noticed before the apple is cut, and when the flesh is exposed, an absence of the potato aromas present in some other apples. Chemically, all this corresponds (roughly) to n-butyl acetate, hexyl acetate, 4-methoxyallyl-benzene, linalool oxide, butanol, hexanol, octanol.

As always when researches of this kind are being reported, faintly bizarre solemnities can be picked up from the scientific abstracts: 'red wine is an inherently unstable system and cannot be kept unaltered as a reference'; 'this paper reports relationships between sensory and chemical quality criteria for carrots studied by multi-variate data analysis'. For that matter, Tony Williams remembers being laughed at ten years ago when he told a biochemical society meeting that flavour and sensory properties were the single most important element in a foodstuff – that however nutritious and hygienic it was, 'it wouldn't do you any good unless you could get it past the barrier of the human palate'. Fellow scientists and commercial sponsors of taste research are less sceptical now. The British cider industry, for instance, which makes a great deal of money with a product duller but also more dependable than what used to be sold in West Country pubs, makes extensive use of Long Ashton findings. But many producers, and for that matter the production-oriented Ministry of Agriculture itself, are scarcely yet touched by this kind of thinking. Both nationally and on thousands of individual farms the uncritical concern with weight, yield and profitability that flooded the market with Maris Huntsman wheat and Moneymaker tomatoes will not vanish overnight. Even thirty years after the abolition of rationing, it is socially unacceptable to insist that *any* nutritious food should be discarded simply for want of taste, though it is permissible to say that some varieties taste better than others.

Even the most mathematically-disposed of taste researchers recognises his or her dependence on the words which people use to fit, and on occasion to shape, their perceptions. The older generation of flavour profilers are highly conscious of the limitations imposed by their vocabulary: no more than 200–300 flavour descriptors in each of the three main European languages. (In Japanese, a language subtly adjusted not merely to the topic of discussion but to the social status of the speaker and his interlocutor, researchers have found 406 terms dealing solely with *texture* and *consistency* in foods. Similar work on *odour* and *flavour* terms has yet to be reported.)[2]

TASTE AND THE CRITICS

To be useful in food criticism, words and phrases need to be descriptive or evocative, as opposed to approving ('delicious') or disapproving ('disgusting'). This is no easy matter: let the reader consider how he or she would convey to a blind person with no botanical knowledge how to find by smell in the herb bed the mint, the basil, and the sage. Other European experience may seem to suggest that English is not unusually poor in odour and flavour words: however, there may be other critical contexts – literature and art for instance – in which English is a singularly rich resource, just as Arabic, for instance, is said to be rich in terms to describe the different shapes, sizes and textures of sand-dunes. Dr R. W. Burchfield, editor of the *Oxford English Dictionary*, describes as 'high and philosophical nonsense' the view held by some scholars that in a language, a variegated and finely nuanced vocabulary for a particular range of objects directly reflects the interests and concerns of the people who speak that language. However, the issue remains a live one. Compare, perhaps, the precise and unexpected range of terms that surround the mating of horses in stud-farming circles, where the sums of money involved leave no room for ambiguity; compare, too, the flight of French slang to food words for male and female private parts (*anguille, asperge, chipolata, flageolet; abricot, baba, figue, mille-feuille*).[3]

To a townsman, a sheep is a sheep, unless it is a lamb; to a Gloucestershire countryman, according to the writer John Moore, it is (or was) a teg, theave, wether or chilver according to age and sex. Moore goes on to describe two groups of youths whom he overheard one evening by his village tench-pond. On his left were 'Birmingham boys so poor in language that they had real difficulty in communicating the simplest ideas and in composing any but the simplest sentences.' On his right were a cowman and a mechanic from the village who not only had plenty of conventional words for their conversation but a subsidiary vocabulary of dialect words for capturing what might be called sensory qualities of a specifically rural kind: 'fidthering' for the rustling noise made by a small creature moving about in reeds or straw, and no fewer than four different expressions to describe the condition of ripeness and over-ripeness of pears in an orchard. ' "Frum" was ripe and in perfect condition; "mawsey" meant soft and woolly; "sapy" suggested the pears had gone sodden-like; "roxy" meant they were altogether decayed.'[4]

Of these epithets, only 'roxy' appears in *OED*, though all are to be found in Wright's *Dialect Dictionary*. Further investigation, coupled perhaps with reference to Dr J. D. A. Widdowson's files at the University of Sheffield's Centre for English Cultural Tradition and Language, might show that most formal English dictionaries since Johnson have been unreliable guides to the language and fine distinctions of farm and kitchen. Words of this kind are too easily dismissed as the unwritten argot of yokels, women, or immigrant, macaronic chefs. Historically, the rise of British lexicography coincided with the beginning of the decline of indigenous British cooking. Chaucer and Shakespeare are much richer repositories of food and drink language than any of their successors – even Dickens, in spite of his keen interest in the sustenance of his characters – presumably in part because the earlier writers lived relatively close to the crafts involved in the production of food and the preparation of meals. Raymond Postgate, when he began to collect the comments of the British eating-out public about the inns they visited, used to complain that most people had little specific to say in praise of dishes they had enjoyed except that the food was 'ample' and 'piping hot'. But that last cliché itself goes back to Chaucer, who must have stood close enough to an oven to detect the whistling noise from air trapped in a very hot dish.

In the nineteenth century, novelists – even female ones – seldom paid cooking that kind of attention. Even in Jane Austen's domestic-scale books, written before Waterloo, it is only the women who can afford little help in the house that feel compelled to take a practical interest in soups and ragouts, as distinct from Mrs Elton's elegant picnicking and strawberry-gathering. We have already seen what effect this dissociation of sensory awareness and social ambition had on British cooking as a craft. But a secondary effect may have been the arrested development of specialised language at the polite or literary level. French may be regarded as a special case, given the vast structure of technical terms and garnishing conventions which make a French menu such an efficient shorthand guide to the extremely complex kitchen processes that underlie it – assuming one knows or has access to the terms employed. Even so, there are familiar examples in French and Italian of technical or textural gradations which cook or eater cannot so easily specify in English: the point of done-ness at which beads of blood appear on a steak or a piece of liver; the stage before the inside of an omelette has coagulated; the residual bite of a vegetable or a strand of spaghetti that has been taken out of boiling water before it has softened. It is surely legitimate to wonder whether linguistic gaps of this kind might have been filled in English if the people concerned with producing effects of this kind had belonged to the same cultural universe as the people they were feeding. Even in twentieth-century novels it is rare to find oneself in the midst of a paragraph such as the following, though it is more successful in conveying character than most passages describing sexual activity ever are:

I have now had lunch (lentil soup, followed by chipolata sausages served with boiled onions and apples stewed in tea, then dried apricots and shortcake biscuits: a light Beaujolais) and I feel better. (Fresh apricots are best of course, but the dried kind, soaked for twenty-four hours and then well drained, make a heavenly accompaniment for any sort of mildly sweet biscuit or cake. They are especially good with anything made of almonds, and thus consort happily with red wine . . .)[5]

Iris Murdoch's Charles Arrowby 'refused with scorn' a friends invitation to initiate him 'into the pleasures of vintage wine'. He would have been a disappointment to Michael Broadbent, who as a professional wine critic, taster and vendor over many years has thought more clearly and deeply than most about the problem of how to taste and now to express intelligibly the outcome of the tasting.

There are reasons why, in English as in other European languages, the vocabulary has been 'stretched' for wine rather than food. Food is a necessity which has only recently become so diverse and abundant in the market that sellers sense a need to draw attention to finer points of discrimination than mere appetite. Wine is optional – at least in Anglo-Saxon cultures – and even when all mystique and snobbery are subtracted, it remains a complex, infinitely various substance. It is sold, as it were, on the nerve endings, as a spark crosses from the verbal evocations of a wine in the vendor's catalogue or advertisement to the first, fleeting impression of the professional taster or the unpredictable impulses of the armchair buyer. Exposure for sale without critical commentary often seems insufficient, because the contents of a bottle are anonymous (despite the label) until the cork is drawn. At the same time, Michael Broadbent's assessment of critical language against statistical analysis has a faintly defensive tone:

The problem is, as usual, to note or convey both subjective and objective impressions, using words which can be understood. The sole *object* of one's concentration should be the wine, but in the ultimate analysis 'I, the taster' am the final arbiter . . . The more similar in quality and style the wines are, the more precisely the basis of judgment must be defined. When it comes to detecting small differences, particularly in wines of neutral character, the sensory thresholds (the level at which elements of smell and taste can be detected) of the judges are important. It would be sensible to test these; and it is possible to do so . . . The French and American academics' partiality to algebra is altogether another thing. The object of the statistician is to reduce the chance element in tasting. In effect, one eliminates as far as possible all the conditions which induce varying subjective impressions, and after testing the tasters, analyses the results mathematically. I concede that with certain types of wine and in certain circumstances there is a case to be made, but it is generally beyond the level of knowledge and out of the area of interest of most wine lovers, in or out of the trade.[6]

TABLE 5: Terms used to describe wine and food

Critical terms (wine)

Words in common use	*Words in common use which should be used in a qualified context*	*Words to use precisely or with care*	*Additional qualitative descriptions*
acid/acidity	aftertaste	astringent	aromatic
aroma(tic)	big	baked	breed, well bred
balance/well-	bland	bite	complex
balanced	body	bitter	distinguished
bouquet	bright	corked	elegant
clean	character	dumb	finesse
dry/medium-	coarse	earthy	flowery
dry etc.	dull	extract	fragrant
fruity	fat	feminine	insipid
grapey	fine	flabby	luscious
hard	finish	flinty	mellow
harsh	flat	forthcoming	metallic
poor	full	green	musty
refreshing	heavy	hot	noble
soft	light	iron	perfumed
sweet	little	maderised	powerful
tannin, tannic	long	mouldy	raw
tough	mature/maturity	nutty	ripe
vinegary	meaty	oxidised	scented
watery	medium	penetrating	sensuous
	neutral	piquant	silky
	ordinary	pungent	smooth
	peppery	robust	spicy
	positive	rough	subtle
	rich	sharp	supple
	round	smoky	unripe
	sour	stalky	velvety
	strong	tang/tangy	vinosity
	varietal	tart	well developed
	weak	vinous	yeasty
	youthful	woody	
		zesty/zestful	

Source: *Michael Broadbent's Pocket Guide to Wine-Tasting* (1982)

TABLE 5: continued

Scientific terms			
Odours	floral	oily	warm
acid	fragrant	petrol, solvent-like	watery
ammonia-like	fruity (citrus)	putrid	waxy
aromatic	fruity (other)	rancid	woody
beery	fresh	resinous	yeasty
broth-like	garlic/onion	rubbery	
burnt	greasy	sharp	*Tastes*
butyric	green	smoky	sweet
camphor-like	hay-like	soapy	acid
cheesy	honey-like	sour	salt
diacetyl	malty	spicy	bitter
dry, powdery	medicinal	sulphurous	
earthy	metallic	sweaty	*Tactile*
estery	meaty (raw)	sweet	astringent
etherish	meaty (cooked)	tallowy	puckery
faecal	minty/peppermint	urinous	cool/cooling
fatty	musky	vegetable (raw)	warm
fishy	musty	vegetable (cooked)	pungent

Source: *Proceedings of Sixth International Symposium on Olfaction and Taste* (Paris 1977)

In Table 5, Broadbent's short-list of English words used in wine description may be compared with scientists' terms, covering taste, odour, and tactile qualities. Neither list is intended to be exhaustive. For instance, 'nutty' does not appear in the scientists' list, although two food scientists who made a special study of the term found over 200 chemical compounds with a nutty smell. Even these researchers did not pause to subdivide for specific nuts, whereas Broadbent (who includes 'nutty' as a word 'to use precisely or with care') later elaborates: 'a crisp rounded flavour associated with full-bodied dry white wines like Corton Charlemagne, or good quality amontillados. Fine old tawny port has a distinct smell of cobnuts'.

Good Food Guide correspondents or inspectors have spontaneously used many of these words about food at one time or another (not necessarily in the same sense: 'hot' and 'green' obviously mean something different for wines and foods). The extent of the correspondences is surprising, remembering that the scientists are trying to find words for

relatively straightforward tastes that are capable of being isolated chemically and identified by different individuals, whereas a wine taster,
restaurant food critic, or ambitious home cook is hoping to be con-
fronted by tastes whose complexity and resistance to synthesis are a
major element in their appeal, like the fifteen different herbs and spices
in the sauce which competing chefs had to identify in Rex Stout's story
Too Many Cooks. However, in leading London restaurants I have myself
not only tasted 'petrol, solvent-like' or 'soap' in particular dishes but
listened to the restaurateur insist, on tasting them, that they fulfilled his
intentions.

A different, perhaps less precise, but more evocative style of reporting
on tastes is presented in the quotations that head this chapter. This kind
of language is closer to the manner recommended to wine *amateurs* by
Broadbent: 'Loosen up: don't be afraid to express an opinion or a
preference: let your imagination roam. Evocative comments help open
up new vistas for others. It is not so much precision that is required but a
vital exchange of reactions and ideas.'[7]

Here, though, a caveat must be entered which applies equally to
'scientific' and 'literary' description. It arises out of the structural
characteristics of English and perhaps other languages. Good writers
who want to convey a vivid impression of a sensual experience are wary
of adjectives, unless the words themselves appeal strongly to the senses,
as did the 'pulpy, slushy, oozy' nectarine that slid down the gullet of John
Keats. Even so, the words in that passage (see page 118) that fix it in the
memory and reveal the master of language are the nouns and verbs
('embonpoint', 'breed'). Notice too how the casual self-portrait of a man
with a pen in one hand and a nectarine in the other erupts into the sexual
comedy of 'I shall certainly breed', suggested by the slithery intro-
mission and the spurt of juice.

Other types of sensory description and criticism obey similar rules.
For a different purpose some years ago, I went through the adjectives in
a record review by a well-known London music critic who perhaps owes
his influence on other people's tastes and choices to his ear, memory,
knowledge and track record rather than to his powers of communication
as such. The adjectives that emerged from the article were 'evocative',
'magnificent', 'vital', 'beautiful', 'skilful', 'mellow', 'under-appreciated',
'striking', 'purposeful' (twice in the same paragraph), 'superb', 'loving',
'devoted', and 'radiantly convincing'. Hardly any of these words say
anything at all about the impression the music made on the critic's
senses except that he liked it: they are the equivalent of 'delicious',

'luscious' and 'super' in restaurant advertising features. It was not by these adjectival appoggiaturas, but by metaphor and characterisation that the late Neville Cardus, for instance, could persuade his readers that they had actually been present in the Queen's Hall listening to Kreisler or at Old Trafford watching Archie Maclaren. Similarly, when another contemporary critic used in a concert notice the phrase 'this great Rolls-Royce of an orchestra swinging down the country lanes and never once scratching its paint', the actual sound the LSO had made in an early Mozart symphony was instantly made audible to any musically experienced reader. 'Polished', 'smooth', 'mellow', 'harmonious' would no doubt have been true descriptions of the sound too, but almost universally transferable epithets of this kind convey no more information than they would if applied to, say, Clos Vougeot '34.[8]

It is the same problem – if the reader will forgive reference to a critical style for which the author has been chiefly responsible – with notices of restaurant meals that have been published in *The Good Food Guide* over the years. 'Delicious' and 'luscious' are not always successfully avoided, and after all these are words people actually use in letters and conversation about food. 'Juicy', 'crunchy', 'garlicky', 'lemony', 'dry', and 'bland' are more usefully descriptive, but become tedious with repetition, as Miles Kington noted in an accurately-spiced lampoon:

When out good food guiding you should keep an eager eye open for the five great qualities in cooking: crispness, freshness, fluffiness, lusciousness and exquisiteness. The five bad things to avoid are: blandness, dryness, tiredness, tinnedness and leftoverness. The greatest quality of all is crispness without, meltingness within . . .

You may call a Cumberland sauce or casserole of kid over-assertive, strident or blowsy, but proprietors with the same qualities should be called attentive or perhaps a soupçon over-friendly.[9]

Personally I share Michael Broadbent's respect for the role of free association in the expression of tastes, but it seems to work more helpfully for wine than it does for food: 'old armour' and 'calf bookbindings' are among impressions particular clarets have evoked from colleagues or myself, but any impression similarly remote and unexpected conveyed by a food stuff would be unlikely to lead to a favourable verdict. (The 'Turkish delight' taste I once detected in a friend's *gravlax* was perhaps on the borderline for an eater who would normally expect to enjoy both these foods, but consecutively rather than concurrently.) There is more to be done with a metaphor, even musical metaphor. If you say of a Lakeland hotel that 'they over-egged the pudding' you are in danger of being taken literally, whereas if you say that 'the salmon and honey represented a lost chord that should never have been found' or that 'the six-course dinner had all stops out, from the *contra bombarde* to the *voix céleste*' the reader familiar with the wilder shores of British catering will begin to feel the precisely appropriate sensations in the pit of the stomach.

The reason for this is that tastes, smells, and sounds of any complexity and distinctiveness normally have a 'profile' which is more like one's memory of a previous occasion on which they have been experienced than they are like a taste, smell, or sound from some other source that may be immediately available for comparison. This is true whether the sensory impression can be taken in isolation, or as part of a blend. A peach is more like your last peach, even if the difference in quality between the two is noticeable, than it is like an apricot, or like synthetic peach flavour. The *sound* of Benny Goodman's clarinet (as opposed to the *sense* of the playing) is more like a schoolboy's clarinet than it is like Leon Goossens playing the same notes on the oboe.

With fine meals, fine wines, fine performances, the battery of sense impressions is too complex to be analysed out in its different particulars. The critic, fortunately for him, is likely to be writing almost entirely for the converted who share these pleasures. There cannot be many who claim to have been converted to burgundy or Berlioz simply by the act of reading, though I would be delighted to be proved wrong. The food critic, like any other critic, has to engage the interest of his reader or listener, and to discuss, if necessary, the techniques employed in procuring, cooking and serving the meal in question. But with tastes as such, he can only hope that his language is accurate and imaginative enough to jog people's memories back to similar tastes and occasions that they can recognise and remember for themselves. Without this sharing of sensory experience, most communication about food fails altogether, although every now and then food writers appear – in our own time notably Elizabeth David and M. F. K. Fisher[10] – whose descriptive and reminiscent powers are more nearly self-sufficient: at their best, one reads under the illusion that one is simultaneously tasting.

Anyone who has got as far as this in these pages is likely to share the writer's view that over and above their nutritive values, both simple and complex combinations of food and drink are capable of engaging the intelligence as well as the appetites and feelings, on the analogy of pictures, concerts, dancing, and other arts and crafts which do not depend on words for their communication. It is of course true that criticism of music and art, for example, normally concentrates upon a kind of formal patterning which lies deeper than the sensual element in sound and colour, and to which even the most ingeniously balanced banquet can only aspire – though such aspiration is not uncommon among chefs. 'Carême wrote, to the great pleasure of Anatole France, that patisserie was a significant branch of sculpture. The Goncourt brothers saw a gentleman with a chisel in his hand in Fremiet's atelier: it was the Rothschilds' *maître d'hotel* learning by modelling how to improve the presentation of his dishes.'[11] But the infinitely diverse sensory qualities of cooked food – the culinary equivalent of painterly values and musicality – persuade me that qualitative criticism of food and drink, whether prepared for daily use or for special occasions, is a useful activity without which we would be worse nourished, as well as very much more shoddily entertained, than we are.

This entails a persistent search for informative and evocative words and phrases. These have to be either so accurate in description that the reader is able to match them to his own memory of familiar tastes and smells and textures, or so evocative that although their meaning is imprecise or metaphorical, he is drawn into the experience as though he were sitting at the same table with the eater or drinker. A genius may use words in both ways in the same breath, as Keats does with his nectarine (and how typical of English scholarship it is that the index to the edition of his *Letters* that I was using to find this quotation has entries for 'fine writers' and 'fagging in schools' but none for 'food' and 'drink', which Keats mentions far more often). A child, likewise, may make imaginative or perhaps more accurately sensual-literalist leaps of language that focus an impression in a different way: at the age of four, invited to help herself from a salad of baby squids, one of my daughters remarked with pleasure, 'It tastes of spiders.'

CHAPTER EIGHT
Eating by numbers
The food technologists

Let us put together an artificial collection of flavours unknown to nature. Beethoven put a collection of sounds together and made a noise better than God ever did. I don't see why I as a food technologist shouldn't make a taste better than God ever made.

Magnus Pyke in the *Guardian*, 14 October 1971.

It is often remarked that the contemporary architects who design high-rise flats and glass-curtained office blocks tend to choose for their own dwellings discreetly converted Tudor cottages, Georgian town-houses, and – more recently – the terraced hutches of Victorian railwaymen. Never mind: it makes them seem more human, like members of the Tribune Group who educate their children privately. For some reason, less curiosity has been expressed about the domestic meals of the men – as with architects, it is usually men – who work to extend the frontiers of food science and technology. Their ultimate aim is modest enough, and humanitarian too. It is to keep the population of this or any other country happily and economically fed without the intervention of anything that looks like an animal or a plant. Dr H. Onrust of International Flavours and Fragrances was very frank:

Our objective is to open new ways of making acceptable and nutritious foods of a pleasant taste and colour, starting from tasteless, colourless material. It is possible to manufacture the raw materials for so-called meatballs and the sauces in a powdered form. All the housewife would have to do would be to add cold water, boil, and make a sauce; or roll out the small meatballs and fry them.[1]

Well, even a house-husband could do it, but this was fifteen years ago and Dr Onrust had not progressed so far in his thinking. It is true that experiment of this kind sometimes runs up against the weakness of the human stomach. The marketing director of Adams Dalkeith, a Scottish firm that was dazzled by the success of its chicken-flavoured sausage and proceeded to whisky, rum and pineapple flavours, called off further development with the comment: 'It just did not seem right sitting down at breakfast and drinking whisky out of a sausage.'[2]

However, even in the virtuous branches of the food industry euphemism is the best sauce. Peter Roberts of Direct Foods: 'We always ask our customers not to pass our Protoveg off as meat. But there is consumer resistance to buying anything described on the menu as Protoveg chunks so they tend to use a generic term like hotpot.'[3]*

Any representative selection of newspaper and trade magazine cuttings on the topic of food product research and development over the past quarter century – a period of intense activity on both sides of the Atlantic, and indeed the Pacific too – not only furnishes plenty of light entertainment but suggests that behind the scenes a cosmic battle is being fought between the good fairy and the bad fairy: the good fairy who with a wave of her magic microbiological wand is keeping just ahead of the global nightmare of mass starvation; the bad fairy who is reversing millennia of dietary progress, and substituting for the traditional foods of European civilisation denatured, chemically flavoured elements which she pretends are just as good for you.

Similar good fairy–bad fairy counterpoints have been familiar features of the technological world we have gained since 1945. Fairy stories are more up to date in their approach than is always realised: to cope successfully with the dangerously open-ended three wishes granted, it was always necessary to take a longer view than the natural man, woman or child in the story could manage.

People in food research and development, whether or not they are working to direct commission from profit-minded manufacturers, cannot be expected to look further into the future than is demanded of them by the general eating public, concerned about where its next meal is coming from. Not surprisingly, the pace of innovation has consistently been two steps ahead of health and safety legislation, and of both public and voluntary forms of consumer protection. For instance, many authorities now believe that it was unnecessary to ban cyclamates as sugar substitutes, as Britain did. But if it *had* been as urgent as say, reducing lead emissions from motor vehicles, the administrative gavotte that

---

* Protoveg lives, I notice from a vegetarian cookery book whose latest edition has just arrived in my household. Cookery books, as a genre of literature, may disguise their sources but never their contents. Deception, if any, is practised only at the next stage, between the recipe-user and the eater.

preceded the ban would have seemed stately to the point of ineptitude.

Sugar itself in recent years has come to be seen as a 'culinary poison', in Frederic Accum's phrase, whose insidious and anonymous role in many manufactured food products highlights the collusive failure of successive British governments to secure adequate labelling from manufacturers and retailers.

However, failures in social control cannot fairly be blamed upon food scientists as such. More basic studies of food production and preservation have occupied British food research institutes and university departments in the past twenty-five years. In quantity, quality and – until the recent checks on overseas student participation – international scope, the work done in this field is unequalled in Europe.* True, the proportion of turnover that the British food and drink industry allots to research and development is modest by other industrial standards, but the total turnover is vast, and after all, most food goes on selling itself without academic intervention. The money available has been sufficient to ensure that most of the questions addressed to food scientists by the industry and its customers or regulators are answered with reasonable despatch, though whether the questions are asked early or forcefully enough is another matter. Apart from isolated examples such as early season apples, soft cheese and unsalted butter, not much food is imported that could easily and economically be produced in this country. 'Foreign' foods that came to be made in British versions as soon as their consumption became statistically significant range from spaghetti to soy sauce. British soy sauce was developed at the University of Strathclyde, and it was also Scots who worked out that a machine which extruded liquorice, a popular Scottish taste, would also extrude pasta. It remains arguable that some of the import substitution that has been achieved has also resulted in objective deterioration of the product sold. The Chorleywood baking process, which enables bread of a kind to be manufactured out of soft British instead of hard Canadian wheats, is the most obvious and emotive example, and the monopolistic pressure of British millers is resented by many specialist bakers who must work to lower standards or look elsewhere for suitable flours.

In the post-war period, a combination of public esteem, government subsidy, and later rapidly rising land prices carried at least a fortunate

* For instance, the Whiteladies campus of the University of Reading now houses side by side the University's food science department, the National College of Food Technology, and the Cadbury-Schweppes Research Institute.

minority of British farmers and market gardeners to a prosperity un-dreamt-of before 1939. Patterns changed but overall profitability did not diminish after British accession to the European Community in 1972, thanks to regulations and subsidies originally designed to protect re-latively inefficient or labour-intensive farmers on the Continent. Euro-pean free trade in farm and garden produce may pose a new threat with the impending accession of Spain to the Community: subsidies are no substitute for the sun. Hitherto, though, the proportion of home-produced food in the nation's diet has remained close to the levels achieved during the 1939–45 war, while the number of people employed in agriculture has drifted steeply and steadily downwards to below two per cent by 1970 – one of the lowest proportions in the world. This labour economy was largely attributable to electrical and oil-driven mechanisation on the one hand, and on the other, to chemical fertilisa-tion and pest-control, with their familiar and unpleasant side-effects. Consumption of nitrogen fertiliser more than doubled during the 1960s, and DDT was proscribed only just in time to preserve from extinction in the British countryside various birds and animals that stand at the end of the food chains where the substance accumulates. But in the context of the national economy, the message was more cheerful: there have been fewer patronising jokes about farmers and yokels in *Punch* since people began half-consciously to compare the productivity of East Anglia with that of British Rail or British Leyland.

A *Financial Times* article in mid-1958 on the 'agenda' for food scien-tists makes a convenient benchmark for the developments of the follow-ing quarter-century.[4] At this time, the frozen food market which Clarence Birdseye had opened up in America thirty-five years previous-ly was in Britain only embryonic: it grew from 100,000 packets of frozen fruit and vegetables in 1954 to 360 million in 1960. The freezing and sealing of fish in distant waters had not yet begun to threaten traditional British fishmongery, but once the wet fish had become the plastic-wrapped cod or plaice fillet it could be sold from any grocer's cabinet freezer, and for a while in the 1970s literally not a day passed without someone somewhere abandoning the fish trade.

Freezing was not the only method of preservation investigated. 'In-teresting experiments have concerned the possible use of antibiotics such as chlortetracycline, oxytetracycline and nisin to preserve poultry, fish and even canned goods.' Desirably or not, these experiments paid off in added value for beef, pork and poultry producers. Irradiation, though a feasible technique of preservation, 'tended to produce changes in colour, flavour and appearance'. In 1964 the Chief Medical Officer's Committee on Medical and Nutritional Aspects of Food Policy reported that the use of ionising radiation for food preservation, within defined limits, would not constitute a hazard to health. But two years later a Labour Minister of Health (Kenneth Robinson) nevertheless ruled against it. In frozen foods, too, the problem of preserving or restoring flavour in meat and fish had been recognised, but at this time few of the aromatic agents necessary had been identified and synthesized, and it was assumed that they would have to be found from natural sources. At this period, some American flavour scientists were thinking of extracting roast beef flavour from a joint as it cooked and bottling it, so to speak, to improve the taste of commercially marketed products. The meat residue, shorn of the flavours concentrated in the browned surface, could then, they thought, be consumed in prisons, psychiatric hospitals and other institutions where complaints would be rare, and if made, disregarded. Fortunately it later proved possible to obtain a battery of synthetic flavours without resorting to such socially obnoxious methods, and it soon became hazardous to ask for a packet of potato crisps in a British pub without specifying 'plain', for fear of being given something purporting to taste of roast pork and apple sauce.

Already in the 1950s, food scientists were exploring lines of research which went behind the age-old problem of how to preserve for later consumption the regional or seasonal gluts of whatever food cultivators could grow or hunters kill. In Britain, especially, scientists were highly motivated, and at this period still far better equipped than their European counterparts, to look for new sources of nutriment. Unlike the Americans, whose equipment and funding were superior but who were surrounded by huge agricultural surpluses, the British had fresh in their memories the near-miss starvation or malnutrition achieved by submarine warfare in two world wars, and the debacle of the 1945–50 Labour government's East African groundnuts scheme, whose promise of abundance had foundered on the intractability of ground, climate, and – above all – human beings. It would have been a triumph, not only for Britain but for the hungry millions of the British Commonwealth in what was not yet known as the Third World, if essential protein could be produced from nothing or nearly nothing in hygienic, controllable laboratories and factories. This was, after all, the period when a controlled fusion reaction was still expected to be the next achievement of atomic science.

At this stage, the new processes of which news reached the papers were usually perceived as mechanisms for bypassing the cow, rather as early motor cars were seen as superior versions of the horse and carriage, and designed accordingly. In 1959, British Glues and Chemicals Ltd announced the arrival of impulse process protein, a powder evolved from grass, maize, peanuts and cottonseed. Unlike cows, this machine could produce 3,000 tons in a year for £300,000, and feed 120,000 people for a shilling a week. It sounded as though Mr W. Heath Robinson would prove the ideal designer for the production model: 'In fifteen minutes whole peanuts emerge as oil protein and carbohydrate after sonic vibration in water to break down cell walls.' On a somewhat smaller scale, the Vegetarian Nutritional Research Centre at Watford was trying its luck with the surplus pods and leaves benignly supplied free by some of the large firms that were by then engaged in packaging frozen and – since 1961 – accelerated freeze-dried vegetables. An admirably British note was struck by one announcement: 'A woman member of the research centre now in her eighties has offered to will her fortune for the production of "plant milk" provided we are able to put on the market within a year of her death a plant milk which is certified as satisfactory from a nutritional viewpoint and whose domestic value is certified by Lady Dowding, who has been interested in the project for some years.' This would indeed have been a notable double: Lady Dowding's husband had won the Battle of Britain in the air, and her fellow vegetarians and spiritualists could be forgiven for expecting his widow to help them win it in the ground.

By the mid-1960s, it had become possible to think commercially about more fundamental solutions than peapod milk to the world's protein deficiency, and vegetarianism itself began to look like a different kind of cause. As Dr Magnus Pyke expressed it with typical pungency to one of his numerous interviewers: 'You can now take any protein you want, cottonseed or peanut or groundnut or fishmeal, purify it, dissolve it in alkali, extrude it through tiny holes, wind it up like a great hank of wool, cut it across the fibres, and lo and behold you have beef, mutton, turkey or smoked salmon according to the flavour you care to give it that day.'[5]

During the 1960s and 1970s, the public mind (including even the Catholic mind) began to take in the implications – long familiar to the scientific community – of the rate at which the world's population was increasing. The reassurance needed by western newspaper readers was provided by progress reports from research that had been started during the 1950s into single cell proteins nourished on fossil fuel feed stocks. In

1972 the head of ICI's food and agriculture research division, John Gow, said that one square mile was all the land needed to produce enough protein for everybody in the world.[6] The waste products would be water, carbon dioxide, and heat. ICI's single cell protein, like a Finnish process based on spent sulphite liquors from paper pulp, was designed for animal feed. A decade later, biotechnology had become a word capable of evoking twitch responses in Parliament and the City as well as in university and commercial laboratories. Rank Hovis McDougall, better known if not better loved for their versions of the British loaf, sounded very sure that in their Fusarium fungus A 3/5, found near their own High Wycombe laboratories, they had a micro-organism of slower doubling-time than ICI's bacterium but of such versatility that it can be converted (according to their research director) into almost any of the foodstuffs to which the British public is accustomed, 'from soups and fortified drinks, through biscuits to convincing replicas of chicken, ham and veal'. A lack of suitable flavouring agents has so far thwarted attempts to develop a beef substitute, in spite of the similarity to steak inherent in A 3/5's ratio of 45 per cent protein and 13 per cent fat. Fish cakes and fish fingers – with a little real fish mixed in – are easier. Roughly speaking, as a converter of starch into protein, A 3/5 is three times as efficient as a chicken or a pig, and ten times as efficient as a cow. Human toxicity trials, which normally take at least three years, are in progress.[7] Any anxieties about the palatability of products of this kind were answered years ago by the Liverpool chemist Jack Tolley, who successfully converted his own excreta into 'something like a rich pudding',[8] and by the then director of Lord Rank's Food Research Centre, who said of the new generation of fermented proteins: 'The new protein will find its way into sausages, hamburgers, and Irish stew. It will produce a meat loaf very similar to one which for thirty years has been a household name.'[9] Exactly as we feared . . .

Across the Atlantic, General Electric have simultaneously been working on a similar process of more immediate potential benefit to the society that devised it. GE's strain of bacterium is activated by a waste product furnished in abundance by intensive animal husbandry – manure. Not that British scientists have missed this potential source of cheap protein. For a similar purpose, the Agricultural Research Council's Rothamsted Experimental Station has been using not a bacterium but a prolific worm, *Eisenia foetida*, which in dried form (as a powder containing 60 per cent protein together with the twenty essential aminoacids and a good range of fatty acids, minerals and vitamins), can be fed directly back to animals. Even the by-product, worm casts, absorb odorous gases from the manure and themselves make a useful and transportable fertiliser for modern farming systems that have separated the cultivation of fields from the generation of the muck that used to be spread on them.

All this is in the future, but not very far into it. By 1980, most people in Britain must have tasted or failed to taste TVP (texturised vegetable protein) under one or other of its brand names, in school meals, supermarket sausage rolls, or freeze-dried packages. Analytically, the substance is said to be hard to distinguish from meat, whatever more subjective human reactions may report. A few years ago, meat-extenders or substitutes of this kind, chiefly derived from the soy-bean until its price was driven up on the world market to unheard-of levels, were novel enough. Several Brave New Dinners were arranged by manufacturers, caterers, newspapers or other interested parties, and invitations were issued to minor celebrities. I vividly recall the sigh of pleasure with which the company in a private room at the Savoy Hotel greeted the (real) French beans that arrived towards the close of an otherwise entirely artificial meal which the Mirror Group had per-suaded Silvino Trompetto of the Savoy to cook: even the Ch. Laville Haut Brion (not available in the Third World) could not persuade us to do more than toy with the texturised smoked salmon. Any one of those present – Dr Pyke included – would have been glad to march up to the Soho Chinatown and sit down to a dish of beancurd made from the same soybean staple by a cottage industry process ecologically superior to the multi-million-pound machinery and vast energy input that west-ern culture tolerates for the sake of making fake steak. Our impressions were confirmed by a similar event arranged by Cecily Williams-Ellis's Cauldron Club at Portmeirion, where the novelist Richard Hughes argued that the new foods could be introduced only with the help of a new generation of witchdoctors.[10]

The first tentative flights of artificial protein may seem a long way from the precious mating calls of contemporary British foodies and the £50-a-plate perfectionism of *les Roux*. But they are a natural develop-ment from the basic nutritional concerns that ruled the lives of rich and poor alike during the 1940s, from Woolton pie to groundnuts. Even in the still-affluent 1980s, some sense of the possible in food science and technology is necessary if one is to balance the instinctive reactions of a child of European food culture against a world citizen's awareness of how things are and will be. This is not just a matter of liberal Anglo-Saxon *angst* about aid budgets, which could be multiplied by ten and still be trivial in relation to the agricultural problems and political inequalities to which they are addressed. In the present context, it is more important to share the thinking of scientists forced to conclude that – failing a wholesale reversal of population trends or a terminally destructive war – global food production a century hence will have to be 800 per cent higher than it is now in order to feed an anticipated world population of over 30,000 million. To a middle-aged man who can remember fifty years, a century does not seem a very long time.

At some point not very far along that road, the role played in human diet by comparatively inefficient protein conversion machines such as cows, pigs and chickens, however intensively bred and farmed, would have to be diminished or abandoned. Here and there, the animals concerned would be relegated to agricultural zoos, to be gazed at with wild surmises by people who obtained their nourishment chiefly from the protein output of those industrious worms, bugs, and funguses, appropriately flavoured. Some of the intermediate stages that can be envisaged are just as off-putting spiritually, if not gastronomically. 'Today the feeling gains ground that three birds in each "nest" of a hen battery is inhumane. Tomorrow it may be technically feasible to use decerebrate hens (that is, hens with their brains removed) which lay eggs just as well and with less fuss.'[11]

The researches that have been all too briefly noticed here, the output of well-funded laboratories in Britain, America and other advanced countries, may go some way towards postponing the population and resource crisis to which the world seems to be driving. But most synthetic food, the product of expensive investment, is confined to the mass market of the country that devised it. Perhaps this is a kind of justice. Poorer peoples usually have a more old-fashioned range of choices: real food, adulterated real food, starvation. Even if the proteins were equally spread round the globe, which seems improbable, they could hardly do more than postpone crisis. Protein alone cannot rescue the wretched of the earth from the high reproduction rates, infantile mortality, unprotected old age and other misfortunes which now belong to the past in societies like our own. It is certainly not obvious that Europeans, blessed with stable or falling populations and sufficient wealth to exercise free choices of diet and leisure, assist the emergence or survival of civilised and 'ecological' diets by embracing uncritically one or other of the directions taken by food technology in the years since plenty returned to our tables in the early 1950s.

On the contrary, if one contemplates various apparently unrelated changes, from the rise of junk food and of food-related psychological illnesses (anorexia and bulimia) to the selective appetite that has appeared here and there in all social classes for 'real' bread and exotic vegetables, it is arguable that Britain is developing its own variation of the north American dissociation between nourishment and pleasurable eating. Up to the period of history covered by this book, at no time had the bulk of the population been more or less equally well (or badly) nourished. Even now, it is possible for a socially competent person to eat well while unemployed, though the nutrient intake of large families has deteriorated more seriously (overall, from 10 to 5 per cent above recommended DHSS levels in 1980, which means that many of the poorest households undoubtedly fall well below).[12] It is still hard to imagine the extent of nutritional inequality in late Victorian and Edwardian London, but whereas the Westminster streetwalkers rescued by Mr Gladstone would in most cases have preferred his food to his benevolence, how many of their contemporary counterparts would think anything to the tables kept by Denis and Margaret Thatcher, or by Harold and Mary Wilson? Social division in the national diet is still real enough, but it arrives not where incomes rise and fall but where some people decide that eating (as opposed to nourishment) is as important to them or their sub-culture as football or golf are to others.

When this point is reached, and food becomes part of the fashion industry, 'ordinary' mass-market food tends to suffer from official neglect and impoverishment, like state schools and health services whose most articulate potential clients have migrated to the private sector. No one of importance – certainly not the generality of ministers and civil servants – cares very much what manufacturers or retailers of food give the population to eat provided that the price can be kept down and scandals avoided. It is only a relatively small community of scientists, food journalists and others who are professionally obliged to taste a range of products that have been surfaced, sequestrated, humected, emulsified, anti-oxided and the rest, and who compare the results with more nearly natural foods, whether from domestic or commercial sources. None of these researchers or commentators enjoys the power to affect the national diet that was conferred on Jack Drummond in 1940, and they are merely left hoping that sooner or later a civilised nation will turn on a food industry whose function of satisfying hunger has been so extensively invaded by the pursuit of the new at the expense of the wholesome, the preservable at the expense of the fresh:

> Transformation for the sake of transformation has become an end in itself. Potato crisps no longer taste of potato but of chicken; chicken tastes of fishmeal; and fish come not with fins but in battered bite-size fingers. Flavour-blur has left creamy soups indistinguishable from creamy puddings ... It is becoming difficult to buy any processed food which does not contain superfluous additives.[13]

Even the articulate bourgeoisie, who during the 1940s ate their baked potatoes and tinned fish on points like everyone else, now occupy different ground: it is a question of asking the fishmonger whether the salmon trout is wild or farmed, and if tins or packets are bought from supermarkets and loaded into the Volvo along with the basic household groceries, they may well be intended for the cat. Only occasionally is a different kind of voice raised, as by M. F. K. Fisher in her introduction to Shizuo Tsuji's book already cited:

> [Shizuo and I] both wish that the staples of our diets could stay honest. In Japan, *udon* noodles in broth can be delicious. In Italy and France and here, pasta can be fine – and so can hamburgers. The problem is to keep them *good*. The great international companies that will have increasing influence on our eating habits do not seem to care much, if at all, about helping our taste buds to stay keen and alive, since if no really excellent food is procurable, they know that we will perforce buy an inferior substitute ... and second rate stuff is cheaper and easier to market anyway.

Food technology needs to be controlled and judged like any other kind of technology – that is, not solely by the unreliable indicator of conditioned public taste – before the age of the bug and the worm are irreversibly upon us. But this cannot happen until there is a general realisation that in common with many other technologies and industrial revolutions, food pollutes. Sometimes this pollution is of a directly physical kind. The embarrassment of surplus manure from intensive farming, and the leaching out of nitrogen fertilisers into rivers, have already been mentioned. The annual weight of additives ingested by every man, woman and (especially) child in this country has more than doubled since 1955, to over 3 pounds. The weight may include, in any combination, any of about 2,500 chemical substances.[15] All of them will have been individually certified as harmless, probably both by British and by American criteria (the latter are usually stricter). But their innocuousness in combination can seldom be finally proved when the question is asked, and although it is certainly true that you can kill yourself with a surfeit of carrots or rhubarb if you try hard enough, it is a different matter when an unpleasant allergy symptom arrives as a result of a personal reaction to an unknown ingredient in a food someone else has thought good for you, or at least profitable to him. The yellow dye called tartrazine is one such substance. Hyperactivity in children may be traceable to the salicylates which most junk-food additives contain. And these are only the short-term effects. But British customers are officially permitted to indulge their preference for tuppence coloured.

Some may think it elitist to classify as a form of social pollution those outputs of the British food industry which are easiest to do without: tinned custard, for instance, or the tinned pork pie which one manufacturer actually took to Lyon, of all places, for exhibition. But what other phrase is appropriate for synthetic turkey made of soya-based meat moulded on to a skeleton of plastic bones for visual effect? Who really needs the 'whitener' called Twinkrema which 'needs no pre-heating, no pre-mixing, does not cool the drink, and dissolves instantly, keeps for a year, takes up less space than cream, doesn't turn sour, and imparts luxury rich flavour in all its applications'? In what respect is a man who succeeds in splitting a £5 note morally inferior to a man who succeeds in selling canned ham with 40 per cent added water? Which trade officials decided to permit manufacturers to reduce, after mid-1983, the meat content of something called a 'country-style' sausage to no more than 10 per cent – considerably lower than the minimum proportion permitted by Ministry of Food regulations during and after the Second World War?[16]

Readers may wonder if these last two examples are merely rhetorical. They are not:

In the late 1960s we learnt about imports of canned hams containing about 80 per cent meat and 20 per cent water; the water was injected along with the curing solution and emulsifying salts (polyphosphate solution which helps water retention). The practice has since spread to poultry, bacon, sausages and cut meats, including ham. When Consumers' Association looked at ham last year we found one sample with over 30 per cent added water; and enforcement officers say there are imports with 40 per cent. Even some fresh meat is now watered, though so far as we know it is used only in the catering trade . . . The buyer can't choose because there is no informative labelling to distinguish the types.   Consumers' Association, *Monthly Review* (internally circulated), December 1980.[17]

New food regulations due to take effect in mid-1983 would legalise debasement to an astonishing degree. Hamburgers would still have to contain 80 per cent meat and beef sausages 50 per cent, but the meat content of 'jumbo' burgers or 'country style' sausages could be as low as 10 per cent.   Richard Milner, *Sunday Times*, 28 March 1982.

Part of the problem is that the definition of meat is loose and getting looser as technology advances. In the draft regulations it is suggested that the term meat shall include the head, heart, kidney, liver, diaphragm, pancreas, tail, thymus and tongue of an animal. Crushed pigs' heads are already used in some pork sausage manufacture, with only the teeth removed. The regulations suggest that cooked meat products should additionally be allowed to contain the feet, intestines, lungs, oesophagus, rectum, spinal cord, spleen, stomach, testicles and udder of an animal without calling for any extra description on the pack. None of this differs greatly from current practice. Rosemary Collins, *Guardian*, 13 April 1982.

Dedicated offal eaters will of course see no individual objection to most of the organs listed in the last example. (See Jean Conil's remark quoted at the head of Chapter One.) In discrete form, and properly processed (unlike the tripe that now appears on the British market, which is useless to a French or Chinese cook) they have their own texture and taste. But beyond the debasement and deception which British legislators are still sometimes willing to permit in a society where most people prefer not to know, place must be allowed for moral and aesthetic disgusts. We shall not be more human when someone works out a humane (and economical) method for persuading the whole beast to walk into the stunner-shredder.

Food manufacturers naturally suppose, and are often supported in their belief by politicians as well as by their own accountants, that all their products, however debased, are economically necessary and socially useful. At a much earlier stage of development the director of the British Food Manufacturing Industries Research Association, Mr A. W. Holmes, was explicit about it: 'Without ready prepared meals, boil-in-bag packs, instant coffee and mashed potato, and many other items, our present industrial life, with one out of every three married women engaged in occupations outside the home, would be difficult if not impossible.'[17]

The assumptions made here – about the role of women, about family structure and time organisation, and about the working speed of a competent cook, are all highly debatable.[18] I am reminded of a friend who found her family reluctant to take her place at the stove even on a self-catering holiday. She put the latest convenience food, pot noodles, in front of them one night and awaited results. It cured them: next night they cooked.

The word 'convenience', used in apposition to 'food', entered the language in the mid-1960s. 'The adjective, with its lavatorial connotation, is well-chosen,' said Raymond Postgate in the preface to *The Good Food Guide* 1969, the last edition that he edited. 'It suggests a certain feeling of disgust in the manufacturers' minds, which one would not have suspected.' He went on to quote one of Heinz Erin's product descriptions: 'The meals provide a high degree of convenience but satisfy the housewife's need to feel she is participating in the preparation.

It is never hard to guy a PR man, especially when he has a psychologist at his elbow, and it is fair to note that by the 1980s, at the upper levels of the mass market, the 'convenience' of the 1960s already seemed primitive: why visit a restaurant if you can buy the same chicken Kiev (from Alveston Kitchens via Marks & Spencer) and eat it at home without exposing yourself to social insecurity in a public place? At the same time, it is possible to criticise many apparently popular food products as a debasement of basic materials and skills which an already well nourished and under-employed society can afford to discourage; and to assert that it is worth paying the marginal extra cost of producing, marketing or making the real as opposed to the ersatz (farmhouse Cheddar for block cheese, free range poultry for factory frozen, crusted hard wheat bread for Chorleywood sliced) because in the long run it makes more people happier, producers as well as consumers.[19]

Serious discussions at academic level of this kind of cultural issue are rare: economists, psychologists, and sociologists seldom talk to each other except at parties about the way different cultures eat. One exception, though, is Tibor Scitovsky's *The Joyless Economy: an inquiry into human satisfaction and consumer dissatisfaction*.[20] Scitovksy, Eberle Professor of Economics at Stanford University, explores the contradiction between the way consumers as economic animals are expected to behave, and how they actually do behave as human beings. Academic detachment often deserts him when he considers American eating habits and the 'puritanism' which (debatably) he blames for them. But he fairly suggests that a desire to save time and effort, as well as expense, underlies the American consumer's want of interest in fresh fruit and vegetables (relative to European cultures) and his or her predilection for short-cuts in almost all food products:

The food-processing industry lives by the consumer's desire to save labour, though usually it also profits by using artificial flavours, inferior raw materials, and cheap fillers ... Most of our labour-saving preparations and processed foods contribute to taking the interest, variety, subtlety, and enjoyment out of our diet, and their effects, of course, are cumulative. One should expect them to have corresponding cumulative effects in saving time, but the data, surprisingly enough, do not quite bear that out.

The internationally comparable time budgets of 1966 show that the average American spends 69.8 minutes a day at meals, almost a half-hour less than the 96.1 minute average of the western European ...* Processed foods, however, are supposed to save not eating time but preparation time, and such savings hardly show up at all in the time budgets ... If one corrected for the greater frequency with which Americans eat out at restaurants, there would be no difference at all in time spent preparing meals. In view of our great reliance on ready-to-eat and almost ready-to-eat meals, this is very puzzling. Could the explanation be that the consumer saves more time than he or she can put to good use, and that time saved in the kitchen is mostly also wasted there?

In other words, not only do convenience foods taste worse than other kinds, and yield numerous unpleasant wastes and pollutions for which someone other than the producer and profit-taker has to pay, but half the time they are not even convenient. They protect the consumer, not from spending time that could be employed on more economic activity, but from acquiring a skill that most civilisations have found useful and some have revered: the skill of cooking palatable meals from simple materials with dexterity and speed. Skill of this kind is likely to remain at a premium when we are all reduced to making chapatis from worm flour – or better, when we have worked out how to make use of the earth's full range of edible plants (thought to number about 75,000, although man has never used more than 3,000).[21]

* S. Giedion, in *Mechanisation Takes Command* (1948) p. 204, explains this by the preponderance in the American diet of foods processed to eliminate the time-consuming effort of chewing them.

CHAPTER NINE
Armoured brigade
Chefs and their customers

A want of long standing still exists in London – and that is the difficulty of finding Restaurants where strangers of the gentler sex may be taken to dine. It is true that some have been opened where gentlemen may take their wives and daughters, but it has not yet become a recognised custom.   *The American Stranger's Guide to London and Liverpool at Table* (1859).

I cannot understand people ordering in restaurants things which they could buy more cheaply in the shops and eat comfortably at home. Gulls' eggs, smoked salmon, prosciutto, oysters, melon, foie gras. How the restaurateurs must glow as they add to their profit margins and think of the labour saved. The reason for eating in a restaurant is to have food which would be cooked less well, or not at all, at home.   Woodrow Wyatt, *To the Point* (1981).

The restaurant is the tank in the warfare of cookery because it has always been a major instrument for smashing old eating habits. Just as competition in the design of weapons sparks off new technological innovations, so the competition of restaurants has been decisive in introducing new tastes . . . Take-away food is the guerrilla of cooking, and a more ancient institution . . . The street vendor is coming back to the West . . . The counterpart to the jeans revolution in clothes is the replacing of good table manners, based on the habits of the rich, by those of the student.   Theodore Zeldin, *Listener*, 15 April 1982.

Micro-technology, which is replacing the old electro-mechanical control system, will allow vending machines previously criticised for being de-human to communicate in a more effective fashion in the area of choice, reliability and personal preference.   David Roberts, chairman of United Vending Traders, reported in *Financial Times*, 22 September 1981.

If historical precedent is any guide, articulation of discontent with British restaurant and hotel provision in the early 1950s may have been sharpened by embarrassments that arose from the 1951 Festival of Britain. A century earlier, within five years of the 1851 Great Exhibition, Sydney Whiting's famously splenetic passage on the odours of London chop-houses had appeared in his *Memoirs of a Stomach*, and Albert Smith had followed suit with *The British Hotel Nuisance* (whose brief text, alas, failed to live up to the promise of the title). The publication during the 1840s of a book as elaborate as Soyer's *Gastronomic Regenerator* argues a taste that had outrun, as in the 1950s, the services available to satisfy it. The rise of British commercial catering begins from this point, when the Victorian middle class became aware of eating out as a source of social pleasure rather than as unavoidable refuelling on long coach journeys, or as the occasion for strictly masculine conviviality in the Pall Mall clubs. But it also soon became obvious, in the hectic growth periods of the 1880s and the 1900s as in the similar post-war spurts of the 1920s and the 1950s, that the British urban lower middle class as a whole lacked taste, talent, or training for serving in restaurants.

It is perilous to generalise about nations, or for that matter classes, as 'good servants' or 'good fighters'. Our social history provides abundant examples of country houses where cooking and service alike depended on impeccably English style and skill, as a contrast to the horrors of institutional catering in army, school and workhouse. Other nineteenth-century industries – from heavy engineering to piano-manufacture – enjoyed periods of British leadership before passing to better-educated and more energetic entrepreneurs in other lands. In British catering, from the beginning until very recent times, both system and panache were qualities that had to be imported from abroad. Soyer, chef of the Reform Club and the most influential gastronomic impresario of his day, rescued British Army catering in the Crimea from disaster by hard work and self-projection on a scale fully equal to Florence Nightingale's in the hospitals. César Ritz and Auguste Escoffier stood behind the eating-out boom of late Victorian and Edwardian London, while Italian immigrants mopped up more popular types of catering, establishing a Franco-Italian control and style that only began to crumble from within after two world wars destroyed its public. (Italians cemented their hold on London catering during the first war, when their French rivals returned home to fight.)

Indian and Chinese family networks, new forms of Mediterranean catering (pizza and kebabs), and later, American system-feeding infiltrated through the cracks in the old structure. They succeeded initially not because the prime materials demanded by the European culinary tradition had become too expensive for common use, though this became true during the 1970s, but because kitchen work in the old styles is labour-intensive to a degree only acceptable (in high wage economies) if a premium price can be charged for meals, or if the hands available are prepared for family or ethnic reasons to accept less money than they could obtain on the 'open' market in wages or social security benefits. The only obvious alternative, now adopted even by various expensive hotels that pretend otherwise, is a shift to capital intensity. This implies food synthesis, central preparation systems, and local mechanisation, which reduce the cost of labour and erode its skills.

The process, and the slight queasiness it provokes even in hardened professional stomachs, is neatly summed up by an exchange in the trade magazine *Caterer & Hotelkeeper* early in 1982.[1] The occasion was an advertising slogan: 'My Veal Cordon Bleu is magic. In just three minutes it can turn 67p into £3.50.' The slogan was explained below:

We chop and reform selected cuts of veal into a tender escalope, and put a layer of quality imported cheese plus a generous slice of ham on top. Then we fold the whole lot in half, egg dip it, and coat it in crisp continental breadcrumbs . . . Cost – at 67p a portion – is very low. Preparation time is nil. Cooking takes only 3 minutes – straight from the freezer . . . And if the result didn't taste every bit as good as it sounds, would customers be happily paying up to £3.50 for a portion?

This pitch was answered in a subsequent issue by a letter from a polytechnic catering officer: 'I believe that advertisements such as the one from Unger Meats do untold harm to the catering world's public relations. At my polytechnic where *Caterer & Hotelkeeper* is filed in the library, this type of headline gives me a very bad time with students and academics alike.'

For the advanced course, 'students and academics' might do worse than analyse not just the public relations and the economics of the offending advertisement, but the seven types of ambiguity in the particular adjectives it employed: 'selected', 'tender', 'quality', 'imported', 'generous', 'continental', and 'as good as it sounds'. Note also the word 'reform'. The other day, in a Birmingham restaurant, I noticed the menu item 'lamb cutlets reformé' – evidently Unger Meats' variation on Soyer's famous Reform Club recipe.

However, developments of this kind only look inevitable after the event. From the perspective of the early 1950s, with the old upper-crust

catering system in exhaustion and disarray, and the new ethnic plural-
ism still well below the horizon, there was a moment of creative optimism, as British as the lovingly revived country inns that housed it and the
army gratuities that paid for it. Both the modest successes and the
ambitious failures of the style that evolved can be studied through the
organic changes reported by customers to successive editions of *The
Good Food Guide* over thirty years: the steak-centred menu, flanked by
increasingly rich and elaborate cold 'starters' (a 1970s neologism) and
sweets, composed the previous day – or week.

It was the nature of these semi-amateur enterprises to die with the
generation that created them. Very few British catering continuities
stretch backwards through the war years. One exception connects the
Robot Café, Bawtry, in 1938 to Fernie Lodge, Husbands Bosworth,
over forty years later. Ishbel Speight explains:

In 1938 my mother bought a small café on the Great North Road at Bawtry (she
had been forced into this because my father could not earn a living). It was a very
hard life for us all (as very small children we had sacks of peas to shell). We were
very embarrassed by the name Robot café (motto, 'Stop, dine and rest') but
traffic lights at this time were still a novelty.

How little change there was in prices between 1938 and 1951: 2s. for lunch in
1938 at a little café in Yorkshire; only 3s. in 1951 at Peter Jones in Sloane Square in
London where my husband was assistant manager after the war. And has there
really been much change in style of eating at the lower end of the market, when
you look at that menu? In 1954, by then re-named the Three Counties, the café
was good enough to get into Raymond Postgate's *Guide* – this was just after I had
left catering college. Then after a break from catering we opened the Old
Farmhouse at Armitage in the mid-1960s, moving to Fernie Lodge ten years
later.

One thing that stands out in our early catering was the cheapness and
availability of fresh fish. Chicken very seldom appeared on café menus.[2]

The patronne of a little hotel in the Pyrenees once described to me a
remarkably similar transport-café-to-bourgeoisie family history. But in
Britain, and especially in southern England, too many operators large or
small found it possible to make quick financial killings, first during the
1960s out of the eating-out boom itself, and later out of playing the
property market in town houses and country hotels. It is patience,
rootedness, and lack of greed that achieve generational transfer in
catering businesses; the difference, perhaps, between making a life and
making a living. Throughout the 1960s and 1970s there were, no doubt,
better restaurants than the Old Farmhouse and Fernie Lodge and

others of their kind (among them, the Arnesen family's regimes at Grange-in-Borrowdale and Caldbeck also spring to mind). But not many offered comparable value for money, or gave their customers from the oldest to the youngest such consistent relief from the pretence and extortion they encountered elsewhere.

Of course, it is not by criteria like these that contemporary British caterers judge 'success' and 'failure', and their achievement must not be underestimated. For instance, no one accuses them of sending people away hungry or wasting their time in queues, as might be the case with their counterparts in eastern Europe; or of being as backward in realised technology as the British urban transport and telephone systems; or of failing to make enough money for their chief entrepreneurs (and if American-based franchise operations have lately penetrated the British market for the ultimate benefit of American rather than native capital, financial know-how has carried Britain's largest catering empire to parts of the world which it could scarcely have reached on the quality of its cooking alone).

But as well try to measure educational success by the output of A levels, or theatrical success by the number of bottoms on seats in the West End. In both these other instances, measurable results matter too, just as there is no future but the bankruptcy court for unprofitable caterers. But cooking and eating is an aspect of a society's culture, and like its happiness or misery, cannot be summed. The success of British hotels and restaurants could be as meaningfully measured by the quality, skills, and stability of its work-force; or by the number of foreign visitors who are tempted to Britain by the prospect of eating well in places where they would previously have been deterred from eating at all; or by the arrival of European delegations, eager to account for the popularity and critical excellence of our school meals and motorway service stations.

This larger perspective is arguably the only one from which it is possible to view British catering whole. The scene is otherwise impossibly diverse, from the Flying Officer Kites who went into steak and chips in the 1950s and have clung to the trade even though young Nigel's in Lazard's now and Fiona's at Newnham and there's a hired chef in the kitchen doing fancy things with raspberry vinegar; to the sharp-suited, calculator-clicking hotel managers turned out by the education-and-training explosion of the 1960s; to the Cypriots or Bangladeshis on urban street corners; to the suave or slapdash Sloane Rangers who groom themselves for matrimony by slipping lemon cheesecake into piggy bankers in City boardrooms at lunchtime; and not forgetting the Mum's Army of school dinner ladies and the Orwellian platoon of easy-come, easy-go kitchen porters who keep the whole inexorable system of cook-and-swallow creaking along the alimentary canal until the next day.

It is an industry, by the way, in which newspaper reports of food poisoning – usually salmonella, the English institutional disease – and of dirty kitchens in restaurants, though far less common than they would be if the environmental health inspectorate had more resources and stronger powers, are far more common than reports of restaurants and hotels closed by industrial action. Garners Steakhouses, Trusthouse Forte – how many other catering strikes does the reader recall in the past decade? In catering, if you don't like the job, you move on. Yet there are few other industries in which levels of basic pay and instances of managerial clumsiness would as readily excuse, locally or nationally, forms of industrial action more drastic than spitting in the *friture* and handing your notice in. Fortunately for its *gros légumes*, British catering is the despair not only of its critical customers but of its trade union organisers too.

Before returning to the islands of merit and hope in the system, and the reasons why they are islands not continents, it is worth noting the system's total size and its directions of flow.[3] About half the adult population buys a meal away from home at least once a week. In 1979, £2,650 million was spent on eating out – 51 per cent more than in 1975 at current prices but 16 per cent less at constant prices. The 1979 Family Expenditure Survey estimated that an average of £3.58 was spent weekly by each household on meals bought away from home – 3.8 per cent of the household's total expenditure. These meals are divided as follows between different types of eating place: take-aways 14 per cent; pubs and pub restaurants 8 per cent; store restaurants 2 per cent; cafés and snack bars 13 per cent; hotels and restaurants 11 per cent; work places 39 per cent; educational institutions 11 per cent; hospitals and others 2 per cent.

The breakdown by socio-economic grouping of the *time* spent over main meals eaten out in the commercial sector is interesting: 70 per cent of ABs spent over 60 minutes (a pity, perhaps, that no secondary category for meal durations of over 120 minutes was included); 66 per cent of DEs spent under an hour and 46 per cent under 40 minutes on similarly structured meals. Short of actually sniffing and tasting the food consumed, there could be no more vivid illustration of the Two Nations at table, and it is hard to imagine similar figures and durations being reported from the other side of the Channel, whatever the inroads of *le fast-food* in Paris.

Still more revealing is one of the earliest reports from the Hotel and Catering EDC ('Little Neddy'), which invited the Tavistock Institute of Human Relations to investigate staff turnover and question people working in the catering industry about the picture they had of it. The Tavvy's psycho-sociological mandarins were taken aback by the results, and wrote with uncommon plainness. The industry appeared to them to combine self-satisfaction and complacency with self-criticism, pessimism, and want of self-respect. It tended to devalue even the skills it clearly possessed, and thought of itself as 'rather un-British'. In 20 units surveyed (an 0.001 per cent sample) the annual rate of labour turnover varied from 28 to 216 per cent. Of 263 kitchen porters interviewed, 75 per cent had left their jobs within three months and 93 per cent within a year. The authors of the report perceived certain psychological stresses on those who provide the public with food, drink, and shelter. They cited the head waiter who started each evening by deliberately annoying his staff to make them hate him rather than the customers. For as any restaurateur – or restaurant guide editor – knows, 'customers may often be unreasonable in their demands and sometimes infantile in their behaviour; for example, giving silent appreciation if gratified and voicing shrill and violent complaints if not'.[4]

Pay and physical conditions in the catering industry had improved out of all recognition in the catering industry – perhaps even in the sweated sculleries of seaside boarding houses and the cockroach-infested kitchens of Soho – since the horrors of the 1930s. Orwell's accounts are familiar enough. But Raymond Postgate, as general editor of a book and pamphlet series called *Fact*, published in 1937 a hotel manager's working hours and conditions on the south coast. It includes a good description of the *tronc* system and hours of duty (seventy hours were normal); and lists the staff dinner menu for seven days in a hotel where the food was always sent down to the linen-room staff in the coal lift; 'a layer of coal dust on the rice pudding and lumps of best Tyneside in the stew being common occurrences':

MONDAY Stew; tapioca pudding TUESDAY Mince; tapioca pudding; WEDNESDAY Fish; tapioca pudding THURSDAY Stew; tapioca pudding FRIDAY Mince; tapioca pudding SATURDAY Mince; tapioca pudding SUNDAY Roast beef; tapioca pudding . . . Supper in this hotel is always cold meat, except for the maids, who receive only a cube of 'staff cheese' – the phrase is eloquent.[5]

Culturally and psychologically, not all that much has changed. In 1982, one reverent observer of the young Anton Mosimann's regime as *chef de cuisine* at the Dorchester Hotel thought it worth reporting that he addressed his kitchen colleagues by name every morning. In an equally famous London hotel, a few years ago, I recall my host (a hotel executive from a different group) ordering a drink from an inexperienced young waiter. When the boy queried it – quite properly, given the notorious Anglo-American ambiguity of the phrase 'dry Martini' – the executive simply repeated the phrase more loudly, in the traditional manner of the Englishman abroad.

Yet it is obvious that the quality of any meal, unless it is prepared, cooked and served by robot mechanisms, depends at some stage on mutual understanding and communication of desires, possibilities and intentions between cook, waiter, and customer. Mutual understanding of this kind has actually lessened since the war in most London hotels and restaurants, because the curse of Babel has been added to their other shortcomings. Throughout Britain, few indeed are the grand hotels and businessmen's restaurants whose chefs and waiters would dream of spending their own money in competing establishments of the same kind, as John Tovey's team at Miller Howe in Windermere sometimes do.

The number and distribution of people employed in catering has been most recently and reliably estimated in *Manpower in the Hotel and Catering Industry* (1977), a report to the industry's training board (see Table 6). In the light of this book's preoccupation with the craft of cooking in British culture it is relevant to observe that in the industry as a whole the number of full-time employees listed with this function – from chefs de cuisine down to apprentices/trainees – is 175,000, easily outnumbered by people listed as managers of one kind or another (268,000). It seems likely that in an industry less preoccupied with *bella figura* most of these 'managers' would be called something else. The largest single defined category is waiters/waitresses (100,000).

Research into the working practices generated by, or expected of, workers in the industry is somewhat older, but from the figures given in *The British Eating Out*[6] it is not hard to see how the various types of fast or convenience foods subsequently came to be seen as an improvement, by caterer and customer alike. In the mid-1960s, only 18 per cent of all hotels and 32 per cent of restaurants cooked vegetables to order, and similar proportions batch-cooked them more than thirty minutes ahead. Just under half of all catering establishments were in the habit of

TABLE 6: Employees in catering

Category of employer	Number of employees	Percentage distribution
Hotels	485,000	22.7
Guest houses	48,000	2.3
Restaurants	209,000	9.8
Cafes	132,000	6.2
Contract catering/industrial catering	176,000	8.2
Public houses	460,000	21.5
Clubs	133,000	6.2
NHS hospitals	45,000	2.1
Education: local authority	383,000	17.9
other	47,000	2.2
Residential hostels	19,000	0.9

Source: *Manpower in the Catering Industry* (HCITB 1977)

roasting meat in advance for subsequent reheating, though in this respect hotels (where 29 per cent reported this practice) had a better record than restaurants (43 per cent), cafés (62 per cent), and canteens (45 per cent).

Findings like these remind the food critic that the different sectors of British catering may differ more in atmosphere and expense than they do in craft technique. The gaudy surfaces and crumbling timbers of jazzed-up Tudor inns are themselves a kind of metaphor for image and reality in British eating-out from the 1950s onwards. Burgeoning demand in the Liebfraumilch belts that surround most big towns and cities expanded the market hugely, and well into the 1970s any youth who could knock two pans together was assured a place on a catering course and subsequently in the industry. Indeed, he could almost spare himself the course, for in 1965 only 9 per cent of all caterers demanded qualifications from kitchen staff, and only 30 per cent provided facilities for outside training. But by 1980, Britain was spending £33 million a year on catering education and training at three universities and 332 other colleges, from full departments at polytechnics to small local day-release institutions. The mock-cream mock-deference culture that bequeathed *Fawlty Towers* to the viewing public easily survived the education and training revolution, and enlivened the private correspondence of *Good Food Guide* inspectors with a regular supply of comic opera vignettes, from the waitress who drew a cork with her teeth in Ipswich and the waiter in Chelsea who escorted a guest to the cloakroom in order to kiss her; to the accountant-*patron*, walked-out on by his staff, who dropped the game-bird he was serving and offered it at half-price 'because it only just touched the floor'. The unseen kitchen counterparts to these visible dining room diversions are best left to the imagination. The ethos of a country's eating yields only gradually, if at all, to formal education, just as the *salons culinaires* at catering exhibitions – polar landscapes in *chaudfroid* sauce, gothic cathedrals in *pommes allumette* – outlive food critics' conviction that sculpture (edible or not) belongs to art school and that the product of a chef exists to be tasted and eaten.

Even in the higher education system itself, in this context, is recognisably divided into two or more nations. Few children of the graduate professional classes (from which *Good Food Guide* voluntary inspectors tend to be drawn) go into catering or are advised to do so, unless they are singularly unlucky with their A levels. Catering college teachers too, like many of the 'professionals' who make a living for a year or two 'testing' restaurants for this or that commercial guidebook, are also normally drawn from within the trade. They have to draw heavily upon their own intellectual resources to avoid perpetuating as teachers the mediocrity of the prevailing standards, when they are faced with students whose own expectations are low. The more thoughtful ones are disarmingly frank:

We get some students who've not even seen a table cloth before. We've got to take them right through from where to put a knife and fork to flambés. The trouble is essentially one of status. It starts with the career master at school who, faced with a not-very-bright student, will say, 'There doesn't seem to be much we can do with you: you'd better go into catering.'

Some hotel owners wouldn't know a good chef if they saw one. The new style of hotel management introduces a strong element of Us and Them, which you never find in France, where they think of cooking as a creative job. There's not much status in being a chef in Britain.[7]

Even in colleges themselves, young people – bright or not – whose earnest ambition is to practise a craft and please people quickly learn that this is generally considered very small beer. The way ahead, for the lecturer as well as the student, opens up for 'portion control', not early mornings at the market; for dark suits, not chef's whites; 'food and beverage managers', not *maîtres d'hôtel*. In any case, technically speaking, very few youngsters emerge from full-time training with more than an inkling of what is being done where in Europe, or even in Britain, by the best practitioners. (Were it otherwise, the Carved Angel in Dartmouth or Les Quat' Saisons in Oxford would be besieged by catering graduates offering their labour free of charge, which is not the case.) They are just about ready to start a serious apprenticeship to food when they are pitchforked into the industry to operate a 100-item menu in a 100-seater restaurant with an absentee proprietor and a chef de cuisine who is drinking himself into early retirement. A caricature, no doubt – but the Hotel and Catering Industry Training Board's recently instituted Craft Achievement awards, for which candidates prepare a simple range of dishes that are then assessed on timing, method, appearance and flavour, had a pass rate no higher than 50 per cent in their first year. John Tovey's assessment of trainees produced at a lower end of the system than this is more caustic: 'I was implored last year to take on an HND student for industrial training. He lasted just over twenty-four hours. In his time at college he had never waited at table, never done any reception work, had done about twelve hours practical cooking and had never made a bed.'8

A different kind of window into British catering education is opened by perusal of the textbooks typically employed. Such books last for many years, pass through numerous editions, and (according to Jill Norman, one of the leading publishers in the domestic arts field) outsell most cookery authors from Elizabeth David downwards. It is perhaps hardly necessary to add that the two genres of book hardly ever refer to each other. The British writer-cooks who have transformed the tastes of a significant proportion of hotel and restaurant customers scarcely exist in the minds of the authors who form the minds of the staff. The brief notices of these textbooks that follow may therefore be considered relevant, perhaps overdue.

Kinton and Ceserani's *The Theory of Catering* (1964, 4th edition 1978) would hardly inspire anyone to put theory into practice: the first picture in the book is of a hotel burning in Brighton. Perhaps in college context it may make sense to start with chapters not only on safety and hygiene but on gas, electricity and water before proceeding to discuss commodities, costing, and menu French. But if catering has a theory, one would expect it to start at the point where a human being consumes the product. As a companion volume to the same authors' *Practical Cookery* the book is useful up to but not beyond the point where a student may be expected to abjure the use of malt vinegar in French cuisine, and to show knowledge of more than a dozen cheeses. The bibliography is inadequate, and for a fourth edition, surprisingly inaccurate in detail.

Cracknell and Kaufman's *Practical Professional Cookery* (1972, corrected 1975) takes for granted the classical French system of kitchen management as it has been understood – more or less – in England since Soyer's day. Students will find its recipes set out with extreme typographical monotony over 500 pages, with minimal illustration. The 'principles of cookery' (to these authors, a matter of technique unaffected by questions of taste) are covered in ten drily written pages, and it is hard to follow the authors' hope that 'the easy-to-follow format will encourage the housewife and mother to serve more adventurous dishes to her family and guests'. However, those who remember that T. S. Eliot counted 'boiled cabbage cut in sections' as an ingredient of English culture will be pleased to find along with the *médaillons de veau maréchale* and the *caneton poêlé aux cerises*, a recipe for *chou à l'anglaise (nature)*: '. . . Boil steadily until cooked (approx. 15–20 minutes) but still slightly firm. Drain in a colander. Place the cabbage between two plates and press firmly to squeeze out most of the liquid. Cut into even-sized portions and dress on vegetable dishes.'

The *'currie de boeuf'* recipe is equally *anglaise*, and includes the elementary if common error of adding curry powder to a liquid without frying it briefly first. There is no guide to sources or further reading, indeed no reference that the reviewer can detect to any other person, cook or author, apart from acknowledgements to fellow polytechnic lecturers in the foreword.

Barbara Hammond's *Cooking Explained* (1963, 2nd edition 1974) represents domestic science rather than catering college teaching. The style and approach are more human and more attentive to kitchen nuts and bolts, albeit excruciatingly economical (with 'margarine or frying oil' suggested as an alternative to butter in scrambling eggs). A raw student would certainly learn something from this book. However, its basic recipe for 'savoury white sauces' (*béchamel*) explains much that has to be endured in British restaurant and institutional dining rooms: it is nowhere indicated that the flour in the sauce needs time to cook after the granules have expanded and thickened the liquid.

Books of this kind – and if these are the successes of textbook publishing, what are the failures like? – can fairly be coupled with the self-congratulatory tone of the weekly trade press. Both present British catering as a closed circuit which cannot be interrupted by ideas derived from other fields of inquiry, and which is therefore harnessed to the mechanical pursuit of the most food for the greatest number in the shortest time for the highest profit. The industry (as distinct from the food science departments of British universities) does hardly any research except of a literally hand-to-mouth kind.

On this analysis, even the accepted commercial successes of the past decade, such as hamburgers for the proletariat and boil-in-the-bag *canard à l'orange* for the fancy market, arise from a cultural nihilism and a breakdown of communication between provider and consumer at a much earlier stage. Zombie-like public acceptance, as well as governmental indifference and the complaisance of large commercial operators, made the motorway service stations into the national disfigurement they were eventually agreed to be when investigated by an official committee (the Prior Committee of Inquiry) powerful enough to insist on comparing them with counterparts in other countries.[9]* With very few exceptions, among them the formula established by Peter Boizot's Pizza Express chain and the conscientious if unimaginative craft training still done by British Transport hotels throughout the post-war period, only restaurants, hotels, and private catering firms small enough to be controlled by imaginative and determined individuals provide young people with models from which it is safe to learn. For much of the food sold to Britons and foreign visitors for consumption in public places is still as horrible as it was when Raymond Postgate launched the Good Food Club in 1949, and when he reviewed progress a decade later:

I wish the law allowed me to publish a book for which members continually clamour, and for which I have an enormous amount of material . . . It would be a *Bad Food Guide*. Reports of dreadful meals which come to my house deal with the spoiling of good food in four general ways – by overcooking it, by failing to season it, by salting it and peppering it excessively, and by leaving it sodden with water. They deal with food which was originally bad, because it was ill-butchered, stale, preserved, or adulterated . . .[10]

Postgate went on to cite specific complaints. Some are dated, but not all, and readers may care to compare the examples with their own more recent experience:

1. False pie crusts. By which I mean the serving of a square of pastry which has had no previous contact with the steak or fruit which accompanies it on the plate . . .
2. Mock cream . . . illegal to serve unless it is described as imitation cream.
3. Mixed butter and marge served as butter.

* I once heard Lord Forte blandly telling an informed audience of journalists, caterers and tourist officials that his organisation had received no more than a couple of complaints that year about the motorway meals for which it was responsible.

4. Bottled mayonnaise . . . The knack of pouring oil into an egg yolk is easily acquired. I know of no bottled mayonnaise that tastes like the real thing, and most seem to me to have a metallic undertaste.

5. Hot plating. Misuse of the hot plate, by which plates of meat and fish are kept drying and curling at the edges, sometimes for twenty minutes.

6. Cold joints sliced thin, covered with hot gravy, and then served as roast meat. This practice was recommended by the Ministry of Food during the war, which is over.

7. Bad coffee. There is a machine called the Espresso which makes it quite difficult to make really bad coffee.

8. A cheese board consisting of a dried and sweaty piece of factory made Cheddar, a wrapped portion of a material called 'processed cheese', and the heel of a stale and chalky Danish blue.

9. Wine sold 'in carafe' with no indication of the contents of the carafe.

Derek Cooper later took up Postgate's challenge and wrote his own *Bad Food Guide* (1967), whose necessarily fictional caricatures of Ray Gunge and the tricks of the trade were – like Basil Fawlty's later on – too funny for their accuracy of detail to be noticed by the trade described. As for Postgate, had he survived another twenty years he would have read without surprise the section entitled 'Not The Good Food Guide' in the 1982 edition: vegetables are less wet, lamb less grey, and some other fakes less blatant than they were in his time, but he did not have to endure the pretensions (and prices) of ersatz *nouvelle cuisine*, or look for flavour in *plats composés* that had spent six months in a deep-freeze, or realise the superiority even of margarine to a meal cooked entirely in rancid butter because no one in the kitchen had been trained to taste dishes before they reached the customer.

In catering as in other forms of vocational education, private enterprise is no substitute for public institutions. But it is still necessary to stress the debt British post-war restaurant-goers owe to particular individuals who entered catering by a variety of back doors in their hurry to satisfy new types of market that native wit – and in many cases, their own healthy appetites – had identified. Here, practice and training shade into each other. The best and most charismatic teachers are usually too busy 'doing' to realise that the skills and attitudes they half-consciously communicate to those who work under them will endure in their pupils' practice, and be transmitted in turn to another generation, so must contain within them seeds of renewal that can be germinated when tastes alter and external conditions change. It was skill and imagination, not previous experience of Army catering, that made

Soyer the dietary saviour of the Crimea. In the past two decades, the demand for 'alternative' catering education, mainly from young women who had no intention of opening restaurants or running industrial canteens but did have their eyes on the lucrative and congenial private catering market, has spawned numerous schools and courses. Their technical limitations are often obvious (the scale is smaller and the pace slower than in fully professional kitchens). But they do foster a more creative approach to food, based on more appropriate texts and practised on a scale that permits human contact and a degree of taste control.

Whose was the face that launched a thousand quiches? She bears a heavy responsibility, and Elizabeth David must often have regretted including in *French Country Cooking* a dish that mothered so many vague approximations in church halls and wine bars. But in turn, the reason why the quiche-and-salad style dominated the wine bars that grew up during the 1970s was not merely its profitability and (in context) 'convenience'. The style spread everywhere because it expressed the tastes of people – often the owner's girl-friends – catering for others of their own age, social status, and even sex: wine and liberation marched together in this period, and in wine bars women could meet, talk, drink and eat without men in tow. Even in the 1980s this remains an uncommon sight in pubs.

If a symbolic figure is sought for the emergent style, both culinary and social, it would have to be Prue Leith, who was born in 1940, brought up in South Africa, taught herself her craft by working doggedly through Constance Spry's book section by section ('suet puddings and all') as lunch-time cook to a prosperous firm of West End solicitors, opened her London restaurant in 1969, as part of a mutual support system that included her out-catering service and cookery school, and a dozen years later was also operating as mother, *Guardian* columnist, and adviser to British Rail. Typically, when another newspaper asked her and other serious restaurateurs to suggest economic but edible improvements upon the American system-feeders' ideas for what you should eat in the street, she was the only one who not only had a practical solution – variants of the beignets of French cuisine – that would not have to sacrifice quality to speed, but also devised a crisp, pop, Americanised brand-name to help sell the product.[11]

However, most sectors of British catering are more specialised and self-contained than this kind of versatility implies. For a restaurant, in particular, to reach the top flight unusual concentration and not just a rich but a knowledgeable public are normally required. At this minority-of-a-minority level, which Leith's itself approached more nearly in price than in critical performance, the outwardly straitened 1970s contributed more than the economically buoyant 1960s had done to the evolution of a high style in the leading restaurants and hotels. The enthusiasms of previous decades had taken deeper root in the culture, and the French innovations christened *nouvelle* – perhaps more accurately, neo-classical – *cuisine* crossed the Channel quickly, abetted by eager British publishers and publicists.

Decades are divisions too short and arbitrary for doing justice to such long-term influences. However, in 1974, after prolonged hesitation, Michelin in Paris published a red guide to Great Britain (and Ireland) for the first time since more occasional publications of this kind between the wars. (When this decision was taken, the exchange rate was working in favour of French tourists to Britain, and although this situation was later reversed, it is still true, according to the British Tourist Authority, that 60 per cent of visitors to Britain and 40 per cent of UK earnings from tourism are European, led by the French and the Germans).

The first few annual editions of the British *Michelin* revealed an imperfect French understanding of what had actually been going on during the dark ages of British *restauration*, notably its conspicuous ethnic and stylistic plurality. But this was to be expected, and later editions – though in oriental restaurants they still took the suit for the man – showed a better sense of where quality was to be found. In any case, the Paris swallow's return had symbolic significance for the kind of European and North American reader who could neither buy nor in the full sense read *The Good Food Guide*: it announced that certain eating places in these islands at last merited the detour even of a Frenchman.

Comparison of the distinction lists printed in 1980s editions of both books reveals a degree of consonance over the two styles of restaurant cooking chiefly admired. The one style is represented by talented and ambitious Frenchmen settled here, whether independents such as Raymond Blanc in Oxford or members and associates of the Roux brothers' *équipe* in London and the Thames valley. Most of these men, joined more recently by an informal group of young British chefs who had in most cases finished their training in France, follow the style developed by Point, the Troisgros brothers, Chapel, Guérard and others. The alternative style, a more eclectic one in the British tradition, belongs to British men – and women – who have in most cases learnt how to cook and run fine restaurants by example, by instinct, by reading, by application, but hardly ever by the kind of professional training or apprenticeship which an ambitious young French chef takes for granted. For instance, Stephen Bull of Lichfield's in Richmond traces his enlightenment about cooking, and the beginning of his self-taught pilgrimages through sound cookery books to *Michelin* and *Good Food Guide* distinctions, to 'the period when I was handling the Olivetti account as an advertising agent, and a particular *risotto milanese* I was given on a business trip to northern Italy'.[12] Paradoxically, it is often these British-run places that offer the best range of wine – even French wine – at the fairest prices, thanks to their owners' superior contacts with the highly competitive British wine trade, and often a breadth of wine experience denied to most Frenchmen.

As Postgate justly pointed out in his time, almost any nation other than Britain, whose administrators long regarded foreign tourists as birthright or windfall rather than as income that had to be earned, would have taken systematic steps to plug the gaps, remove the worst excrescences, and build upon individual initiatives in British catering. But even now, short perhaps of the party associated with the slogan 'claret and chips' gaining an overall majority at Westminster, a development of this kind remains improbable. A necessarily arbitrary list of chefs and restaurateurs who best represent both these styles of cooking – the imported and the more nearly indigenous – is appended at the end of the book, and may serve as a form of recognition normally denied them in a country whose politicians and civil servants award honours to each other instead.

Behind most of these names lie stories worth telling. There is room only for one, chosen because it is the key not just to an individual but to a whole network of teacher and disciples. George Perry-Smith, for twenty years proprietor of the Hole in the Wall restaurant in Bath and since 1972 of a smaller *restaurant avec chambres* in Cornwall, is not the earliest or longest-serving of the names listed. (Francis Coulson, still active at the time of writing, was serving quixotically extravagant teas at his Sharrow Bay Hotel, Ullswater, as long ago as 1949). He would also be the first to admit that by 1982, several other tables in Britain, including at least two kept by his own relatives or ex-pupils, bettered his own. His influence as a chef-patron never depended on an articulated system, and he has published no book. Only a tiny proportion of the *prominenti* in the London catering trade ever visited him, even in his heyday: compare, perhaps, the pilgrimages French chefs and London foodies feel obliged to make to Vienne or Roanne or Eugénie-les-Bains. But few eaters whose experience spans both sides of the Channel have failed to recognise in the work of the Perry-Smith connection a European idiom of cooking filtered through a more personal and English style of cooking and restaurant management, rather as – *mutatis mutandis* – certain English musicians and artists have found it possible to express nationality through a language evolved elsewhere. (In his own cooking, Perry-Smith seldom strays far from Elizabeth David's recipes, drawn as they are from France, Italy, Britain and the Near East.)

A second list appears in Appendix Three, of the dozen or so restaurants and restaurateurs known to *The Good Food Guide* that have branched from this parent tree. All stemmed from a man who claims never to have learnt to chop an onion properly. Like the present writer, he learnt much about cooking in the Friends' Ambulance Unit, in his case 'from a madman called Eric Green who eventually fetched up in Shepheard's Hotel in Cairo'. After a post-war French degree at Cambridge he spent a year 'reading and eating' in the *Quartier Latin*. When he abandoned academic life and opened the Hole in 1952 with a former Canadian Mountie as chef, the proprietor was deliberately named as 'G. Perry-Smith MA', 'because at that time it was not thought very high class to run a restaurant'. They offered, as well as 'omelettes and eggs whenever we are allowed to serve them', the modish continental dishes of those gastronomically innocent times: bouillabaisse, ravioli, risotto, Hungarian goulash, chile con carne, quiche Lorraine. Twelve French and English cheeses, three kinds of coffee, and five kinds of tea were also listed. 'Dishes which the chef definitely has available have marked against them a price which we shall always try to keep as low as we can; oddly enough, we are interested at least as much in doing our job well, that is to give you pleasure, as in making money out of it.'

The last theme still crops up in Perry-Smith's conversation:

A lot of the girls who worked for us were sent by parents who liked the way we did things. There is no regular training system in England that instils and elicits restaurant skills. We had the advantage of being very interested in eating, where most catering colleges are preparing you to run a business. We have always insisted that everyone does some waiting and some cooking, to eliminate the division between kitchen and front of house. When the doors are open the place belongs to the customers and no one else. Of course this is easier in a restaurant with no more than fifty covers, which is as many as we can manage. A good restaurant is an extension of home cooking, without that restauranty taste that makes people feel full to the eyebrows. You mentioned that wonderful French kitchen maxim 'rien se perd': it's a wise restaurateur who never cooks a dish without having a plan for it if it's not eaten.

Further comments can be added from the affectionate reminiscences of his pupils:

'Never buy anything in bulk,' George used to say. 'Otherwise you'll have to find a use for it, whether it's good or not.' Many's the time I've had to dash out at six o'clock for a tin of tomatoes.

I teach cooking myself now, and I've always found it quite easy to transmit what I think of as the verbs of cookery – the 'active' techniques of chopping, steaming, whatever. What's hard to teach is the adjectives: the sense of flavour, of what will go with what.

Up here in north-east England, restaurant customers are easily impressed by vulgar display and pretentious menus. We are looking for what we learnt about in Bath: real cooking in a white-washed room.

CHAPTER TEN
Quality of the common need

[After describing how calf's foot and wine jelly was made for an invalid over two nights and two days]: Few would care to take that trouble for the sake of a few spoonfuls of jelly in these days. Laura's aunts delighted in such cookery and her mother would have enjoyed doing it had her means permitted, but already it was thought a waste of time in many households. On the face of it, it does seem absurd to spend the inside of a week making a small jelly, and women were soon to have other uses for their time and energy, but those who did such cookery in those days looked upon it as an art, and no time or trouble was thought wasted if the result were perfection.   Flora Thompson, *Lark Rise to Candleford* (1945).

To eat well in London it is necessary to know and to love real English cooking, which is excellent when it is done slowly, with modesty and according to the old recipes. It is killed by hastiness in young families, the indifference of housewives, too much refrigeration, and the great number of restaurants which serve imitation French food.   Paul Morand *A Frenchman's London*. Translated by Desmond Flower (1934).

Let no man snub his stomach. Come, be very kind to the stomach. You had better. . . . Living with your stomach is not unlike living with a petulant spouse upon whose bounty you must depend.   Richard Selzer, *Mortal Lessons* (1981).

Short of nuclear cataclysm, or siege economy, the dietary discontinuities of the next forty years may be less abrupt than the ones my own generation has lived through. The technology of food preservation, processing, synthesis and distribution will certainly alter again and again, not at the leisurely pace of the century that elapsed between the tin-can and the deep freeze, but at the more hectic pace dictated by molecular biology and electronic communication. But there is perhaps less reason to anticipate, and certainly no way to predict, social changes as far-reaching in their effects on how we eat and cook as the arrival of dietary egalitarianism and the disappearance of domestic service in the 1940s, followed by large-scale immigration in the 1950s and 1960s, and by accelerating Europeanism or globalism in the 1970s. Every age thinks it is a new one, but it is still true that some changes are followed by periods of digestion.

Furthermore, even revolutions do not always affect basic nutrition and food supply. Indeed, at such times people may depend on their meals as islands of stability in the wrack, as Jack Goody suggests:

The relative conservatism of specific dishes could be a reflection of their relative lack of entailment with the rest of the socio-cultural system. It would then be the autonomy of certain aspects of cooking that gave it a very special importance for individuals in situations of social change, especially of rapid, revolutionary change. The continuity of borsch may provide some thread of living to those passing through the years following the October Revolution, just as the hamburger clearly states to many an American that he is home and dry. Oatmeal may have bridged the gap between Catholic freedom and Puritan restraint in sixteenth century Scotland. The persistence of these elements is not inconsistent with radical change in others.[1]

By twentieth-century global standards, British changes and temporary privations have been modest. But wartime diaries, documents and memories tend to support this view. Comparable Soviet documents are not available, at least to me, and is it ideology or incompetence that restricts the publication of cookery books in Moscow, even the classic *Gift to Young Housewives* which Elena Molokhovets brought out in the same decade as Mrs Beeton and at similar length? Verbal and regional craft tradition in Russian cookery might well surface again if the materials returned. Ice cream, which was allowed to make the transition from the nobility to the populace, still has 'a purity and creaminess that constantly astounds Western visitors' (as well it might, when they are British ones).[2]

It is not as though food and the cooking of it lie below the threshold of class consciousness and ideological awareness. The sumptuary laws often adopted in ancient Rome and mediaeval England have their counterparts in the explicit revolutionary 'puritanism' that in our own time has assailed such fundamentally food-loving peoples as the Russians, the Chinese, and the Vietnamese. The original offence, brought home daily at table, is that the few have more and the many less on their plates. But once that kind of consciousness has been raised, radical politicians, like enthusiastic priests before them, have a second hurdle to surmount. They are often disconcerted to realise that at least half their potential audience is never completely tuned to what they are saying, because it is thinking about the next meal or watching the bread rise. This is partly why the rhetoric of food politics about the 'starving millions', or (in British depressions) the 'submerged tenth' who are living on bread and scrape, comes from the left, while practical suggestions for alleviating the material misery require a different use of time and thought, and usually derive from unacceptable bourgeois or official sources. The wartime Ministry of Food, run by the former manager of a department store, did more for British popular nutrition than the Left Book Club ever contemplated.

In any case, contemporary ideologies – whether socialistic or capitalistic – are often at a loss either to explain or alter people's food-ways, because these are formed in a prior stage of social development, and remain subject to events and influences that are popularly perceived as politically neutral, whether they are or not. Thus, Goody points out that throughout Eurasia, the main line of hierarchical division in cuisine normally falls between those who eat a lot of meat and those who eat very little. (Young contemporary British vegetarians may be trying to reassert this division in a complicated society whose 'lower' classes have lately tended to consume more meat, of better cuts, than the 'upper'.) 'Throughout the forms of European literature, tension is expressed between the styles of life of rich and poor, some admiring the achievements of haute cuisine, others sympathetic to the morality of denial, of poverty, of the simple life.'[3]

But two distinct civilisations, the Chinese and the African, represent alternative approaches, relatively untouched by this dualism which in the West keeps both Christians and Marxists in a permanent state of agitation and self-reproach. 'The world's finest, most elaborate cuisine, that of China, was created on the basis of a much more sparing use of animal flesh, both at the top and at the bottom of the social scale. One Scottish observer in the 1850s found that "the poorest classes in China seem to understand the art of preparing their food much better than the same classes at home".'[4] (Much the same is true of India, notwithstanding the divide, originating in conquest, between meat-eating Muslim and vegetarian Hindu.) In West African societies, the sense of community at table is preserved in a different manner. A professional (male) craft of chef seems never to have emerged in Africa, as it did in China and Mogul India, where it turned the domestic culinary repertoire into a typically masculine form of public display. In West Africa, even in the house of the tribal chief, 'the cook is also the sexual partner'.[5] At a Gonja festival 'there is no *grande bouffe*, no extravagant blow-out, no meal of many courses. The actual content of the meal is that of everyday life. For some there may be more meat, but it is at most a question of more rather than different . . . There is a minimal differentiation, not only between festival and weekday, but between the various states of this stratified community.'[6]

A society cannot gain what it has never lost, or lose what it has never gained. In Britain, hierarchical differentiation in cuisine has been exceptionally well marked since 1066, when an alien conqueror's highly articulated food culture became, and remains to this day, a powerful instrument of social control. The English themselves had to wait seven centuries for the opportunity to exert comparable influence as conquerors-in-residence, and were then not at all deterred from doing so by the unsuitability of the theatre they chose for their culinary campaign – the barrack towns and hill stations of India.

The Norman culinary invasion ensured that all subsequent breaks and divisions in British food culture would tend to be expressed in terms of social class and status, rather than of food as such. Dorothy Hartley has imagined Norman counts talking to each other about 'something these Saxons make rather *well*'.[7] But it is a romantic vision, perhaps. The commanding heights of Norman-French cuisine, as in the Roux brothers' London restaurants today, often include peasant dishes either transmogrified (*pieds de porc farçis au foie gras*) or even left undisturbed in something that approximates to their original painstaking simplicity (*pot au feu sauce Albert*). But the indigenous dishes and foodstuffs of the English rural poor mostly stayed both poor and rural until in very recent times various *amateurs*, converted to French kitchen philosophy by literature and travel, took them up and exclaimed at their merit: 'This is something Mrs Pennyfeather grows in her garden/showed us how to cook.' Tom Jaine and Joyce Molyneux at the Carved Angel in Dartmouth recently reported their 'discovery' of local samphire. We are only now arriving at the point where it would occasion no surprise if a consciously English restaurant in Lincolnshire reproduced for paying customers the traditional funeral fare of the county, as described by John Widdowson: 'seed bread, made with caraway or tansy seeds, apple pies with chopped bacon fat in the bottom of the dish, plain oven bottom cakes containing either chopped parsley or sage, and currant cakes rather like Eccles cakes but made in three tiers'. Elsewhere in the same article, Dr Widdowson neatly makes a similar socio-historical point about the shadow of the Conquest on our food-ways:

> Just as it is no accident that the English can distinguish by name the living animal (sheep, ox, pig, deer) from the cooked one, borrowed from French (mutton, beef, pork, venison), so we feel equally at home in a *café* or *restaurant* where the *cuisine* and the *menu*, whether *table d'hôte* or *à la carte*, might perhaps include items as remarkable as the classic *oeuf sur toast*. The use of such terms and, more important, their pronunciation or mispronunciation, continues to divide the *gourmet* from those with less expertise in food (and French), just as 'acceptable' or 'unacceptable' table manners provide a means of social stratification.[8]

Thirty years ago, it was part of the received wisdom (transmitted by Postgate among others) that Britain forgot how to cook at the time of the Enclosures and the Industrial Revolution; that when large migrations to towns and factories emptied the land, young adults became separated not only from the unwritten lore of their older kin, but from the staple materials of the regions they had quitted for ever, and from the rural rhythm of seasonal food preservation and processing: bacon in the rafters, jellies and preserves on the shelves. (*Quaere*, in the context of food preservation, why the Jutes and the Saxons did not bring *sauerkraut* to these shores.)

This interpretation has a respectable history as far back as Cobbett, and is probably correct in essence even if it is hard to demonstrate in detail.[9] But it omits other factors of importance: among them the hand-to-mouth existence of pre-industrial farm labourers, who had never had a chance to acquire the food accumulation techniques practised by their employers; and the emergence during the nineteenth century of food factory products which the mass public was easily persuaded to prefer to the memory of more 'authentic' but troublesome or unreliable rural counterparts. (Compare the popularity of wrapped sliced bread in contemporary Africa and Sri Lanka.)

We have approached again the subject-matter of the first chapter, but I hope with a different sense of the directions British food has taken in the past forty years, and the probabilities or possibilities that can now be projected – or rejected. We shall not know, except impressionistically, exactly what is being eaten when and how in contemporary Britain until a successor to the 1938 and 1958 Crawford surveys is run and published. But basic data of this kind, though indispensable, do not reveal the way people treat food in their own conscious or unconscious minds, and in the privacy of their family circles. In Britain – and in this respect, other countries much more conservative about their food are likely to be no different – the contents of the shopping basket may change from decade to decade, and times of meals alter with patterns of work and entertainment, but there are constants which reveal themselves to more minute types of sociological or anthropological investigation.

Mary Douglas's work 'on deciphering a meal' and other themes is well known, and it would be impertinent to attempt to summarise it. But her essay, *Food as a system of communication*, based on research by Michael Nicod, has particular interest here.[10] It was commissioned by the Department of Health and Social Security in the early 1970s, at much the same time that the DHSS thought it worthwhile to ask *Good Food Guide* inspectors to visit various NHS hospitals. An early account of Douglas and Nicod's research, published in *New Society* magazine, even drew a Parliamentary question challenging the then Minister (Sir Keith Joseph) to justify squandering money on studying food habits when there was real hunger to be relieved. By contrast, the authors insist that 'when it comes to understanding the social factors affecting presentation and acceptability of new food, practically no work has been done and certainly no general principles are established'. They take food as a medium through which a system of relationships within the family is expressed. The content of meals may vary without affecting their structure and the social cohesion they express and seek to preserve:

Take the main course, which is generally called the dinner. It always consists of a serving of potato, a 'centrepiece' which on Sundays is always meat, 'trimmings' (which word designates one or two green vegetables) and a sousing in rich brown thickened gravy (here called 'liquid dressing') ... When the second course is examined we find a repetition of the rules of combination for course one, except that everything is sweet.

One of the structural rules of this food system is progressive desiccation and geometrification of forms through the day ... This progressive desiccation allows of the shift from forks and spoons to fingers. (The British biscuit, 'geometrically shaped, with a layer of jam or cream in the middle and coated with icing, at a sufficiently modest price to permit them a regular place in the daily menu', is the logical conclusion to this desiccation; hence its popularity, unmatched anywhere else in the world).

In the very simplicity and economy of the working-class dietary system we are able to see at work universal principles of recognition and stable structuring ... Each significant unit in which food is served must be complex enough to show in its structure the pattern of all meals ... This lays bare the basis of conservatism in taste and explains its exclusion of novel units from its structure ... It also explains the attachment of the British housewife to the round of beef ... Whether it is chicken, leg of lamb, turkey or round of beef, the culinary treatment is the same: oven roast ... At this high point of the week's menu, Sunday dinner, the meat is produced as one unitary piece which is not to be cut into until the meal is assembled; stew is impossible on Sundays.

Conclusions are drawn and predictions made. Douglas and Nicod conclude that it would be a waste of breath for a middle-class dietician to appear on television and advise the hard-pressed blue-collar public that stew instead of a roast and fresh fruit instead of pudding would be more economical of time or money. But cheap labour-saving substitutes can readily be introduced into the 'unstructured' parts of the system, even in families which protect the structured dinner against powdered potato and other corruptions, and indeed upgrade its elements as affluence rises: 'more meat, better meat, more varied vegetables, richer gravy, more dressings, mint jelly, redcurrant jelly, apple sauce'.

Related research by Anne Murcott 'on the social significance of the "cooked dinner" in South Wales'[11] fills out further details of what constitutes a 'plateful', in which the gravy performs a double role: not only does it link together the necessary three or more components (meat, potatoes, and a green vegetable), but it makes it easier to 'put up' a dinner on a working day for a latecomer or series of latecomers, with whatever dire results for the food itself. Sex-typing is reinforced:

The nature of the dinner, its mode or preparation, demand that the woman be in the kitchen for a required time before her husband's homecoming – and that not too infrequently, even daily, she has been shopping. Otherwise, the cooked dinner, clearly composed of appropriate items, could not be ready on time. If a job defines how a man occupies his time during the working day, to which the wage packet provides regular testimony, proper provision of a cooked dinner testifies that the woman has spent her time in correspondingly suitable fashion.

Is it possible, in a time of renewed mass unemployment, to explode these expectations or at least secure a change of roles within them, without shattering the security of the family which they express? The question may have been answered already, by different social groups in the same region, or by similar social groups in other regions. For instance, many British families with both partners working have in recent years come to accept a sit-down family meal as a weekly rather than a daily event. Television watching, and leisure activities outside the home, will have reinforced this trend. But it is clear that severe constraints are built into food systems like the ones described, and these constraints may in turn help to explain why among housewives interviewed by Ann Oakley, cooking was disliked by 23 per cent. True, it was actively enjoyed by 60 per cent, and among the other tasks of an (on average) 77-hour working week, it was preferred to ironing, washing-up, cleaning, washing and shopping. Perhaps only restless food writers are perturbed by the notorious predictability of family meals through the week in traditional working class homes, for predictability seems to have its own appeal in the milieu for which *The Sociology of Housework* is written:[12] ' "Thinking what to eat" is an endless duty, however creative the actual task may be. Thus one latent function of the creative cookery ideal is the production of dissatisfaction. Standards of achievement exist of which the housewife is permanently aware, but which she cannot often hope to reach due to the other demands on her time.'

It is curious, surely, that an intellectual researcher should find the 'doing' more likely to be 'creative' than the 'thinking'. The sense of pressure from 'creative cookery' is understandable, but the very pervasiveness of the ideal supports, rather, Theodore Zeldin's argument that the future of cooking and eating, in this as in other advanced countries, is unlikely to rest with the protein and flavour substitutions of the technological nightmare. Class eating, like class voting, may be tending at last to break up. There is no precedent in British history, even at crucial periods such as the mediaeval opening of the spice routes and the Victorian revolution in food transport and preservation, for the present sense of *potential* in the composition of our diet. This notion includes the scope for differentiation between the diets of a dozen houses in the same street, and the number of people who take an active interest, both intellectual and sensual, in the mathematically inexhaustible combinations of substance and flavour within their reach. As Zeldin remarks, 'the world today uses only 3,000 plants for its food and grows only 150 on any scale. There remain millions of others whose potential is unappreciated'.[13] Again, 'a most important change of the last few decades which is bound to be accentuated is the disappearance of the self-imposed taboos that make people stick tenaciously to their national or local food'. However, if taboos were self-imposed they would not be taboos. Culture moves at its own pace, and it will surely be some time before the south Wales families studied by Murcott scour the Gower for *Entermorpha intestinalis, Laminaria saccharina* and other edible seaweeds advocated by the *Observer*, whether or not they retain an ancestral taste for laverbread.[14]

If the production of worthy or worthless cookery books and food-related titles (about 2,000 annually in the British publishing trade) proves anything except the optimism or avarice of publishers, Dr Zeldin's expectations for the future of food should be amply fulfilled. In some ways, the appearance of the books may have anticipated by several years the opportunity to exploit them. Not until the electronics revolution has sent office-bound commuters back to cultivate their homes and gardens in the intervals of other work will it be possible to take full advantage of the productive resources of the average middle-class home, whose machinery deploys more horse-power than a small nineteenth-century factory, and which will soon have by computer-telephone link the research capacity available to Karl Marx in the British Museum Reading Room. However, past experience of British food culture reminds us that all this capacity can be used to deaden and deteriorate our dietary future just as easily as it can be used to quicken it. This is why I am concluding this book with three variations on themes previously heard.

DIFFERENTIATION IN TWENTY-FIRST-CENTURY BRITISH CUISINE

Historically, as we have seen, differentiation in British food culture has been determined by social hierarchy rather than by regional geography. It would be naive to suppose that this class bias to cooking in Britain is likely to disappear altogether or – with the Soviet Union's example in mind – that it would be to our dietary advantage if it did. Only in *1984*, not in 1984, can the feat be accomplished of imagining a society without a past, only a present. Since the seventeenth century, most of the technical advances made and branching paths taken in our cooking have owed something to the endemic tension between bourgeois and aristocratic – or Puritan and Royalist – ways of regarding food and drink and the crafts associated with both. The Royalists after the Restoration published the household book of Elizabeth Cromwell, wife of the Lord Protector, to draw attention to the mean household they thought she kept: mercantile society responded to the excellence of the recipes the book contained by demanding successive editions.[15]

Raymond Postgate, a labour historian, when criticised by fellow-socialists for the preoccupations of his *Good Food Guide*, invariably appealed to the uncompromising standards of the Rochdale Pioneers in their selection of butter and cheese for the first co-operative shops. But this political stance ensured that his guide, which for some became an emblem of indulgence, never quite caught on with *Daily Telegraph* readers in Camberley and Cowes. The very refusal of the British to complain vigorously in restaurants which rob them of the quality of cooking they are entitled to expect for the price they pay does not derive only from native reserve (where is that reserve on sporting occasions?) but from bourgeois fear of being branded as hagglers by open-handed aristocrats. Restaurant criticism in the London glossies, in the style originally set by Quentin Crewe before he turned restaurateur himself, is often instructive in this connection: it is not good form, on the nursery slopes of social climbing, to question value for money too closely, or demand accurate itemised bills, as would be done automatically if £100 were being spent on consumer durables at Harrods.

The best cooking in Britain has always been domestic, at least since the dissolution of the monasteries, because its characteristic scale and style evolved in the prosperous households of Puritan merchants as well as in the professional kitchens of court and courtier. The legal exclusion of Dissenters from public life and institutions after 1662 perhaps further inclined people of this sort to hold celebrations in small family or professional groups at their own hearthstones rather than at large banquets and routs. But this left the whole middle class, when it 'came out' in the early nineteenth century, dependent upon foreign craftsmen and entrepreneurs for restaurants, hotels and banqueting rooms, that is, for the whole public dimension of eating and entertaining that was forced upon people 'in trade' by their position in Victorian England. Mercantile society also neglected seriously, to its own ultimate cost, the diet and the dietary education of the newly urbanised working class whose labour and surplus value they exploited so profitably.

In this last respect, the record of the aristocracy, more deeply rooted in the countryside and its traditions, was markedly better. The feeling for quality expressed in our own time by the catering at certain National Trust houses and even Women's Institute stalls may rest in part on this localised sense of a tradition never quite lost, so capable of being revived. In large towns and cities, by contrast, a tradition and style in which to cook decently and personally for paying customers was beyond the reach of department store owners, even when they recognised the demand by opening in-store cafés and restaurants.* Their horizons were

---

* Of Scottish department store catering a *Good Food Guide* inspector once wrote (1963/4 edition, p. xviii): 'Women as fashionably dressed as the mannequins who parade before them sit cheerfully putting up with lukewarm food, dirty crockery, dirty cutlery, and dirty habits. I wonder what their own kitchens are like.' A colleague who remembers Edinburgh at the same period puts in a kinder word for the teashops attached to bakery stores.

limited and their chief preoccupations lay elsewhere. The mechanistic British caterers who succeeded them were worse, and a style for small-scale catering had to be invented in our own time by the graduates of small private cookery schools, or imported along with cultures fortuitously lodged in our own: Italian, Indian, Cypriot, Chinese.

Socially as well as gastronomically, the significance of this last development is that it introduces to British cuisine a non-hierarchical form of stylistic differentiation. Even vegetarianism, when professed from within a family hitherto entirely unused to thinking about what it eats, thus becomes a tentacle of taste, extended laterally to global food-ways that lie outside the British tradition. Vertically in society, still, genuine communication is clogged: throughout the food and catering trades, you may watch the rich giving rubbish to the poor and the poor giving rubbish back to the rich, whenever either can get away with it.

However, immigrants in Britain, at least recent ones, are less fussy about the social status of the people they feed and serve. At student level in university cities, the unwaged punk and the heir to a Georgian manor are equal before the kebab and the biriani. If it proves possible to interest the education system – the high, the middle, and the low – in this aspect of 'food as a system of communication', and if the new growths can be protected from the commercial gigantism which is the foe of all quality in cooking and catering, Britain is capable of becoming the most highly differentiated food culture in the world, to the immense advantage of its economy while it is losing much of its manufacture to more industrious societies and some of its primary food production to sunnier lands afar. As Jill Tweedie returning from her summer holidays has fairly pointed out, Europe is full of countries which cook very well what they cook, but know no other way. We are becoming the country that knows other ways, and is prepared to practise them.

HOMES AND RESTAURANTS: A BARRIER BROKEN?

The reader will know by now why British cooking, both in public and in private, is better than it was but no better than it should be; why the foreign visitor to these shores is well advised to procure invitations to the private houses of natives whose company he enjoys, rather than eat in the generality of hotels and restaurants; and why such a high proportion of the hundred or two shining exceptions to this rule are run by men and women who have come late to catering after success or failure in other walks of life. But it is important to think of these present realities as still subject to the fluxes and changes that have made the past forty years so diverting for a reasonably curious eating man. There is no First Law of Frigidynamics that compels British-run restaurants to choose between espousing technological cynicism of one kind or another, and pricing themselves outside the financial and social range of the family parties that sustain French restaurants in France and, more relevantly perhaps, ethnic restaurants in Britain.

With the restaurants of the British Isles, there is always the possibility of something quite extraordinary emerging, in human if not invariably gastronomic terms. The great restaurants – and there are a few that can be called that – are a matter of public record, but places equally remarkable for other qualities also have something to teach: the proprietor who gave an agog dining room a blow by blow account of the power failure in the kitchen and his wife's state of mind during it; the restaurant whose proprietor won a bet with his head waitress that he would not walk through the dining room without his trousers on; the patronne – formerly an antique dealer – who summed up British restaurant decor in the sentence, 'I hate everything all matching and simultaneous, as though someone had come into money'; and the London market café (in its way, the best place that it would never have been sensible to put into any *Good Food Guide*) whose owner gets up – usually – just early enough to roast a couple of huge joints, undercook his vegetables, and uncork his claret, with the backing of a resting actress or music student to wait at table and experiment in spare moments with recondite English puddings.

Restaurants such as these are models for nobody, because nobody could copy them. Yet they are the kind that do most to restore the missing element of domestic conviviality in public eating. (British – or at any rate English and Welsh – public *drinking* has always had this ingredient.) Such conviviality, arising out of shared pleasure in the technical prowess of a performer, the cook, is normally stunted by the poverty of guests' expectations and the deficiency of their sense-education. It seldom breaks through the expensive crust of mutual embarrassment that is palpable elsewhere when meals are purveyed for profit in an artificial environment. But the basic culinary techniques of our own and several other nationalities are now being taught, well or ill, to mass audiences on television. Enterprises that made use of these acquired skills on a modest cooperative basis might here and there do something to help roll back the miseries consequent on mass unemployment in post-industrial cities. Gastronomy in Gateshead? All things are possible.

Theodore Zeldin's coupling of restaurants and street-vendors as 'tanks and guerrillas in the smashing of old eating habits' is at once useful and misleading. It is useful, in that a continuum between indoor and outdoor was formerly indigenous to British eating culture but has been tending to disappear with the decline of fish and chip shops and ice cream parlours and the rise of the formal restaurant, until take-aways and street-vending were re-imported from the Near and Far East. But it is also misleading, because the very aggression of Zeldin's chosen imagery somehow suggests that food systems are self-contained and self-referent. Styles of public eating need to be examined for the function they perform in a civilisation that may adopt certain tastes and practices because it has been deprived of something else: for example, social assurance, contact with the physical world, ready access to the conversation of friends. In France, the public restaurant was a by-product of the Revolution; in mid-twentieth-century Britain, of imperial decline. In many places where restaurants have flourished extremely, they have done so as a kind of comment on the defects of housing or town planning: in Hong Kong, the want of living space; in London, the travelling time and distance between friends and colleagues who cannot easily eat with each other at different ends of the Great Wen; in Los Angeles, the un-neighbourliness of the suburb, the freeway, and the defended private space.

In the Britain of 1980, the interpenetration of home and restaurant cooking is now palpable. I first became aware during the 1970s that some of the best country restaurants were farming out their sweet courses to local housewives whose enthusiasm was easy to arouse and whose standards they could control. The influence of serious cookery writers on restaurants of particular genres has already been noted: its counterpart is the six-figure sales of *Good Food Guide* cookery books based upon restaurant recipes, and the seven-figure television audiences commanded by a Carrier or a Tovey. The rise of ethnic cooks with similar technical and communicative powers is only just beginning. The process may accelerate if people can learn to modify the model of a restaurant that they hold in their minds, and couple it with the single-cell outlets with which public eating in Britain began: pie shops, tripe shops, later fish and chip shops, later still salt beef bars and smoked fish counters. Paul Morand, the shrewd French traveller in London who is quoted at the head of this chapter, clearly realised that the best cooking to be found in Britain depended essentially on this modesty of scale; on doing one thing well, rather than several things badly. Indians, Italians and Chinese could profit from the same perception.

APOLOGIA PRO GULA SUA

At an elemental level, the way a person cooks and eats is a form of autobiography. Throughout the writing of this book, it would have been hard to forget that the period it covers is roughly the period of my own apprenticeship to the miraculous transformability of food, from dried-egg omelettes and class-room experiments with cocoa and margarine in the 1940s, to the armoury of dishes and flavours from *aalsoep* to *zwiebel-sauce* that in the 1980s awaits an active restaurant critic if he also keeps one foot in his own kitchen.[16]

I cannot remember a time when I did not appreciate good food and feel offended by bad, for my mother's standards were high and they were thrown into relief by a succession of boarding-school cooks. (At this distance, knowing how little they had to work with at the time, I can sympathise with their shortcomings more easily than I can forgive contemporary chefs who want for nothing but spoil everything.) Several of my forebears were preachers or teachers in another hemisphere, which may explain why missionary zeal, as well as self-interested gour-mandism, affects the tone of what has here been written on topics that in Britain used to be left to the women.

Even in those days, allowances were made for bachelor dons of epicurean or epicene inclinations, who were expected to take a minute and particular interest in the food that accompanied their Margaux '23 or Richebourg '37. Examples of this endangered species still survive, not all of them in Oxbridge. But remarkably few of them dared to carry their interest in food through to their scholarly work even where it would have been appropriate, in history, sociology and other subjects. One excep-tion, the historian J. H. Plumb, recently retired from the Mastership of Christ's after a Cambridge career spanning half a century. At its outset, one Fellow of King's was still breakfasting on beer and a mutton chop, virtually every don had his own cook general to boil his brown Windsor soup and over-roast his meat, and college feasts lasted a full nine courses. Today, the competitive spirit of academics extends to the kitchen ('what has he cooked lately?') and the college chef holds Polish or Brazilian nights to keep up the interest of his staff. 'He does it very well, but when I was young my senior colleagues would have been furious.'[17]

A British Brillat-Savarin or in modern times Curnonsky ('Prince élu des gastronomes') would not have got very far in our culture – till now perhaps – though there may exist a niche for them in the Foreign Service, judging by the activities of Sir Harry Luke and Alan Davidson. Still, one of the minor social changes recently noticeable has been the appearance of men in high streets as food-shoppers (or should it be hunter-foragers?) and also in the kitchen as cooks, on ordinary rather than one-dish-special occasions. Since it is also predominantly men who eat in restaurants, and sometimes notice what they are eating, this development must in its turn have accelerated the cross-fertilisation between private and public eating which was discussed in the previous section.

There have been other consequences for kitchen style and culture from this still very incomplete readjustment of sexual roles. Many feminists, for instance, affect to despise or actually do despise cooking, on the grounds that it keeps them in political subjection, chained to sink and oven. Some of the men who take their place, regularly or intermittently, wonder what tasks of comparable variety and intellectual complexity await these women at the electric typewriter, the ward meeting, or even in boardroom and senate. Women reply, fairly enough, that this is their business, and remark the coincidence that men only began to take an interest in kitchen work when machines removed much of its drudgery. Perhaps both sexes should simply note that 'small is beautiful' advocates have become suspicious of the ideology clustered round the concept of 'labour-saving'. In a factory, the now-familiar process of de-skilling – the reduction of craft-work to machine-minding – is generally thought to be inevitable if the product is to remain competitive in a high-wage economy. Hardly a day passes without this ideology being reasserted by politicians, businessmen, journalists, and advertising agents, and for want of experience in making value judgements where food and cooking are concerned, gullible or self-interested commentators and salesmen transfer the ideology entire to the family kitchen, even though in this context different choices exist:

Marx argued that machinery is a means of creating surplus value correspondingly devaluing the human labour involved, both in terms of wages and the alienation of the worker who lost skill, creativity and control over work . . . Domestic technology may also be a means of creating surplus value by 'allowing' a woman to go out of the home to work, as well as (unpaid) rear the children and keep house. In the process her labour may be devalued and she may lose skills and the creativity of cooking.[18]

The force of Anne Murcott's argument is modified but not destroyed when household roles are redistributed between man and woman on a more equal basis. If skills are permitted to diminish in both workplace and home, or even if they diminish in the one and are enriched in the other, a normally ingenious man can be trusted to emerge with the best package available.

Once in the kitchen, domestic or even semi-professional, a man – whatever the reasons – usually cooks differently from a woman. His mediaeval function as hunter-carver has been reborn as forager-barbecuer. He tends to season with more temerity, and refer to recipes more readily (research suggests that in social classes where household lore depends on verbal tradition, a woman's use of recipes is an implicit admission of deficient upbringing).* He may also be less troubled by the overbearing moral and psychological imperatives that pervade house-hold and child-rearing literature. (Few things worry a woman more than a child's refusal to eat, however transparent the perversity or blackmail.) A psychologist might be found to explain male amateur cooks' relative lack of interest in baking puddings and cakes not by their want of a sweet tooth (after all, who eats the lethal gateaux in London lunchtime trattorias?) but by a latent confusion of the act of baking with the process of gestation. Certainly, today's male couples, whose emergence from the social purdah to which they were previously confined has contributed much to the improvement of British restaurant and small hotel cooking, often confirm this hypothesis by showing particular strength in patisserie. Above all, within the historical period covered by this book, it is relevant to observe that when a mother cooks, her sons, prisoners of the peer culture, have to make a positive effort to imitate her, while her daughters have to make an equally positive effort not to. When a father cooks, the behaviour of daughters is unaffected, but sons are more often liberated to imitate him.

Throughout these pages, I have assumed that food, and the manner in which it is transformed and consumed, belong to a value system to

---

* 'There is considerable feeling that an experienced housewife ought not to need recipes' – *Food and Cooking in England: changing habits and changing attitudes* (1964): a report commissioned by J. Walter Thompson & Co. Of course, twenty years may have changed attitudes further since this research was done. In 1960, but not in 1980, most active cooks would have learnt the craft before the war and its output of Kitchen Front recipes.

which words such as 'style' and 'culture' are no less appropriate than they are to other value systems perceived by different senses. If this is elitist, never mind; anyway, I would choose to quote in this context Hannah Wright's apostrophe to *New Statesman* colleagues who apparently took the priggish view that even in the *advertisement* columns of the magazine only 'intellectual' material should be offered.

Higher education elevates and develops the mind, unconsciously promoting the attitude that the brain is a sovereign state controlling and drawing fuel from a large but subservient colony called the body . . . There is hardly a degree to be found that cannot be got with first class honours by a person completely lacking in the senses of taste, smell, and interior sensation of all kinds . . . If intellectuals, defined by the *Dictionary of Modern Thought* as 'the culture-bearers of the nation', continue to consider food and drink an unworthy subject for creative and critical thought, we will have less and less culture to bear for a sadder and sicker nation. Our national diet, national health and national brain power will be left to the disintegrated and self-interested attentions of farmers, food manufacturers and retailers.[19]

If this is accepted, I am free to think about food culture in terms of gain and loss, atrophy and renewal, the sectional and the shared. I stress the last of those pairs. The exquisite gastronauts whose skills are now readily marketable in London and New York as well as in Paris all too easily forget that in this branch of culture, as in others, high art depends on the quality of what is held in common. Jeremy Seabrook, a chronicler of material and spiritual poverty in modern working class life, insists:

Our mothers were conjurors, they could make a meal out of next to nothing, some bits of offal – of course, they couldn't do it now, it all goes to the factories for pet food.

There is a dynamic relationship between the decay of human resources in everyday life and the growth of production; and this leads to an indefensible waste of our substance. It is a double prodigality: not only do we squander the perishable commodities on which the economies of the West depend (that is an old story) but at the same time the positive abilities that poor societies had called forth are also being eaten away; and these are things that we should treasure beyond price.[20]

In a culture, writers depend on readers, composers on listeners and amateur performers, and cooks on eaters who share their 'vocabulary' of food and are capable of criticising their use and extension of it. Bernard Levin – he reminds us – once began a dyspeptic report from Tel Aviv, after a series of hideous meals in Israel, with the line 'Doesn't anyone here have a Jewish mother?'[21] Emotion of this kind is seldom deployed by British gentiles in defence of their birthright, which is one reason why deteriorated or adulterated products so easily edge their way into the national shopping basket.

As Flora Thompson said of the calf's foot and wine jelly, in the passage quoted at the head of this chapter, 'few would care to take the trouble in these days'. There is no necessity. But suppose there were no necessity, opportunity, or incentive for man, woman or child to do the following: make bramble jelly or marmalade; skin a rabbit or pluck and draw a chicken; make a batter pudding; bake potatoes in the ashes of a bonfire; taste a farmhouse cheese made of unpasteurised milk; be offered cucumber sandwiches at teatime; pick sloes for gin or find a pub selling scrumpy cider? These are a few food or drink events whose frequency has almost certainly diminished in recent years, some of them to the point of invisibility; not because everyone has lost a taste for them, but as a result of independent changes in farming methods, commercial and industrial practice, administrative regulation, or socio-economic redistribution. Damage to the quality of the common material or action is not made up by the accessibility – to some – of *magrets de canard*, or *pesto* in little pots.

Elsewhere in the same article, Levin suggests that you do not have to compare bouillabaisse with Beethoven or a well-made matelote with Mozart in order to maintain that the pleasures conveyed by good performances of both food and music have something in common. He then muddles the issue by pretending that the two kinds of aesthetic delight approach each other more nearly if marginally less distinguished composers are substituted – say, the Mendelssohn of the Italian Symphony. This confusion of quality with genre suggests that Levin addressed the topic rather too soon after visiting one of the Bayreuths of French gastronomy. He also fails to disentangle art from craft and creation from performance, but that is a complex task which had better be left to other minds and other books. It is nearer the truth, perhaps, to say that any performer who moves easily between the written and the improvised – be he dancer, theatrical director, or jazz pianist – has or ought to have an instinctive affinity with a chef of similar calibre. All are occupied with touching sense and emotion by constructing patterns in media whose very essence is their ephemerality. They depend as they do so on the imagination which they share with all artists, and on the conscience, similarly shared, that prevents them from presenting 'what Jones will swallow' and no more. It is in this sense that food transcends nutrition, as even the most self-indulgent of columnists transcends the birth and death notices. It is for this reason that cooks deserve to be admired, criticised, and remembered, just as actresses and violinists had to be remembered in the days before the film and the gramophone record partially atrophied that most ancient of cultural skills, the skill of remembering and building a tradition upon the remembrance.

This may point to a further reason why the chef in our society is beginning to acquire a touch of the shaman. Colour photography and televised demonstrations are part of it, of course. But it is also true that in the age of mechanical reproduction, sacredness clings to what cannot be readily reproduced, to the one-off. A 'memorable meal' is a meal that can be remembered but not reproduced in all its nuances. As eaters and drinkers, we are caught up in a war whose lines we may cross and re-cross several times a day: carbon-copy food for lunch, perhaps, and a hand-written tea where the cake that husband or wife, son or daughter, has baked may emerge differently from the version by another hand in another home, even if it is made with the same ingredients, utensils and temperatures. And if it is objected that this is a sentimental vision of a lost ritual – cucumber sandwiches, and seed-cake on a filigree stand – this too belongs to my argument. Access to artefacts of this kind is now in practice much harder to secure than it is to fill the room with the sound of a first-rate string quartet or symphony orchestra, a sound which within living memory even the keenest musician considered himself lucky to hear more than once or twice a year. But at this point the philosopher of taste, gourmand and violinist, had better be allowed to make his own *envoi*:

Two married gourmands have a pleasant opportunity to meet at least once a day; for even those who sleep apart (and there are many such) eat at the same table; they have a subject of conversation which never grows stale, for they talk not only about what they are eating, but also of what they have eaten, what they are about to eat, what they have observed at other houses, fashionable dishes, new culinary inventions, etc. etc.; and such chit-chat is full of charm.

No doubt music too has strong attractions for those who love it; but it must be played, and that requires an effort. Besides, a cold, a lost music-book, an instrument out of tune, or even a headache, and there is no music.

But a common need calls man and wife to table, and a common inclination keeps them there; they naturally show each other those little courtesies which reveal a desire to please; and the manner in which meals are conducted is an important ingredient in the happiness of life.[22]

Appendix one

The following list of tinned foods obtainable in London before the Second
World War was assembled by Ambrose Heath for his *Open Sesame: two hundred
recipes for canned goods* (Nicholson & Watson, 1939). The scope of the list, he
wrote, was 'portentous, if horrific'. Forty years on, the reader may be surprised
not only by its ambition and catholicity, but also by probable disappearances
(tripe and onions, boiled mutton, samphire, . . .) I have not attempted to amend
confusions of content or lay-out.

Soups
Alexandra
Artichoke
Asparagus
Bean, Black
  Golden
Beef Broth
  Tea
Cauliflower
Celery
Chicken Broth
  Consommé
  Cream
  Noodle
  with Rice
Clam Bouillon
  Chowder
Cock-a-leekie
Consommé
  Arctique
  Julienne
  Madrilène
  Royale
  Trile
Crécy
Game
Giblet
Gravy
Grouse
Hare
Haricot
Hotch-Potch
Kidney
Lentil
Lobster

Macaroni
Minestrone
Mock Turtle
Mulligatawny
Mushroom
Mutton Broth
Normandie Cream
Onion
Oxtail
Oyster
Pea, Green
Potato
Printanière
Purée de Gibier
Russian Borsch
Scotch Broth
Shrimp
Spinach
Summer
Toheroa
Tomato
Turtle
Vegetable
Vermicelli

Fish
Anchovies
  and Pimiento
  and Pignole
  and Pistachio
  in Piquante Sauce
  with Capers
Bloaters
Bombay Duck (Bummaloe
  Fish)

Botargo
Brisling in Oil
  in Tomato
  Sauce
Caviare
Clams
  Minced
Cockles
Cod Fish, Curried
Crab
  Dressed
Crawfish
Crayfish
Danefish (Balls)
Escargots à la Bordelaise
Fish Flakes
Fundies
Haddocks, Smoked
Herrings à la Sardine
  and Anchovy Sauce
  and Mustard Sauce
  and Shrimp Sauce
  and Tomato Sauce
  Fresh
  Grilled and Filleted
  in Mayonnaise
  in Oil
  Kippered
  Red
  Smoked Fillets in Oil
    (*Gendarme*)
  Roes
Kippers
  Fillets
  Snacks

Lax (Smoked Salmon in Oil)
Lobster
  Curried
Mackerel Fillets
  au vin blanc
  Fresh
  in Tomato Sauce
  Soused
Ormers
Oysters
Pastes (various)
Pike, quenelles
Pilchards in Oil
  Fillets
  in Tomato Sauce
Plaice, Fried Filleted
Prawns
  Curried
Salmon
  Roll
  Smoked in Oil (Lax)
Sardines (various)
Shad Roe
Shrimps
Sild in Oil
  in Tomato Sauce
Snails
Sprats in Sesame Oil
Sturgeon in Tomato Sauce
Thon in Oil
Toheroa
Tunny Fish
  Fillets *aux achards*
  with Mushrooms
  with Peas
  with Tomato
Turtle Meat
Whitebait
Whiting, Fresh
  Smoked

Meat
Bacon, Sliced
Beef *à la mode*
  Boiled
  Brisket, in Slices
  and Tongue
  Whole
Collared
  Corned
  Corned Beef Hash
  Jellied with Ham

Loaf
  Pressed
  Roast
  Scotch Round
  Seasoned
  Silverside, Boiled
  Spiced
Black Puddings
Boar's Head
Brawn
Calf's Head
  and Bacon
  in Tomato Sauce
Camp Pies, Chicken and
  Ham, Chicken, Ham and
  Tongue
  Chicken and Tongue
  Turkey and Tongue
  Veal and Ham
Cassoulet Gastro
Chicken
  à la King
  Boneless
  Breasts
  Curried
  Cutlets
  Loaf
  Meat
  Paprika
  Quenelles
  Roast
  Tamales
Chile con Carne
Chop Suey
Coq-au-vin
Duck and Green Peas
  Roast
Enchiladas
Foie gras, Pâté
  Purée
Fowl Boiled
  Curried
  Roast
Galantines, Beef and Ham
  Beef and Tongue
  Chicken
  Chicken and Ham
  Chicken, Ham and
  Tongue
  Chicken and Tongue
  Game
  Ham and Tongue
  Pheasant

Pork
  Turkey and Tongue
  Turkey
  Veal, Ham and Tongue
  Veal, Truffled
Game, Quenelles
Gammon, Cooked
  Boneless
Goosebreast, Hungarian
Grouse, Whole Roast
Haggis
Ham, Boneless
  Loaf
  Sliced
  Smoked Raw (*Jambon de Parme*)
  Spiced
  York
Hare, Jugged
Kidneys, Devilled
  Stewed
Lamb and Green Peas
  Brains
  Cutlets
  Py Dumpy
  Roast
  Sweetbreads
  Tongues
Liver and Bacon
Meat Rations
Mixed Grill
Mutton Boiled
Mutton Chops
  Curried
  Cutlets
  in Tomato Sauce
  Haricot
Lancashire Hot Pot
  Roast
  Seasoned
Ox Cheek
  and Vegetables
  Curried
Ox Tail, Braised
  Curried
Pastes, various
Pâtés, various
Partridge, Whole Roast
Pheasant, Roast
  and Sausage, Roast
Pork
  and Beans
  Pressed

Puddings, Beefsteak
  Steak and Kidney
Quails, Stuffed, in Aspic
Rabbit and Pork
  Cooked
  Curried
  Haricot
  Stewed
  with Onions
Ravioli (stuffed with chicken)
Rice Birds
Rolls, Beef and Ham
  Beef and Ham (Spiced)
  Chicken and Ham
  Cumberland
  Ham
  Ham and Egg
  Ham and Tongue
  Liver and Bacon
  Ox Tongue
  Partridge and Ham
  Roast Chicken and
    Tongue
  Roast Pork and Stuffing
  Roast Turkey and Ham
  Savoury
  Steak and Kidney
  Turkey and Tongue
  Veal, Ham and Tongue
  York
Sausage and Mashed
  Potato
  Toad-in-the-Hole
Sausages, Beef
  Bologna
  Breakfast
  Cambridge
  Chipolata
  Cocktail
  Frankfort
  Luncheon
  Mortadella
  Oxford
  Pork
  Smoked
  Tomato
  Vienna
Sausages with Beans
Shepherd's Pie
Steak and Kidney
  Pudding
  Stewed Rump
Sweetbreads

  with Mushrooms
  with Tomatoes
Tamales
Tongue, Brawn
  Calves'
  Lamb's
  Lunch
  Ox
  Pig's
  Sheep's
  Tripe and Onions
  à la mode de Caen
Turkey
  Breasts
  Minced
  Roast
Veal and Ham
  and Peas
  Curried
  Cutlets and Bacon
  Cutlets and Tomato
  Jellied
  Loaf
  Minced
  Quenelles
  Roast
  Spiced, in Aspic
  Stewed
  Stewed with Peas
  Stuffed
Venison Liver Paste

Vegetables
Artichoke Bottoms
  (*fonds d'artichauts*)
  Hearts
    in French Dressing
Artichokes, Whole
  Whole Green (*carciofi*)
Asparagus
  Tips
Aubergines, Stuffed
Bamboo Shoots
Beans, Baked in Tomato
  Sauce (with or
    without Pork)
  Broad
  Butter, Curried
    in Tomato Sauce
    in Gravy
  Curried
    in Gravy
  Golden

  Golden Wax
  Green Stringless
  Kidney
  Lima
  Red Kidney
  Scarlet Runners, sliced
  Stringless Runners,
    Whole
Beetroots,
  Diced
  Sliced
  Whole
Brussels Sprouts
Carrots, Diced
  Sliced
  Whole
Cauliflower
Celery, Cut
  Hearts
  and Pea Purée
Cèpes au naturel garniture
Champignons
Corn-on-the-Cob
Corn, Sweet (Maize)
Flageolets
Hominy
Macédoine
  in Mayonnaise
Morilles
Mushrooms
  Black
  Grilled in Butter
  in Cream Sauce
  White
Okra (Ladies' Fingers)
  and Strained Tomatoes
Olives
  Black
  Stuffed with Anchovies
Onion Powder
Palm Hearts (*cœurs
  de Palmier*)
Parsnips
Patal
Peas, Green
  à la Paysanne
  and Carrots
  in Butter
Petits pois
  Sugar
Peppers, Green
  Red, Stuffed
  Small Venetian in Vinegar

Pimientos, Red (Spanish)
  Paprikas (Hungarian)
Potato Crisps
  Salad with Mayonnaise
  Sticks
Potatoes, New
  Sweet
Pumpkin
Ravioli, Stuffed with
  Spinach
Sauerkraut
Sea Kale
Soups
Spinach
  Leaf
  Purée
Sprouts, Chinese
Squash
Succotash
Tomato Juice
  Purée
Tomatoes, Peeled
Truffle Peelings
Truffles
Turnips
  Diced
  Mashed
  Quartered
  Whole
Vegetable Salad in
  Mayonnaise
  in Tomato Mayonnaise
Vine Leaves, Stuffed
Water Chestnuts

Fruit
Apple Sauce
Apples, Baked
  Sliced
  Solid
  Whole, Cored and
    Peeled
Apricots
  Whole
  Sliced
Bilberries
Blackberries
  and Apple
Black Currants
Blueberries
Cantaloup Melon
Cherries, Black
  Morello

Red
White
Chestnuts in Syrup
  Marrons glacés
Cranberry Sauce
Custard Apples
Damsons
  (Prune)
Figs
Fruit Cocktail
  Juices, various
  Salad
  in Jelly
Goldenberries
Gooseberries
Gooseberry Purée
Grapes, Peeled
Greengages
Guavas
Jams:
  Apricot
  Cape Gooseberry
  Fig
  Guava (Jelly)
  Melon and Lemon
  Orange Marmalade
  Peach
  Pineapple
  Plum
  Quince
  Raspberry
Lichies
Loganberries
Loquats (Japanese
  Medlars)
Mandarines
Mangoes
Marrons glacés
Mirabelles
Nectarines
  Whole
Passion Fruit
Paw Paw
Peaches
  Whole
  Spiced
Pears
  Red
  Stewed
  Whole
  Spiced
Pineapple
  Juice

Plum Purée
Plums, Golden
  Purple Egg
  Red
  Victoria
Prunes, Dry
  in Loganberry Juice
  in Syrup
Puddings:
  Apple (Suet crust)
  Date Sponge
  Fig Sponge
  Gooseberry (Suet Crust)
  Mixed Fruit
  Plum (Suet Crust)
  Raspberry Sponge
  Strawberry Sponge
Quinces
Raspberries
  and Red Currants
Red Currants
Rhubarb
Strawberries
Strawberry Purée
Tangerines
Whortleberries
Youngberries

Sauces
Apple
Béarnaise
Brown (Chinese)
Cranberry
Financière
Genevoise
Gratiné
Madère
Meat (Bolognese)
Périgueux aux truffes
Poivrade
Royale
Tomato

Miscellaneous
Apple Juice
Beer
Casserole Preparation
Chocolate Syrup
Cinnamon Toast
Coffee
  and Milk
Cooked Rice (Chinese)
Cream

Dripping, Beef
Ginger, Stem, in Syrup
Grapefruit Juice
Honey
Lard
Macaroni
  in Cream Sauce with
    Cheese
Maple Butter
  Sugar
  Syrup

Milk
Mincemeat
Molasses
Noodles (Chinese)
Nutmeats, various
Orange Juice
Poppadums
Porridge
Puddings:
  Chocolate Sponge
  Christmas

Marmalade Sponge
Treacle Sponge
Ravioli
Samphire
Spaghetti
  à la Bolognese
  à l'Italienne
  with Cheese and
    Tomato
  with Tomato

Appendix Two

See Chapter Nine, pages 162–3

France has a title, *Meilleur Ouvrier*, that is bestowed on the most creative and influential of her chefs. In the perspective of thirty years of restaurant and hotel cooking in Britain, the following names are suggested. These are not claimed as 'the best post-war chefs': if achievement were related to career opportunities and conditions prevailing at the time, a very different list might emerge. If the Republic of Ireland were included, two or three more names would be added (Declan Ryan for example); and if non-European restaurants were included, several more.

Imported talent
Raymond Blanc: Les Quat' Saisons, Oxford
Michel Bourdin: Connaught Hotel, London
Louis Carini: Old Deanery, Ripon†
Robert Carrier: Carrier's, London; Hintlesham Hall, Essex†
Maurice Ithurbure: Chez Maurice, Eastbourne†
Pierre Koffmann: Tante Claire, London
Jean Labat: Malmaison Restaurant, Central Hotel, Glasgow†
Nico Ladenis: Chez Nico, Dulwich† and Battersea
Anton Mosimann: Dorchester Hotel, London
Albert and Michel Roux: Le Gavroche, London; Waterside, Bray
Franco Taruschio: Walnut Tree Inn, Llandewi Skirrid

Indigenous talent
Kenneth Bell: Elizabeth, Oxford†; Thornbury Castle
Hilary Brown: La Potinière, Gullane
Stephen Bull: Lichfield's, Richmond
Francis Coulson: Sharrow Bay Hotel, Ullswater
Tim and Sue Cumming: Crane's, Salisbury†; Hole in the Wall, Bath
George Fuller: Vineyard, Colerne†
William Heptinstall: Fortingall, Glen Lyon†
Mary Johnson: Tullythwaite House, Underbarrow
Marion Jones: Lavender Hill Restaurant, London†; Croque-en-Bouche, Malvern Wells
Joyce Molyneux: Hole in the Wall, Bath†; Carved Angel, Dartmouth
David Partridge: French Partridge, Horton

† indicates that the citation is historical, not current (January 1983).

Appendix Three

See Chapter Nine, page 163

Restaurants/restaurateurs derived from the work of George Perry-Smith, presently or formerly appearing in *The Good Food Guide*:

Tim and Sue Cumming: Crane's, Salisbury; Hole in the Wall, Bath
Elaina Gardiner: Bowlish House, Shepton Mallet
Tony Gulliford: The Laden Table, Bath
Tom Hearne: La Chandelle, Marlow; Hole in the Wall, Bath
Simon Mallet: Mallet's, Ramsgate
John Marfell: Cleeveway House, Bishop's Cleeve
Stephen Markwick: Bistro 21, Bristol
Michael Milburn: The Undercroft, Durham
Joyce Molyneux: Hole in the Wall, Bath; The Carved Angel, Dartmouth
Penny Ross: Popjoy's, Bath; Homewood Park, Hinton Charterhouse
David Tearle: Tearle's, Limpley Stoke; Claret, Bath; Tearle's, Bristol
Michael Waterfield: Wife of Bath, Wye
Colin White: White's, Lincoln

Even this list omits people who have made substantial catering careers outside the genre of '*Good Food Guide* restaurant': Angus Lamont (The Crown, Chiddingfold); Michael and Monique Manners, who run a 100-seat restaurant in New South Wales; Annie Volpe in private catering; among many others who may be similarly employed but whose whereabouts are unknown to George Perry-Smith and his partner Heather Crosbie.

George Perry-Smith: Hole in the Wall, Bath†; Riverside, Helford
Richard Shepherd: Capital Hotel, London†; Langan's Brasserie, London
Sonia Stevenson: Horn of Plenty, Gulworthy
John Tovey: Miller Howe, Windermere
Michael Waterfield: Wife of Bath, Wye†

Notes

PART ONE: CHAPTER ONE

1 – J.-A. Brillat-Savarin tr. Anne Drayton, *The Philosopher in the Kitchen* (1970), pp. 135–6.
2 – Sarah Freeman, *Isabella and Sam* (1977), p. 168.
3 – N. Newnham-Davis, *Dinners and Diners* (1899), p. 83.
4 – A. Escoffier, *A Guide to Modern Cookery* (1907), p. vii.
5 – *Simple French Cooking for English Homes* (1923).
6 – X. M. Boulestin, *Myself, My Two Countries* (1936).
7 – Michael Bateman, *Cooking People* (1966) pp. 164–74.
8 – Florence White, *Good Things in England* (1932), p. 11.
9 – Raymond Postgate in *Sunday Times Magazine*, 8 January 1967.
10 – Constance Spry and Rosemary Hume, *The Constance Spry Cookery Book* (1956) p. xi.
11 – John Burnett, *Plenty and Want* (revised edition 1979) pp. 317, 319.
12 – *The Road to Wigan Pier* (1937) p. 15.
13 – *The New Survey of London Life and Labour* (1928–35), vol. IX, *Life and Leisure* (1935), pp. 413–14.
14 – *ibid.* pp. 141, 11–2.

CHAPTER TWO

1 – J. C. Drummond and Anne Wilbraham, *The Englishman's Food* (revised Dorothy Hollingsworth), 1958, p. 459.
2 – See Table p. 26.
3 – Mancur Olson, Jr. *The Economics of the Wartime Shortage* (Durham, N. Carolina, 1963), p. 142.
4 – J. C. Drummond and others (1940).
5 – André L. Simon, *In the Twilight* (1969), p. 121.
6 – *DNB Supplement* 1951–60.
7 – *The Nation's Larder* (op. cit.) p. 17.
8 – Lord Woolton, *Memoirs* (1959) pp. 190–94.
9 – ibid. p. 251.
10 – See Elizabeth David, *English Bread and Yeast Cookery* (1977), pp. 32–6. 'National' flour was not discontinued until the Flour (Composition) regulations of 1956.
11 – Woolton, *op. cit.*, p. 249. For Woolton pie recipe see p. 37.
12 – Irene Veal, *Recipes from the 1940s* (1944) pp. 43–5.
13 – *ibid.* p. 241.

14 – See R. J. Hammond, *Food* (Civil History of the Second World War) Vol. 2 (1956) pp. 65–81.

15 – Woolton *op. cit.* p. 241.

16 – W. S. Churchill, *The Second World War*, Vol III p. 753.

17 – Woolton *op. cit.* p. 242.

18 – Ministry of Food Bulletin, 10 November 1942.

19 – Frederic Accum, *A Treatise on Adulterations of Food and Culinary Poisons, exhibiting the fraudulent sophistications of bread, beer, wine, spirituous liquors, tea, coffee, cream, confectionery, vinegar, mustard, pepper, cheese, olive oil, pickles, and other articles employed in domestic economy, and Methods of Detecting them* (1820). The full title indicates the scope of a book which earned its author the concerted odium of the trades (and individuals) named in its pages. The reminder of the ambiguity inherent in the phrase 'sophisticated tastes' is also useful.

20 – Hammond *op. cit.* Vol II p. 321.

21 – Theodora FitzGibbon, *With Love: an autobiography 1938–1946* (1982) pp. 54, 124.

22 – In conversation with the author.

23 – Churchill *op. cit.* Vol II p. 663.

24 – Mario Gallati, *Mario of the Caprice* (1960) pp. 95–7.

25 – Veal, *op. cit.* p. 215.

26 – Gerald Priestland, *Frying Tonight: the saga of fish and chips* (1972) p. 83.

CHAPTER THREE

1 – Susan Cooper in Michael Sissons and Philip French (editors), *Age of Austerity* (1963) p. 41.

2 – P. L. Simmons, *The Curiosities of Food: or, the dainties and delicacies of different nations obtained from the animal kingdom* (1859) p. 120.

3 – Raymond Postgate in *Leader Magazine*, 23 June 1949.

4 – Cooper *op. cit.* p. 51.

5 – Unpublished letter in the writer's possession.

6 – David Marquand in *Age of Austerity* (*op. cit.*) p. 180.

7 – *ibid.* (David Hughes) p. 95.

8 – Magnus Pyke, *Townsman's Food* (1952) p. 63.

9 – Tom Laughton, *Pavilions by the Sea* (1977) p. 145.

10 – *ibid.* p. 167.

11 – Nicolas Freeling, *Kitchen Book* (1970) pp. 97 and 103.

12 – *Leader Magazine* 20 May 1950.

13 – Retrieved by Neil Rhind and Hope Chenhalls for an (unpublished) history of *The Good Food Guide* (to 1970).

14 – *Leader Magazine* 23 April 1949.

16 – *The Good Food Guide* (1951) pp. 7, 15–16, 25.

17 – Elizabeth David, *French Country Cooking*, pp. 74–5.

Notes

18 – In a letter to 'Hilary Fawcett', editor of *The Good Food Guide* Dinner Party Book (1971).
19 – Elizabeth David, *Mediterranean Food*, p. vi.
20 – *French Country Cooking*, pp. viii–ix, 21–2.
21 – Peter Jones, *Good House Design* (n.d., *c.* 1950) p. 21.

CHAPTER FOUR

1 – *Which?*, February 1982.
2 – 'Michael' in David Lodge, *How Far Can You Go?* (1980), a fictional evocation of the period.
3 – *Guardian*, 6 March 1982.
4 – *ibid.* 2 March 1982.
5 – James P. Johnston, *A Hundred Years Eating* (1977) p. 118.
6 – Burnett *op. cit.* pp. 337, 362.
7 – Geoffrey Warren, *The Foods We Eat* (1958).
8 – *ibid.* p. 117.
9 – *Encounter*, September 1955.
10 – *Observer*, 28 February 1982.

PART TWO: CHAPTER FIVE

1 – *Guardian*, 20 April 1966.
2 – Lincoln Allison, *Condition of England* (1981) p. 189.
3 – In James L. Watson (editor) *Between Two Cultures* (1977) pp. 246–51.
4 – *ibid.* pp. 181–211.
5 – In K. C. Chang (editor) *Food in Chinese Culture* (1977) p. 360.
6 – See Watson *op. cit.*, pp. 23–4 (Roger and Catherine Ballard) and 181–211.
7 – Lalita Ahmed, *Indian Cooking* (1981).
8 – A. H. Sharar, *Lucknow; the last phase of an oriental culture* (translated and edited by E. S. Harcourt and Fahir Hussein, 1975) pp. 165–6.
9 – Rosemary Brissenden, *South East Asian Food* (1969) p. 14.
10 – Shizuo Tsuji, *Japanese Cooking: a simple art* (Tokyo, New York and San Francisco, 1980) p. 21.
11 – *ibid.* p. 23.
12 – *ibid.* p. 14.
13 – Fay Maschler in *New Standard*, 29 June 1982.
14 – Quoted in Elizabeth David, *Spices, Salt and Aromatics in the English Kitchen* (1970) pp. 160–61.

CHAPTER SIX

1 – *Changing Food Habits* (1964) pp. 136–7.
2 – *English Food* (1974) p. 235.

Notes

3 – Jack Goody, *Cooking, Cuisine and Class* (1982) p. 84.

4 – *Manchester Guardian*, 19 February 1941.

5 – Michael Balfour and Judy Allen, *The Health Food Guide* (2nd edition 1972) p. 244. Lesley Nelson's *Vegetarian Restaurants in England* (1982) is a more recent account of cooks and customers in this genre.

6 – 4 July 1971.

7 – November 1970.

8 – Robert Moore, *The Social Impact of Oil* (1982) p. 157.

9 – Paul Levy, *Observer*, 7 March 1982.

10 – Tom Jaine of the Carved Angel restaurant in Dartmouth (see pp. 157, 169) refers in his monthly circular *Twelve Times a Year* (August 1982) to the varieties listed in John Abercrombie and Thomas Mawe, *Every Man his own Gardener*, which went through eighteen editions between 1767 and 1800.

11 – *Memoirs of a Public Baby* (1958) p. 42.

12 – Richard Selzer, *Mortal Lessons* (1981) pp. 53, 54.

13 – Richard Olney, *Simple French Food* (1981) pp. 278–82.

14 – Harold Wilshaw (*Guardian*, 18 January 1974).

15 – D. Elliston Allen, *British Tastes* (1968), especially Chapters. 5 and 8.

16 – *ibid*. pp. 117–19.

17 – Dorothy Hartley, *Food in England* (1954) p. 20.

CHAPTER SEVEN

1 – *Spectrum* (C.O.I.: British Science News) No. 155/1978.

2 – The references are for German, Wagner (1950); for French, Le Magnen (1962); for English, Harper (1958, 192, 1971); for Japanese, Yoshikawa and others (1970).

3 – R. W. Burchfield interviewed by Bernard Levin on BBC 2, July 1982; Dennis Barker on horse-breeding terms, *Guardian*, 12 February 1983; Larousse *Dictionary of Argot and Popular French*.

4 – John Moore, *You English Words* (1961) pp. 164, 180.

5 – Iris Murdoch, *The Sea, The Sea* (1978) p. 16. I do not quite follow the argument about apricots, almonds, and red wine.

6 – Michael Broadbent's *Pocket Guide to Wine Tasting* (1982) pp. 93–4.

7 – *ibid*. p. 94.

8 – In this paragraph I have drawn on a radio talk of mine previously published in *More Words* (BBC, 1977).

9 – *The Times*, 28 April 1982.

10 – For M. F. K. Fisher, see her essays collected in *The Art of Eating* (1963), to be republished later this year (1983).

11 – Robert Courtine, *La Gastronomie* (Paris, 1970), p. 121.

Notes

CHAPTER EIGHT

1 – *Observer*, 1 December 1968.

2 – *Guardian*, 16 December 1970.

3 – *Guardian*, 13 January 1973.

4 – 23 June 1958.

5 – *Guardian*, 14 October 1971. See also Magnus Pyke's *Technological Eating, or, Where does the fish-finger point?* (1972), *passim*.

6 – *Guardian* 13 April 1972.

7 – John Elkington in *Guardian*, 17 June 1982.

8 – *Guardian*, 22 November 1974.

9 – *Guardian*, 9 September 1971.

10 – *Guardian*, 4 May 1971.

11 – Magnus Pyke, *op. cit.* p. 60.

12 – Chris Pond, *New Society*, 3 December 1981.

13 – Derek Cooper in *Observer Magazine*, 10 January 1982.

14 – Tsuji, *op. cit.*, pp. 10–11.

15 – Derek Cooper reporting Dr Jim Thomson, *Guardian*, 27 May 1974

16 – See page 45.

17 – *Guardian*, 8 July 1968.

18 – See page 172.

19 – For the sensory hell of working in a chicken factory, see Merrilyn Winterborn, *New Society*, 23/30 December 1982. Of course, as many witnesses have testified, old-style abattoirs and knackers' yards were often worse.

20 – Scitovsky (1976) pp. 189–90.

21 – Norman Myers in *Guardian*, 3 February 1983

CHAPTER NINE

1 – 14 January; 18 February 1982.

2 – In a letter to the author.

3 – *Market Assessment*, February/March 1981. See also *Trends in Catering* (Hotel and Catering EDC) and regular Gallup surveys.

4 – *Staff Turnover* (Hotel and Catering EDC) 1969.

5 – *Behind the Swing Doors* (1937) 'by a manager'.

6 – A report from the National Catering Inquiry, sponsored by Smethursts Foods Ltd (1966).

7 – College and Polytechnic lecturers quoted by Martin Leighton in an unpublished paper.

8 – *Catering Times*, 10 June 1976.

9 – Committee of Inquiry into Motorway Service Areas: report (2 vols., 1978).

10 – Preface to *The Good Food Guide*, 1959–60.

11 – *Sunday Telegraph Magazine*, 19 July 1981.

12 – In conversation with the author.
13 – In conversation with the author.

CHAPTER TEN

1 – Goody *op cit.* p. 152.
2 – Lesley Chamberlain, *The Food and Cooking of Russia* (1982) pp. 13, 290.
3 – Goody *op. cit.* p. 133.
4 – *ibid.* p. 134.
5 – *ibid.* p. 88.
6 – *ibid.* p. 92.
7 – Hartley *op. cit.* p. 27.
8 – *The Things They Say About Food: a survey of traditional English foodways* in *Folk Life*, Vol. 13 (1975).
9 – See E. P. Thompson, *The Making of the English Working Class* (1963), pp. 211–12, 289–90, 314–18; Raymond Postgate's comments in *The Good Food Guide* 1965/6 p. 10, and John Burnett's critique in *Plenty and Want* (*op. cit.* pp. 9–11).
10 – Report to the DHSS reprinted in Mary Douglas, *In the Active Voice* (1982) pp. 82–116.
11 – *Social Science Information* 21 (4/5) 1982, pp.677–96.
12 – Ann Oakley, *The Sociology of Housework* (1974) pp. 49, 59. For a different perspective on the under-explored topic, see Caroline Davidson, *A Woman's Work is Never Done* (1982).
13 – *Listener*, 15 April 1982. 'Millions' is a large exaggeration: see the last sentence of ch. 8.
14 – Roger Phillips in *Observer Magazine*, 12 September 1982.
15 – Michelle Berriedale-Johnson, *Olde English Recipes* (1981) p. 28.
16 – I take these items from Theodora FitzGibbon's useful encyclopaedia *The Food of the Western World* (1976). It will be interesting to see whether Alan Davidson's *Oxford Companion to Food* (forthcoming) manages to stretch the alphabet even further.
17 – In conversation with the author.
18 – Murcott *op. cit.*, and see her essay, 'Cooking and the Cooked: a note on the domestic preparation of meals' in Anne Murcott (ed.), *The Sociology of Food and Eating* (1983).
19 – *New Statesman*, 27 March 1981.
20 – *Listener*, 2 September 1982.
21 – *Guardian*, 21 August 1982. Apropos of pet food and wasted substance, the manufacturers of Chum and Whiskas, in the same newspaper's advertisement columns (17 February 1983), offered food scientists a 'multi-disciplinary research challenge' and a £16,000 starting salary under the heading 'New approaches to palatability'.
22 – J.-A. Brillat-Savarin *op. cit.* pp. 138–9.

Bibliography

This does not pretend to be a work of exhaustive scholarship in any single corner of the wide field it covers. However, the field itself has not been overtilled, except by writers of cookery books as such. It would be easy to list numerous titles, especially in the social sciences, that sound promising but turn out to pay no attention whatsoever to how people eat and drink. I have therefore clustered my principal printed sources (many of which are mentioned in the main text), under four heads. I have also added brief comments here and there, perhaps especially where a title is essential reading, or simply obscure. For articles and reports, see the notes on page 206. Almost all the books listed I am lucky enough to have either on my own shelves or on long loan from the patient London Library. A more comprehensive historical collection of food-related books, especially Victoriana, is to be found in the Brotherton Library of the University of Leeds. I have cited cookery books selectively, where their authors, or in some cases particular titles by a notably prolific author, seem representative of a style or interesting on other grounds. Another book could be written, and no doubt eventually will be, from primary sources: the records and catalogues of food firms; the comments of consumers recorded in diaries, letters, and the archives of institutions ranging from Mass Observation to *The Good Food Guide*; and a fuller range of social survey data. At the time of writing, a Sunday newspaper polling organisation is planning to re-run in some form the 'Crawford' surveys (1938 and 1958) referred to in the text. But data on taste as opposed to nutrition are haphazardly collected as yet.

HISTORY AND BIOGRAPHY

Frederic Accum, *A Treatise on Adulteration of Food and Culinary Poisons, etc.*, 1820
J.-P. Aron, *The Art of Eating in France*, 1975. (*Le Mangeur au XIX Siècle*, 1973)
Janet Barkas, *The Vegetable Passion: a history of the vegetarian state of mind*, 1973
Georgina Battiscombe, *English Picnics*, 1949
John Burnett, *Plenty and Want: a social history of diet in England from 1815 to the present day*. Revised edn. 1978 (1966 q.v.) The best book of its kind since Drummond & Wilbraham

Bibliography

K. C. Chang (ed.), *Food in Chinese Culture*, 1977. Indispensable for any thorough understanding of the Chinese diet from pre-history to modern times.

C. I. Cutting, *Fish Saving: a history of fish processing from ancient to modern times*, 1955.

Elizabeth David, *Spices, Salt and Aromatics in the English Kitchen*, 1970

– *English Bread and Yeast Cookery*, 1977. See also under Section 3, where these books too could equally well appear.

Caroline Davidson, *A Woman's Work is Never Done*, 1982

Dorothy Davis, *A History of Shopping*, 1966

J. C. Drummond and Anne Wilbraham, revised Dorothy Hollingsworth. *The Englishman's Food*, 1929, 1958. The pioneer study. The revision includes an account of Drummond's own work at the Ministry of Food, 1939–45.

Sarah Freeman, *Isabella and Sam: the story of Mrs Beeton*, 1977

R. J. Hammond, *Food* (in the Official History of the Second World War Series). Vol. 1. *The Growth of Policy*, 1951. Vol. 2. *Studies in Administration and Control*, 1956

John Hampson, *The English at Table*, 1944. A title in the 'Britain in Pictures' series.

Dorothy Hartley, *Food in England*, 1954. A practical, rural, quirky but accurate account of the culinary world we have lost.

Eugene Herbodeau and Paul Thalamas, *Georges Auguste Escoffier*, 1955

Harry Hopkins, *The New Look: a social history of the forties and fifties in Britain*, 1963

James P. Johnston, *A Hundred Years Eating: food, drink and the daily diet in Britain since the late 19th century*, 1977. Less comprehensive than it sounds.

Arthur Marwick, *British Society since 1945* (Penguin), 1982

– *Class: image and reality in Britain, France and the USA since 1930*, 1980

Raynes Minns, *Bombers and Mash: the domestic front 1939–45*, 1980

Helen Morris, *Portrait of a Chef: the life of Alexis Soyer*, 1938

Derek J. Oddy and Derek S. Miller (eds.), *The Making of the Modern British Diet*, 1976. Essays by many hands on particular topics in nutrition and trade history.

Mancur Olson, *The Economics of the Wartime Shortage*, Durham, N. Carolina, 1963

Philippa Pullar, *Consuming Passions: a history of English food and appetite*, 1970

Marie Ritz, *Cesar Ritz: host to the world*, 1938

A. H. Sharar (trans. E. S. Harcourt and Fakhir Hussain), *Lucknow: the last phase of an Oriental Culture*, 1975

Michael Sissons and Philip French (eds.), *Age of Austerity, 1945–51*, 1963

H. Llewellyn Smith (ed.), *The New Survey of London Life and Labour*, 1935

Reay Tannahill, *Food in History*, 1973

Derek Taylor and David Bush, *The Golden Age of British Hotels*, 1974

Irene Veal, *Recipes of the 1940s*, 1944. Included in this section for its account of institutional practice in the period.

C. Anne Wilson, *Food and Drink in Britain*: from the Stone Age to recent times, 1973. Scholarly domestic history, leaning heavily upon the collection of cookery books in the Brotherton Library, Leeds.

Woolton, Lord (Fred Marquis), *The Memoirs of the Rt. Hon. the Earl of Woolton*, 1959

– (ed.), *Food Facts for the Kitchen Front*, n.d.

Theodore Zeldin, *France 1848–1945*, Vol. 2, 1977. There exists no equivalent book about Britain in this period by a historian whose interests include food and drink, and who is capable of raising the question (p. 745): 'One of the great problems in the history of cooking is why England, which was a richer country than France and had a vastly richer aristocracy capable of spending without limit to obtain the best food, did not develop as sophisticated or as varied a style of cooking as France did.'

SOCIAL SCIENCE AND OBSERVATION: CONSUMPTION AND TASTE

D. Elliston Allen, *British Tastes* 1968. Throughout this text, which is organised by regions not by topics, tastes in food and drink are hard to disentangle from tastes in other spheres that are also of interest to market researchers. But the effort is well worth while.

Lincoln Allison, *Condition of England*, 1981
   Rambles round Britain in the Priestley tradition.

T. C. Barker, J. C. McKenzie and John Yudkin, *Our Changing Fare*, 1966

Michael Bardsley, *Common Man and Colonel Bogus*, 1944

Richard Boston, *Beer and Skittles*, 1976

Hilde Bruch, *Eating Disorders*, 1974. Worth the attention of anyone who regrets that discussion of anorexia, bulimia and other aspects of dietary pathology had to be omitted from the present book.

Derek Cooper, *The Bad Food Guide*, 1967
– *The Beverage Report*, 1970

Jilly Cooper, *Class: a view from Middle England*, 1979

Robert Courtine, *La Gastronomie*, Paris, 1970. A short, useful book in the *Que-sais-je?* paperback series by *Le Monde*'s food critic.

W. Crawford and H. Broadley, *The People's Food*, 1938. The first 'Crawford' survey.

E. C. Crocker, *Flavor*, New York, 1945. A text from the early days of taste science before specialisation set in.

Mary Douglas, *Implicit Meanings*, 1976
– *In the Active Voice*, 1982

J. C. Drummond and others, *The Nation's Larder and The Housewife's Part Therein*, 1940

Henry T. Finck, *Food and Flavor*, New York, 1924. Pre-scientific, by comparison with Crocker (q.v.), but practical and concerned.

Jack Goody, *Cooking, Cuisine and Class*, 1982

Roland Harper, *Human Senses in Action*, 1976

Jessica Kuper, *The Anthropologist's Cookbook*, 1977

Judith Listowel, *The modern Hostess*, 1961

David Mabey (with Richard Mabey), *In Search of Food: traditional eating and drinking in Britain*, 1978. Concentrates on food markets. Uneven geographically.

Stephen Mennell, *The Sociology of Taste: eating in England and France*, (forthcoming).

Robert Moore, *The Social Impact of Oil*, 1982. A study of the Aberdeen district.

Anne Murcott (ed.), *The Sociology of Food and Eating*, 1983

Ann Oakley, *The Sociology of Housework*, 1974

George Orwell, *Down and Out in Paris and London*, 1933
– *The Road to Wigan Pier*, 1937

Magnus Pyke, *Townsman's Food*, 1952
– *Food and Society*, 1968
– *Technological Eating*, 1972

Tibur Scitovsky, *The Joyless Economy*, 1976

Bibliography

Ashley Smith, *A City Stirs*, 1939 (rev. edn 1951)
James L. Watson (ed.), *Between Two Cultures*, 1977
Geoffrey Warren, *The Foods We Eat*, 1958   The second 'Crawford' survey.

COOKING AND CATERING:
RECIPES, REFLECTIONS, GUIDES, REMINISCENCES

Eliza Acton, *Modern Cookery*, 1845
– *The English Bread Book*, 1857
H. Pearl Adam, *Kitchen Ranging*, 1928
Anon., *The American Stranger's Guide to London and Liverpool at Table*, 1859
Elizabeth Ayrton, *The Cookery of England*, 1974
Michael Balfour and Judy Allen, *The Health Food Guide*, 1970–2
Adie Ballantyne, *Choose Your Kitchen*, 1944
Michael Bateman, *Cooking People*, 1966
Isabella Beeton, *The Book of Household Management*, 1861
X. Marcel Boulestin, *Simple French Cooking for English Homes*, 1926
– *What shall We Have Today?* 1931
– *Myself, My Two Countries*, 1936
– (ed. Robin Adair) *Ease and Endurance*, 1948
Gregory Houston Bowden, *British Gastronomy*, 1975
A. J. Brown, *Farewell High Fell*, 1952
Osbert Burdett, *A Little Book of Cheese*, 1935
– *Memory and Imagination*, 1935
Thomas Burke, *Dinner is Served, or, eating round the world in London*, 1937
Mike Bygrave and Joan Goodman, *Fuel Food*, 1973
L. C. R. Cameron, *The Wild Foods of Great Britain: where to find them and how to cook them*, 1917
Campaign for Real Ale, Good Beer Guide, 1971–
Susan Campbell, *English Cookery New and Old*, 1981
– (with Alexandra Towle), *Cheap Eats in London*, 1975
Robert Carrier, *Great Dishes of the World*, 1963
H. L. Cracknell and R. J. Kaufman, *Practical Professional Cookery*, 1972
Fanny Cradock, *Something's Burning*, 1960
Fanny and Johnny Cradock, *Around Britain with Bon Viveur*, 1952
– *Bon Viveur in London*, 1953
Elizabeth Craig, *Cookery Illustrated and Household Management*, 1936
Rupert Croft-Cooke, *English Cooking*, 1960
Daily Express, *Wartime Cookery Book*, 1939
Elizabeth David, *A Book of Mediterranean Food*, 1950
– *French Country Cooking*, 1951
– *Italian Food*, 1954
– *Summer Cooking*, 1955
– *French Provincial Cooking*, 1960
Alan Davidson, *North Atlantic Seafood*, 1979
Christopher Driver (ed. 1970–82), *The Good Food Guide*

Bibliography

Auguste Escoffier, *A Guide to Modern Cookery*, 1907
Hilary Fawcett and Jeanne Strang, *The Good Food Guide Dinner Party Book*, 1971
– *The Good Cook's guide*, 1974
Hilary Fawcett, *The Good Food Guide Second Dinner Party Book*, 1979
M. F. K. Fisher, *The Art of Eating*, 1963 (*see also* Tsuji *below*)
Theodora FitzGibbon, *The Food of the Western World*, 1976
– *With Love: an autobiography 1938–46*, 1982
John Fothergill, *An Innkeeper's Diary*, 1931
Nicolas Freeling, *Kitchen Book*, 1970
Mario Gallati, *Mario of the Caprice*, 1959
Doris Grant, *Your Daily Food*, 1973
Patience Gray and Primrose Boyd, *Plats du Jour* (Penguin), 1957
Jane Grigson, *Fish Cookery*, 1973
– *English Food*, 1974
– *Vegetable Book*, 1978
– *Fruit Book*, 1982
Barbara Hammond, *Cooking Explained*, 1963
Jack Hampton, *Canteen Cookery*, 1953
Philip Harben, *The Way to Cook*, 1945
– *Traditional Dishes of Britain*, 1953
Philip and Katharine Harben, *Entertaining at Home*, 1951
Ambrose Heath, *Good Food*, 1932
– *Open Sesame*, 1939
– *Meat dishes without Coupons*, 1940
– *Good breakfasts*, 1940
– *Kitchen Front Recipes*, 1941
– (unsigned) *Patsy's Reflections: learn to cook by pictures*, n.d. (1949)
William Heptinstall, *Hors d'Oeuvre and Cold Table*, 1959
Vere Hodgson, *Few Eggs and No Oranges*, 1976
Josie A. Holtom and William H. Hylton, *The Complete Guide to Herbs*, 1979
Jocasta Innes, *The Pauper's Cookbook*, 1971
– *The Country Kitchen*, 1979
Elizabeth Jordan, *As Cooks Go*, 1950
Sheila Kaye-Smith, *Kitchen Fugue*, 1945
Elizabeth Kent, *Country Cuisine: cooking with country chefs*, 1980
R. Kinton and V. Ceserani, *The Theory of Catering*, 1964
Tom Laughton, *Pavilions by the Sea: the memoirs of a hotel-keeper*, 1977
T. A. Layton, *Dining Round London*, 1947. A tiny booklet, but possibly the first of its kind to
  appear after the war.
C. F. Leyel and Olga Hartley, *The Gentle Art of Cookery*, 1925
Sir Harry Luke, *The Tenth Muse*, 1962
Richard Mabey, *Food for Free*, 1972
F. Marian McNeill, *The Scots Kitchen*, 1929
Vicomte de Maudit, *They Can't Ration These*, 1941
Clara Milburn, *Mrs Milburn's Diaries*, 1979
Lesley Nelson, *Vegetarian Restaurants in England*, 1982
N. Newnham-Davis, *Dinners & Diners*, 1899
  Perhaps the most evocative restaurant criticism written in English.

Bibliography

Richard Olney, *Simple French Food*, 1981

Frances Partridge, *A Pacifist's War*, 1979

Raymond Postgate, *The Plain Man's Guide to Wine*, 1951

— (ed. 1951–69) *The Good Food Guide*

Gerald Priestland, *Frying Tonight: the saga of fish and chips*, 1972

Peggie Rafferty, *Food for the Duke*, n.d. (1981)
   Reminiscences of her pub, the Duke of York, at Iddesleigh.

Patrick Rance, *The Great English Cheese Book*, 1982
   Our nearest equivalent to Pierre Androuet's *Guide du Fromage* (English translation 1983)

Cyril Ray (ed.), *The Compleat Imbiber*, 1956–67
   Though chiefly devoted to wine, these annual (or near-annual) volumes also make room for the food tastes and reminiscences of their contributors.

— *The Gourmet's Companion*, 1963

Claudia Roden, *A Book of Middle-Eastern Food*, 1968

Egon Ronay, *Guides* (to restaurants, hotels, pubs, cafés etc.), latterly coupled with the names of various sponsors. 1957–

Penelope Seaman, *Little Inns of Soho*, 1948

P. Morton Shand, *A Book of Food*, 1927

André Simon, *In the Twilight*, 1969

Edward Spencer, *Cakes and Ale*, 1897

Constance Spry, *Come into the Garden, Cook*, 1942

Constance Spry and Rosemary Hume, *The Constance Spry Cookery Book*, 1956

Tom Stobart, *Herbs, Spices and Flavourings*, 1970

Susan Strong, *'Feed the Brute!'* or *cookery for the million*, 1942

'Syllabub' (Aidan Philip), *Syllabub in the Kitchen*, 1961
   The blurb of this delightful book (collected from columns originally published in the *Observer*) includes what must be an early use of the term 'gastronaut'.

Marika Hanbury Tenison, *Deep-Freeze Cookery*, 1970

Flora Thompson, *Lark Rise to Candleford*, 1945

Shizuo Tsuji (intro. M. F. K. Fisher), *Japanese Cooking: a simple art*, Tokyo/New York/San Francisco, 1980

Colin Tudge, *Future Cook*, 1980

Isabelle Vischer, *Now to the Banquet*, 1953
   Collected from talks on the BBC's Third Programme

Florence White, *Good Things in England*, 1932
      Flowers as Food, 1934
      The Good Food Register or New Traveller's Guide, 1934–36
      A Fire in the Kitchen (autobiography), 1938
      Good English Food, (posth.) 1952

In the following sub-section, I have assembled sound, and in most cases, fairly accessible examples of cookery books covering the main cuisines that have established themselves in British urban taste since 1945 (see Chapter Five). Authors in this genre whose contribution to British style as a whole seems more important have already been listed (e.g. Elizabeth David, Jane Grigson, Claudia Roden). But it may be thought useful to be able to compare the repertoire of ethnic restaurants in Britain with the repertoire of the same countries set out in London-published books. For some Far Eastern countries it may be better to seek out American publications, for instance the Time-Life series.

Bibliography

CHINA (Cantonese, Pekinese, Szechuanese)
Kenneth Lo, *Chinese Food* (Penguin), 1972
– *Regional Chinese Cookbook*, 1981

FRANCE ('*nouvelle*')
Paul Bocuse, *The New Cookery* (trans. Colette Rossant and Lorraine Davis), 1978
Michel Guérard, *Cuisine Minceur* and *Cuisine Gourmande* (ed. Caroline Conran), 1977 and 1978
Jean and Pierre Troisgros, *Nouvelle Cuisine* (ed. Caroline Conran), 1981
Roger Vergé, *Cuisine of the Sun* (trans. Caroline Conran and Caroline Hobhouse), 1978

GREECE (including Cyprus and islands)
See David in above section
Theonie Mark, *Greek Islands Cooking*, 1978

HUNGARY
Fred Macnicol, *Hungarian Cookery* (Penguin), 1978

INDIA (Bangladesh, Pakistan)
Lalita Ahmed, *Indian Cooking*, 1981
Dharamjit Singh, *Indian Cookery* (Penguin), 1970
Meera Taneja, *Indian Regional Cookery*, 1980
Madhur Jaffrey, *Indian Cookery*, 1982

INDONESIA (Malaya, Singapore)
Rosemary Brissenden, *South-East Asian Food* (Penguin), 1969

ITALY
See David in above section

JAPAN
Peter and Joan Martin, *Japanese Cooking* (Penguin), 1970
See also Tsuji in above section

JEWISH
Florence Greenberg, *Jewish Cookery* (Penguin), 1947

NEAR- and MIDDLE-EAST (Cyprus, Turkey, Lebanon, Egypt, etc.)

See Roden in above section

PORTUGAL
Carol Wright, *Portuguese Food*, 1969

SPAIN
Elizabeth Cass, *Spanish Cooking*, 1957
Anna MacMiadhacháin, *Spanish Regional Cookery* (Penguin), 1976

Bibliography

WEST INDIES

Rita G. Springer, *Caribbean Cookbook*, 1968

Elizabeth Lambert Ortiz, *Caribbean Cooking* (Penguin), 1975

UNCLASSIFIED

Kingsley Amis, *The Green Man*, 1969

Jean-Anthelme Brillat-Savarin, *The Philosopher in the Kitchen* (Penguin), (trans. Anne Drayton) 1970

Michael Broadbent, *Pocket Guide to Wine-Tasting*, 1982

Richard Burnet, *The Lean Years: politics in the age of scarcity*, 1981

Daniel Green, *The Politics of Food*, 1975

Abraham Hayward, *Art of Dining, or, gastronomy and gastronomers*, 1853

Timothy Mo, *Sour Sweet*, 1982

Doris Langley Moore, *Pleasure*, 1953

Iris Murdoch, *The Sea, the Sea*, 1978

Henry Smith, *Making Money in the Catering Business*, 1955

Thomas Walker, *The Original*, 1835 (new edn 1850). The advice of Victorian cooks is familiar enough. Walker, the metropolitan magistrate, and Hayward (above) represent the quirkier views of Victorian eaters.

PERIODICAL AND OTHER PUBLICATIONS

These cannot be listed in detail, but apart from newspapers and magazines, the following should be cited: *Social Trends*, the National Food Survey, commercial polls or analyses summarised in the food and catering trades press, and *Wine and Food* Quarterly (1934–1963). Among recent newcomers, two that concern the micro-economy of the kitchen deserve particular mention: *Petits Propos Culinaires*, edited by Alan Davidson at 45 Lamont Road, London SW10 0HU (booklets intermittently published since February 1979, with a strong penchant for the recondite); and *Twelve Times a Year* edited by Tom Jaine at the Carved Angel, 2 South Embankment, Darmouth, Devon (a cyclostyled diary of a fine restaurant's provisioning, cooking, and serving).

Index

Index

Index